DETAIL
& PATTER

ESSAYS FOR COMPO

D0937394

SECOND EDITION

DETAIL & PATTERN

ESSAYS FOR COMPOSITION

ROBERT BAYLOR

Department of English
Mt. San Antonio College

McGRAW-HILL BOOK COMPANY

NEW YORK   MONTREAL
ST. LOUIS   NEW DELHI
SAN FRANCISCO   PANAMA
DÜSSELDORF   RIO DE JANEIRO
JOHANNESBURG   SINGAPORE
KUALA LUMPUR   SYDNEY
LONDON   TORONTO
MEXICO

This book was set in News Gothic by Monotype Composition Company, Inc., and printed and bound by The Maple Press Company. The designer was J. E. O'Connor. The editors were Robert Fry, Alison Meersschaert, and Paula Henson. Sally Ellyson supervised production.

DETAIL AND PATTERN: Essays for Composition

Library of Congress Catalog Card Number 77-172651

07-004135-0

2 3 4 5 6 7 8 9 0 **MAMM** 7 9 8 7 6 5 4 3 2

Acknowledgments

Stewart Alsop, "Dr. Calhoun's Horrible Mousery," reprinted from *Newsweek*, August 17, 1970, with the permission of the publisher.

Donald Barthelme, "Game" from *Unspeakable Practices, Unnatural Acts* by Donald Barthelme. Copyright © 1965 by Donald Barthelme. First appeared in *The New Yorker*. Reprinted with the permission of Farrar, Straus & Giroux, Inc.

Bruno Bettelheim, "Business as Usual" from *The Informed Heart* by Bruno Bettelheim. Copyright © 1960 by The Free Press, a Corporation. Reprinted by permission of The Macmillan Company.

Brigid Brophy, "Monogamy" from *Don't Never Forget* by Brigid Brophy. Copyright © 1966 by Brigid Brophy. Reprinted by permission of Holt, Rinehart and Winston, Inc.

Claude Brown, "We Got Soul, Baby, Aren't We Beautiful?" from *Manchild in the Promised Land* by Claude Brown. Copyright © 1965 by Claude Brown. Reprinted by permission of The Macmillan Company.

Art Buchwald, "A Head Start on Brain Inventory." First appeared in the *Los Angeles Times*, June 19, 1965. Reprinted by permission of the author and World Publishers.

Estelle Changas, "Love Story: A Minority Point of View," reprinted from *The Los Angeles Times*, January 17, 1971, with the permission of the author.

Shirley Chisholm, introduction from *Unbought and Unbossed* by Shirley

Chisholm. Reprinted by permission of the publisher, Houghton Mifflin Company. Copyright © 1970 by Shirley Chisholm.

Frank Conroy, "Finally Free," from *Stop-Time* by Frank Conroy, copyright © 1965, 1966, 1967 by Frank Conroy. All Rights Reserved. Reprinted by permission of the Viking Press.

Robert Coles, selections from remarks by Robert Coles in *The Writer's World*, published by the McGraw-Hill Book Company, and copyright © 1969 by The Author's Guild and the author.

William Faulkner, "Nobel Prize Acceptance Speech" by William Faulkner. Copyright 1954 by William Faulkner (Random House, Inc.). Reprinted from *The Faulkner Reader* by William Faulkner.

Paul Goodman, "A Useful Job" from *Growing Up Absurd* by Paul Goodman. Copyright © 1960 by Paul Goodman. Reprinted by permission of Random House, Inc.

Joseph Heller, "Catch-22" from *Catch-22* by Joseph Heller. Copyright © 1961 by Joseph Heller. Reprinted by permission of Simon and Schuster, Inc.

Ernest Hemingway, "I was always embarrassed" excerpt reprinted with the permission of Charles Scribner's Sons from *A Farewell to Arms*, p. 191, by Ernest Hemingway. Copyright 1929 by Charles Scribner's Sons. Renewed copyright © 1957 by Ernest Hemingway.

Steven Kelman, "You Force Kids to Rebel" from *The Saturday Evening Post*, November 19, 1966. Reprinted by permission of the author.

Martin Luther King, Jr., "I Have a Dream." Copyright © 1963 by Martin Luther King, Jr. Reprinted by permission of Joan Daves.

Daniel Lang, from *Casualties of War* by Daniel Lang. Copyright © 1969 by The New Yorker Magazine, Inc. Used with permission of McGraw-Hill Book Company.

John Lardner, "Titanic Thompson" from *The World of John Lardner* edited by Roger Kahn. Copyright © 1961 by Hazel Lardner. Reprinted by permission of Simon and Schuster, Inc.

Jeremy Larner, "Hector Warms Up" from *Drive, He Said* by Jeremy Larner. Copyright © 1964 by Jeremy Larner and used by permission of the Delacorte Press.

Marshall McLuhan, "Murder by Television" from *Understanding Media: The Extensions of Man* by Marshall McLuhan. Copyright © 1964 by Marshall McLuhan. Used by permission of McGraw-Hill Book Company.

Jean Mayer, "Destruction of Vietnam Crops Doesn't Help Win the War" by Jean Mayer. Appeared in *The Los Angeles Times*, May 29, 1966. Reprinted by permission of the author.

Don McNeill, "The Seranos: Linda Cusamano, reprinted by permission of *The Village Voice*. Copyright by the Village Voice, Inc., 1967.

Willie Morris, "I Think I Must Have Been Listening," from *North Toward Home*, by Willie Morris. Copyright © 1967 by Willie Morris. Reprinted by permission of the publisher, Houghton Mifflin Company.

Newsweek, "Eichmann in Jerusalem—Can One Know the 'Whole' Truth?" Appeared on June 17, 1963. Reprinted by permission of *Newsweek*.

Newsweek, "The Message of Marshall McLuhan" taken from *Newsweek*, March 6, 1967. Reprinted by permission of *Newsweek*.

Gordon Parks, "My Mother's Dream for Me" from *A Choice of Weapons* by Gordon Parks. Copyright © 1965, 1966 by Gordon Parks. Reprinted by permission of Harper & Row, Publishers.

John Riley, "Saga of the Barefoot Bag on Campus" from *Life*, March 17, 1967. Copyright © Time Inc. Reprinted by permission of *Life*.

James Reston, "Joe Namath, the New Anti-Hero," from *The New York Times*, August 21, 1970, copyright © 1970 by the New York Times Company. Reprinted by permission.

Eugene Schoenfeld, "Kill Speed," from *Dear Doctor Hippocrates: Advice Your Family Doctor Never Gave You*, copyright © 1968 by Eugene Schoenfeld. Reprinted by permission of Grove Press, Inc.

Eric Sevareid, "What Really Hurts," from *Maybe Nobody's Been Listening*, copyright 1970 by Time, Inc., reprinted by permission of the Harold Matson Company, Inc.

Gloria Steinem, "What Would It Be Like If Women Won," reprinted from *Time*, The Weekly Newsmagazine; Copyright Time, Inc. with the permission of the publisher.

Studs Terkel, "Cesar Chavez," from *Hard Times*, by Studs Terkel. Copyright © 1970 by Studs Terkel. Reprinted by permission of Pantheon Books, a Division of Random House, Inc.

Time, "Crime: The Madman in the Tower" including "The Symptoms of Mass Murder." Copyright Time Inc. 1966. Reprinted by permission from *Time*, The Weekly Newsmagazine.

Time, "Protest: Memoirs of Diana," from the issue of March 30, 1970. Reprinted by permission from *Time*, the Weekly Newsmagazine; Copyright Time, Inc. 1970.

Mark Twain, "The War Prayer," from *Europe and Elsewhere* by Mark Twain. Copyright © 1923, 1951 by the Mark Twain Company. By permission of Harper & Row, Publishers, Inc.

John Updike, "Central Park" from *Assorted Prose* by John Updike. Copyright 1956 by John Updike. Reprinted by permission of Alfred A. Knopf, Inc. Originally appeared in *The New Yorker*.

Martin Weinberger, "The Double Standards," reprinted from *The Claremont Courier*, September 3, 1969, with the permission of the author and the publisher.

Frances Power Weisemiller, "To Ralph Nader with love: History, segregation, manners and the automobile," reprinted from *The Claremont Courier*, February 6, 1971, with the permission of the author and the publisher.

Katherine Whitehorn, "A Fine Time to Be Alive" from *The Observer Weekend Review*, *The London Observer*, January 3, 1965. Reprinted by permission of *The Observer*.

Tom Wolfe, "Clean Fun at Riverhead" from *The Kandy-Kolored Tangerine-Flake Streamline Baby* by Tom Wolfe. Copyright © 1963 by New York Herald Tribune Inc. Reprinted with permission of Farra, Straus and Giroux, Inc.

CONTENTS

10 BIOGRAPHICAL DATA   209

11 AN APPENDIX OF PHOTOGRAPHS   213

A NOTE ON THE SECOND EDITION

The changes in this edition were made with the advice of students and teachers familiar with the original. Introductory essays have been expanded to include more examples and illustrations. More relevant selections—by such members of the new writing generation as Frank Conroy, Robert Coles, Gloria Steinem, Estelle Changas, and Don McNeill—have replaced those that tended to date. More photographs are used to allow teachers to make more assignments based on visual perception. Many of the longer essays have been cut in favor of shorter essays with the result that, with no increase in the length of the book, the selections have been increased from thirty-eight to forty-three. None of the changes, however, alters the purpose of this edition, which remains the same as that stated in the Preface.

Robert Baylor

PREFACE

Detail and Pattern exemplifies Marshall McLuhan's pun, the medium is the massage, in that every item—including gag lines, song lyrics, photographs, wrong-choice answers in the vocabulary tests, and assignments—is useful in achieving the goals of writing with clarity and reading with understanding.

The book is designed to interest the student in every way. The subject matter of the essays and stories is oriented toward genuine student concerns: sexual conduct and attitudes, peer-group relationships, the generation gap, the search for identity. The massage may be fun, irritating, shocking, mysterious, amusing, nonsensical, personal. If it is one of these or all of these to each student, it will be educational. The writing student will become aware of the need to employ specific detail to clarify writing assignments. The reading student will learn to see the patterns implied by cumulative detail in the information. Once this has been achieved, the massage will then become the message, and the medium will have served its purpose.

Robert Baylor

... it is always delightful when a great and beautiful conception proves to be consonant with reality.

Albert Einstein

To write with clarity, to read with understanding, is to observe and to comprehend the detail in the pattern. A tourist gallops through the Louvre to gaze at the "Mona Lisa" as an object that will become a detail in his account of his trip when he returns home. A painter sits for hours studying the "Mona Lisa," noting each individual brush stroke, the color gradations, the subtle balances. These details of method and technique he then puts to use in his own work. A doctor sees in the "Mona Lisa" a woman with symptoms of adenoid infection. A little girl who has been told by an aunt that her smile is as enigmatic as the Mona Lisa's peers at the painting and tries to transpose the subject's smile to her own features to understand what "enigmatic" means.

A communication involves information that is received, comprehended, and understood. Jazz musician Louis Armstrong, asked by a fan what a composition of his meant, said, "Man, if you have to ask, you ain't never going to know." To know, Louis implied, you first had to feel (comprehend). When you listen to a musical composition, you hear it (receive it) and, if you are dancing, catch the beat (comprehend it). There is no need to understand it in intellectual terms unless you are a musician.

A skin diver discovers a sunken ship. He taps on the hull and hears a tap-tap-tapping in return. He comprehends, then, that one or more men are trapped within. If he and the trapped man have studied Morse code, the skin diver can understand the details of the situation.

Our feeling (comprehending) response to a film or a happening or a piece of writing is often in terms of "I like/don't like it." This book, however, and your other textbooks, as well as most of your college writing assignments, involve expository writing. Receiving and comprehending are not sufficient. You must understand. You must write with clarity so your reader can understand. In exposition the writer seeks to explain his subject in such a way that his reader will not only comprehend it, but understand it. You comprehend a general statement, "The costumes of the natives are colorful, but brief." You understand a general statement only when it has been detailed; only when you know how colorful is colorful and how brief is brief and what country the natives are native to. The detail verifies, clarifies, illustrates, makes concrete. Memorization plays little or no part in arriving at understanding in this sense. If you understand the detail, you will understand the author's point. If the detail in your own writing is precise and concrete, your generalization and thus your explanation will be understood by your reader.

The following poem makes a universal point quite easy to comprehend: that all men present, in different ways, masks to the world about them; that all men hide some part of themselves, their ideals, their personalities, from exposure to strangers. A popular song says it in the line "Laughing on the outside, crying on the inside."

The addition of one biographical detail about the author of this poem, however, gives us a concrete understanding of it. Paul Laurence Dunbar was the son of a slave who lived his life as a black in white America.

WE WEAR THE MASK   PAUL LAURENCE DUNBAR

(1872–1906)

We wear the mask that grins and lies,
It hides our cheeks and shades our eyes,—
This debt we pay to human guile;
With torn and bleeding hearts we smile,
And mouth with myriad subtleties.

Why should the world be over-wise,
In counting all our tears and sighs?
Nay, let them only see us, while
     We wear the mask.

We smile, but, O great Christ, our cries
To thee from tortured souls arise.
We sing, but oh the clay is vile
Beneath our feet, and long the mile;
But let the world dream otherwise,
     We wear the mask!

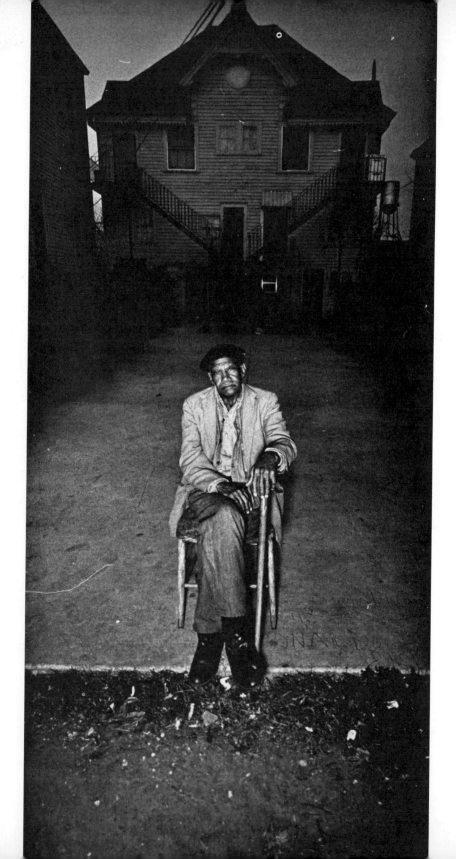

It was a heavenly place for a boy, that farm of my uncle John's. . . . In the summer the table was set in the middle of that shady and breezy floor, and the sumptuous meals—well, it makes me cry to think of them. Fried chicken, roast pig, wild and tame turkeys, ducks, and geese; venison just killed; squirrels, rabbits, pheasants, partridges, prairie-chickens; biscuits, hot batter cakes, hot buckwheat cakes, hot "wheat bread," hot rolls, hot corn pone; fresh corn boiled on the ear, succotash, butterbeans, string-beans, tomatoes, peas, Irish potatoes, sweet potatoes; buttermilk, sweet milk, "clabber"; watermelons, muskmelons, cantalopes—all fresh from the garden; apple pie, peach pie, pumpkin pie, apple dumplings, peach cobbler—I can't remember the rest.

Mark Twain

To write with clarity and to read with understanding is to understand the use and significance of specific detail. Mark Twain's recollection of the meals of his childhood gives details as to why his uncle's farm was "a heavenly place."

To write well requires a conscious effort to perceive experience in specific terms. To read well requires a conscious effort to understand the implications of the detail the writer develops. Here are several general statements. "The movie was fascinating/dull." "She/he is cute." "The speaker gave a witty talk." "Babe Ruth is the greatest home-run hitter of all time." To clarify these statements, the writer specifies details and examples from the film that define his standard for describing it as fascinating or dull. "Cute" is broken down into specifics related to the appearance, intelligence, athletic ability, figure, and unique attributes he/she seeks in a date. "Witty talk" is specified by citing witty details from the talk. Babe Ruth's greatness as a homer hitter is verified by one key detail, the official record book statistic that shows he hit more home runs than any other major league baseball player.

Reporters learn to get the details of a story by asking who, what, where, when, why, how. They train themselves to develop concrete detail. This is an apt technique for beginning writers to imitate. A reporter does not simply see and hear a singer. He sees the color of her eyes and hair, the style and color of her clothing, the mannerisms and gestures peculiar to her, and the quality and clarity of her voice and diction.

The average fan at a football game is aware of its general flow. He knows who has the ball, who is winning, and what the score is. A football scout viewing the game perceives it in a specific and highly detailed way. He keeps a chart on which he indicates field position, yards to go, down, and each play called. He charts every play that is executed. He knows who handled the ball, which specific offensive hole the ball carrier ran through, what defensive men were blocked and by whom. He notes the different offensive patterns used, the spacing of the line, and the positioning of the backfield. At the end of the game he will have sufficient specific information to discover, perhaps, an unconscious pattern which the play caller has fallen into.

A professional develops the ability to perceive specific details which clarify the generalizations he makes in the course of his daily work. A surgeon's decision to operate is based on a great deal of specific information about the patient: symptoms, pulse rate, blood count, general physical condition, mental attitude, and the results of x-ray and laboratory studies.

The writer's task is to train himself to see and think in concrete terms and to avoid the easy, but often empty, generalization. The reader's task is to train himself to draw implications from the specific detail the writer develops. Even a listing of concrete words without the context and structure of a sentence can convey meaning and tone if the reader is perceptive. If a writer describes a desk, for example, on which copies of the *Wall Street Journal, Business Week,* and the *Kiplinger Report* are scattered, the titles of these periodicals tell the reader something about the man who uses that desk. Suppose *Sports Illustrated, Field and Stream,* and *Rod and Gun* had been listed? *Good Housekeeping, Ladies' Home Journal,* and *McCall's?*

The examples that follow begin with several listings of words and phrases and end with an Art Buchwald article made up of thirty-six individual details. Note in the first two sections how a tone—serious, satirical, sad—can be implied by a list of items standing alone.

At the height of the Roaring Twenties and prohibition, Edmund Wilson compiled a list of words "denoting drunkenness now in common use in the United States." Prohibition has ended. The Roaring Twenties are only a romantic myth. But booze and the state of being resulting from imbibing it remain of sufficient interest to fill a full page in the Americanized edition of *Roget's Thesaurus*. Note how the following listing of these words has, simply as a listing, a developing tone.

ebriosified	gravy-eyed
ginned up	black-eye-pea—eyed
lit up	giddy
flushed	stinko
merry	stinking
gay	blotto
nappy	gone
high	shot
elevated	stiff
squiffy	stoned
tight	sodden
tipsy	blacked-out
lushy	titillated
sozzled	tickled
soused	splificated
soaked	half-seas over
pickled	three sheets in the wind
oiled	one over the eight
boiled	ripe
fried	mellow
frazzled	full as a tick
potted	loaded for bear
canned	embalmed
honked	buried
plowed	lit up like Times Square
smashed	lit up like a church
overtaken	slopped to the ears
blasted	stewed to the gills
plastered	to have a slant on
maudlin	to have a skinful

fuddled	to have the jumps
muddled	to have the zings
muzzy	to have the horrors
woozy	to have the jim-jams
obfuscated	to have the heebie-jeebies
glazed	to have the screaming meemies
glassy-eyed	to have a grog-blossom nose
pie-eyed	to have the dt's
cock-eyed	to have the whoops and jingles
bleary-eyed	to burn with a low blue flame

DISCUSSION | APPLICATION

1. What differentiates the words and phrases on this list from the more formal words *intemperance, intoxication,* and *inebriated?*
2. Can you add any words to the list that are currently being used?
3. Most of these words are metaphors. They express a direct comparison: *boiled, blotto, stoned.* Others are similes. They express a comparison introduced by *like* or *as.* Select three of the words or phrases and be prepared to explain their derivation, that is, their origin as used in this context.

AFTER THE BATTLE
SAMUEL WEAVER

(Editor's note: On July 1, 2, and 3, 1863, the decisive battle of the Civil War raged outside the village of Gettysburg. For three days Robert E. Lee attacked across a sunny valley of wheat fields, apple and peach orchards. For three days the Union forces, ensconced on a series of ridges and hills overlooking the valley, repelled the Confederate attacks. On July 4, General Lee withdrew. The Union Army moved out a few days later. They left a valley ripe no longer with the smell of peach blossoms and fresh-growing wheat. They left a valley reeking of gunpowder, destruction, and death. For almost four months the field remained essentially as the two armies had left it. On October 27, 1863, the site having been designated a national cemetery, work began on the exhumation and identification of the bodies. Samuel Weaver directed the work. On March 19, 1864, it had been completed and he submitted his report to the Governor of Pennsylvania.)

Report of Samuel Weaver

The work has been protracted much beyond our original anticipation . . . by the number of bodies exceeding our first calculations.   1

The number taken up . . . is thirty-three hundred and fifty-four (3,354). Of these, nine hundred and seventy-nine were bodies nameless, and without any marks to designate the state from which they volunteered.   2

* *

Before we commenced our work, the battle field had been overrun by thousands of sorrowing friends in search of lost ones, and many of the graves opened and but partially closed. Many of the undertakers who were removing bodies also performed their work in the most careless manner, invariably leaving the graves open, and often leaving particles of the bones and hair lying scattered about.   3

The bodies were found in various stages of decomposition. On the battle field of the first day, the rebels obtained possession before our men were buried, and left most of them unburied from Wednesday until Monday, when our men buried them. The consequence was, that but few on the battle field of July 1st, were marked. They were generally covered with a small portion of earth dug up from along side of the body. This left them much exposed to heat, air, and rains and they decomposed rapidly, so that when these bodies were taken up, there was nothing remaining but the dry skeleton.   4

Where bodies were in heavy clay soil, or in marshy places, they were in a good state of preservation. Where they were in sandy, porous soil, they were entirely decomposed. Frequently our men were buried in trenches—a shallow ditch—in which they were laid side by side. In several instances the numbers in a trench amounted to sixty or seventy bodies.   5

In searching for the remains of our fallen heroes, we examined more than three thousand rebel graves. They were frequently buried in trenches, and there are instances of more than one hundred and fifty in a trench. 6

It may be asked how we could distinguish the bodies of our own men from those of the rebels. This was generally easily done . . . the rebels never went into battle with the United States coat on. They sometimes stole the pantaloons from our dead and wore them, but not the coat. The rebel clothing is made of cotton and is of grey or brown color. The clothing of our men is of wool, and blue; so that the body having the coat of our uniform on was a pretty sure indication that it was a Union soldier. But if the body were without a coat, then there were other infallible marks. The rebel shoes were differently made from ours. The rebel cotton underclothing gave proof of the army to which he belonged. In no instance was a body allowed to be removed which had any portion of the rebel clothing on it. I here most conscientiously assert, that I firmly believe that there has not been a single mistake made in the removal of the soldiers to the cemetery by taking the body of a rebel for a Union soldier. 7

*600 words**

(Editor's note: Appended to Samuel Weaver's report was a "list of articles taken from the bodies of the soldiers removed to the Soldier's National Cemetery." Note how the concrete naming of these articles indicates something about the dead man and gives an implicit tone to the listing.)

Capt. G. D. Smith, Co. I, 20th Regiment, gold plate with artificial teeth.
Unknown, fish hook, Testament, a letter signed Anna Grove.
G. W. Sprague, the grape shot that killed him, two knives, a comb.
Unknown, diary with name Agnes Jones, Pittsburgh, Pa.
Unknown, cavalryman, very light hair, spoon, needle.
Unknown, black thread, ring, pin cushion, pipe.
Unknown, knife, gun wrench, comb and (magnifying) glass.
Unknown, two cents, comb, and pencil.
Unknown, jet heart.
Unknown, piece plaid blanket—colors, white, blue, green.
Charles Sets, pocket book, hair of father, mother, sister, and brother.
Unknown, snuffbox.
Unknown, German Testament from Catherine Detanpafer.
Unknown, book: "Morning Exercises."
Thomas Shanahik, rosary.
Unknown, golden ear-rings, the minnie ball that killed him.
Sgt. L. Lee, two combs, diary, the bullet that killed him.
Unknown Corporal, ambrotype of female.

* See Reading Speed Chart on the inside back cover.

DISCUSSION | APPLICATION

1. We have all read about battles in history books and seen and heard descriptions of battles on television. What do the details of Weaver's letter and list tell you about the Battle of Gettysburg? About war?

Assignment

1. Develop a list of items and objects accumulated in the aftermath of an event: a stadium after a big game, a house after a party, the souvenirs collected in your desk drawer from senior year in high school, or the day's accumulation of cigarette butts, bottle caps, etc. in a cafeteria ash tray. Your listing should be arranged in such a way as to give some element of significance and tone to the items listed. Do not restrict yourself to the suggestions.

I was always embarrassed by the words sacred, glorious, and sacrifice and the expression in vain. We had heard them, sometimes standing in the rain almost out of earshot, so that only the shouted words came through, and had read them, on proclamations that were slapped up by billposters over other proclamations, now for a long time, and I had seen nothing sacred, and the things that were glorious had no glory and the sacrifices were like the stockyards at Chicago if nothing was done with the meat except to bury it. There were many words that you could not stand to hear and finally only the names of places had dignity. Certain numbers were the same way and certain dates and these with the names of the places were all you could say and have them mean anything. Abstract words such as glory, honor, courage, or hallow were obscene beside the concrete names of villages, the numbers of roads, the names of rivers, the numbers of regiments and the dates.

175 words

DISCUSSION | APPLICATION

Ernest Hemingway expresses the frontline soldier's distrust of abstract, emotionally loaded words and his feeling that only concrete descriptive words have dignity. Find, in a current periodical (newspaper or magazine) or in the preceding letter by Samuel Weaver, some examples of "expression(s) in vain" as Hemingway uses the term or list several such expressions in current use.

MARY HAWORTH'S MAIL

Dear Mary Haworth:

I wish you would help me understand my wife. I think she is insane. She is a terrific pianist and could make big money, but she won't work at it. It comes natural; she never had a lesson, but practices very much when I am not home. She turns down offers to play in night clubs, or to go to Hollywood, saying she wouldn't be able to call her life her own. She has always been poor.   1

I want a better house, now that we've paid for this not-so-good one. But she won't leave her trees and flowers; says nobody would care for them as she does. Yet one night she telephoned me and said, "Goodbye, I am sick of you and your television." She was bicycling to New York City, with no money and no headlight. The police brought her home.   2

She doesn't like women, says they are too catty and bore her to death; and has no female friends. At times she cooks with genius; other times I can hardly eat it. Last week she stuffed and baked a big turkey, placed it before me and said, "Here, it's all yours." It was wonderful. Sometimes she leaves the dishes for days, neglecting to comb her hair likewise. Other times she looks like a *Vogue* model.   3

Once she divorced me; then two weeks later called me to come home, saying she couldn't live without me. She spent four months crocheting a rug eight feet square. It cost more than if we'd bought one, but she said it would be an heirloom. When my relatives came unexpectedly to visit, she entertained them royally, then got drunk next day and said they were sly, deceitful and a bunch of bums, and didn't like her.   4

She loves our old Ford, says, "It's better than a Cadillac." She would rather do without clothes and nice things than work as a musician. I don't think she's happy. How could she be, suppressing a talent like hers? I'd give my right arm to play as she does; to which she says, "Silly, then you couldn't play!" She has contemplated suicide. Frankly, she worries me to death. Help! Help!   5

(Signed) G. B.

375 words

DISCUSSION | APPLICATION

1. Are sentences one and two in paragraph 1 contradictory? If the husband wants to understand his wife, is it a help or a hinderance to think she is insane?

2. Is this woman sane? Is this man rational? Can this marriage be saved? In one cogent paragraph, discuss what might happen if you tuned in next week.

3. Is insanity a state of mind or a series of actions; i.e., if a person hears voices, is he insane even if he does not act on what they say to him?
4. The husband uses several general words and phrases which he fails to specify. Note two of these and be prepared to give your conception of the specific details that would verify or clarify the generalization. For example, what are the "nice things" she would rather do without? What *does a Vogue* model look like?
5. Look up the word "suppressing." Is it used correctly in the context of paragraph 5? How does the context define the word?
6. Do you empathize with the husband or the wife? Why?
7. What details of their home environment do you get directly or indirectly from the letter?

Theme Assignment

Write Mary Haworth's answer to this letter.

CENTRAL PARK
JOHN UPDIKE

On the afternoon of the first day of spring, when the gutters were still heaped high with Monday's snow but the sky itself was swept clean, we put on our galoshes and walked up the sunny side of Fifth Avenue to Central Park. There we saw: 1

Great black rocks emerging from the melting drifts, their craggy skins glistening like the backs of resurrected brontosaurs.   2

A pigeon on the half-frozen pond strutting to the edge of the ice and looking a duck in the face.   3

A policeman getting his shoe wet testing the ice.   4

Three elderly relatives trying to coax a little boy to accompany his father on a sled ride down a short but steep slope. After much balking, the boy did, and, sure enough, the sled tipped over and the father got his collar full of snow. Everybody laughed except the boy, who sniffled.   5

Four boys in black leather jackets throwing snowballs at each other. (The snow was ideally soggy, and packed hard with one squeeze.)   6

Seven men without hats.   7

Twelve snowmen, none of them intact.   8

Two men listening to the radio in a car parked outside the Zoo; Mel Allen was broadcasting the Yanks-Cardinals game, from St. Petersburg.   9

A tahr (*Hemitragus jemlaicus*) pleasantly squinting in the sunlight.   10

An aoudad absently pawing the mud and chewing.   11

A yak with its back turned.   12

Empty cages labelled "Coati," "Orang-outang," "Ocelot."   13

A father saying to his little boy, who was annoyed almost to tears by the inactivity of the seals, "Father [Father Seal, we assumed] is very tired; he worked hard all day."   14

Most of the cafeteria's out-of-doors tables occupied.   15

A pretty girl in black pants falling on them at the Wollman Memorial Rink.   16

"BILL & DORIS" carved on a tree. "REX & RITA" written in the snow.   17

Two old men playing, and six supervising, a checkers game.   18

The Michael Friedsam Foundation Merry-Go-Round, nearly empty of children but overflowing with calliope music.   19

A man on a bench near the carrousel reading, through sunglasses, a book on economics.   20

Crews of shinglers repairing the roof of the Tavern-on-the-Green.   21

A woman dropping a camera she was trying to load, the film unrolling in the slush and exposing itself. 22

A little colored boy in aviator goggles rubbing his ears and saying, "He really hurt me." "No, he didn't," his nursemaid told him. 23

The green head of Giuseppe Mazzini staring across the white softball field, unblinking, though the sun was in its eyes. 24

Water murmuring down walks and rocks and steps. A grown man trying to block one rivulet with snow. 25

Things like brown sticks nosing through a plot of cleared soil. 26

A tire track in a piece of mud far removed from where any automobiles could be. 27

Footprints around a KEEP OFF sign. 28

Two pigeons feeding each other. 29

Two showgirls, whose faces had not yet thawed the frost of their makeup, treading indignantly through the slush. 30

A plump old man saying "Chick, chick" and feeding peanuts to squirrels. 31

Many solitary men throwing snowballs at tree trunks. 32

Many birds calling to each other about how little the Ramble has changed. 33

One red mitten lying lost under a poplar tree. 34

An airplane, very bright and distant, slowly moving through the branches of a sycamore. 35

500 words

DISCUSSION | APPLICATION

John Updike's listing is composed, with the exception of the exotic zoo animals, of sights one might see in a walk through any big city's public park. It is the concrete way in which he reports them that gives tone and vivid interest. In addition to sight he exploits the sense of touch and of hearing: "The snow was ideally soggy," "Two men listening to . . . Mel Allen broadcasting." Often one key word implies the tone: squinting, supervising, overflowing, exposing, murmuring.

Theme Assignment

Write a theme using Updike as a guide. List details observed and experienced in all the senses on a walk around campus at noon or your daily drive or ride to the campus. Perhaps the activity of the teacher and your classmates during a class period might serve also. Be specific. Use concrete words. Seek active-voice verbs to impart the tone of any one item, as Updike does in this fragment: "Two showgirls, whose faces had not yet thawed the frost of their makeup."

Vocabulary:

Note how the following words are used in the context. Look up those you do not understand.

Paragraph

2. resurrected
   brontosaurs
5. balking

8. intact
30. treading

indignantly
32. solitary

A HEAD START ON BRAIN INVENTORY
ART BUCHWALD

Psychological testing in the U.S. government has come under fire from several congressional committees, who feel that asking job applicants a series of questions to gauge their personalities is an invasion of privacy. 1

The test that has come in for the most criticism is the Minnesota Multiphasic Personality Inventory, a 566-question true or false quiz. 2

As an answer to the MMPI, one of its critics has developed the North Dakota Null-Hypothesis Brain Inventory, which the reader is invited to take right now. Answer true or false:

1—I salivate at the sight of mittens.
2—If I go into the street, I'm apt to be bitten by a horse.
3—Some people never look at me.
4—Spinach makes me feel alone.
5—My sex life is A-OK.
6—When I look down from a high spot, I want to spit.
7—I like to kill mosquitoes.
8—Cousins are not to be trusted.
9—It makes me embarrassed to fall down.
10—I get nauseous from too much roller skating.
11—I think most people would cry to gain a point.
12—I cannot read or write.
13—I am bored by thoughts of death.
14—I become homicidal when people try to reason with me.
15—I would enjoy the work of a chicken flicker.
16—I am never startled by a fish.
17—My mother's uncle was a good man.
18—I don't like it when somebody is rotten.
19—People who break the law are wise guys.
20—I have never gone to pieces over the weekend.
21—I think beavers work too hard.
22—I use shoe polish to excess.
23—God is love.
24—I like mannish children.
25—I have always been disturbed by the size of Lincoln's ears.
26—I always let people get ahead of me at swimming pools.
27—Most of the time I go to sleep without saying good-by.
28—I am not afraid of picking up door knobs.
29—I believe I smell as good as most people.
30—Frantic screams make me nervous.

31—It's hard for me to say the right thing when I find myself in a room full of mice.

32—I would never tell my nickname in a crisis.

33—A wide necktie is a sign of disease.

34—As a child I was deprived of licorice.

35—I would never shake hands with a gardener.

36—My eyes are always cold.

Now for the results. If you have answered more questions true than false, you should work for the Labor Department.

If you have answered more questions false than true, you should try for the Peace Corps.

If you answered 18 true and 18 false, you should apply for work with the Voice of America.

If you refused to answer some of the questions, you might work for the White House.

If you talk about this test to anybody else, then you could never get a security clearance and you'd better stay where you are.

DISCUSSION | APPLICATION

Art Buchwald uses satire, a tone which makes fun of something in order to improve it, to attack personality tests by making up a pseudo personality test of his own. He poses questions to which the answers are obvious (5, 9, 18) and questions which are ridiculous (1, 2, 4, 28) or inane (25, 32, 33). Buchwald's approach is to emphasize the rational content of the questions in a manner that contrasts them with the irrational factors that make up an individual's "personality."

In Harlem idiom a square is a lain, a doe, a John, a mark—in other parlance
a fool, a chump, a sucker, a simpleton. A five-cornered square is a square so
square as to have an extra corner; a five-cornered square is a square's square.

Chester Himes
Pinktoes

When a word or phrase becomes part of our vocabulary, we use it
with confidence that the person we are speaking to or writing for will
understand the meaning of the word as we understand it. His definition of the word will be the same as our definition. Quite often, however, his definition will not coincide with ours. Then we consult a
dictionary. That may settle the question if the dictionary definition is
clear and the word in question quite concrete—man, woman, car,
house. If the word is abstract—truth, beauty, honor, happiness—it
may take a further exchange before each of us understands what
limits we agree upon for the word in question.

Ernest Hemingway defined courage as "grace under pressure."
In his writing he develops and illustrates this definition with graphic
descriptions of bullfighters, big-game hunters, and boxers. The mata-
dor passing the bull, the big-game hunter facing a charging lion, the
boxer moving out at the bell—each is aware of the risk he takes.
Hemingway's definition of courage concerns this conscious awareness
of risk combined with a performance that implies grace in both the
physical and the spiritual sense.

In the following paragraph a definition of "hydroplaning" clarifies the possible cause of an auto smashup. Indeed, as the context
indicates, if the writer had known the definition beforehand it's likely
the accident would have been avoided.

I was driving a straight stretch on a high-speed, limited-access
highway outside Tulsa, Oklahoma, known as the Skelly By-Pass.
Like most highways in Oklahoma Skelly is made of macadam with
a heavy oil base. In wet weather, the natives told me later, the
water and oil mix in patches. If you drive more than 50 mph you

risk a phenomenon known as hydroplaning. Your tires no longer touch the highway when this occurs, but glide along on a thin layer of water and oil. I think this is what caused the car to spin. I was doing 65 mph.

Writers strive to define their terms to assure clarity of expression. A reader must be aware of how words are being used in the particular article he is reading. If a singer's words go out over a microphone, bounce off the auditorium walls, and return to be amplified again, the resultant echoing is called "feedback." In the newspaper profession, however, feedback describes reader response to particular stories or cartoons. Radar, to cite another example, involves feedback from radio impulses which bounce off solid objects impinging on the steady flow of the impulses. A politician, on the other hand, makes a statement hinting that he has changed his position on a key issue. He then waits for the feedback—letters and telegrams, newspaper editorials, poll results on the issue—before making his position absolutely clear and definite.

When a writer uses a word with several definitions, he defines it with a specific definition or by the context in which he uses the word. A *New York Times* editorial of July 7, 1968, exemplifies a careful writer's approach to defining "ecology."

> To explain a recent multimillion-dollar grant to promote the study of ecology. . . Gordon Harrison of the Ford Foundation tells a story of pest control in Borneo.
>
> Modern chemical sprays were introduced to eliminate mosquitoes —which they did. But shortly thereafter, the roof fell in. The spray also killed a wasp that preyed on caterpillars. The caterpillars multiplied and consumed the palm-thatched roofs of Borneo's village houses.
>
> If an ecologist had been consulted, this disaster might have been averted.
>
> Ecology is a too-long-neglected science that deals with the interrelations of living things with their environment and with one another.

The opposite of "normal" is "abnormal." Warren G. Harding campaigned for the Presidency in 1920 using the slogan "I will return the country to normalcy." He won. What did his slogan mean? What does normal mean? There are nine definitions listed in the *American College Dictionary.* Look the word up in your dictionary. *Roget's Thesaurus* lists the following synonyms: average, median, typical, sane, regular, right.

"Normal" and its synonyms typify words that need definition almost every time they are used. We all know the definition of "insanity." Or do we? Is insanity a description of a mental process or a physical action? Are legal and medical definitions of insanity identical? If a person hears mysterious voices, is he insane? If the voices tell him to strike the stranger waiting at the bus stop with him, is he insane if he listens to them, but sane if he does not?

"Define your terms," cries the debater. The writer lacks the debater's opportunity to clarify after the fact. He is not present when what he has written is read. He must anticipate difficulties and clarify the meanings of key words that require definition. He must define them by the way he uses them or by direct definition.

The items that follow illustrate several aspects of the process of definition. Eugene Schoenfeld defines "speed" in terms of both its medical and nonmedical usage, with examples of results from the latter. Brigid Brophy defines "monogamy" in a way that challenges the accepted definition of the word. The erratic definition of "Catch 22" is developed by comic dialogue that constantly circles back on itself. William Faulkner defines what he believes must be the concerns of writers in our era.

Tell us about "speed." What happens to the body and brain when "meth" (crystals and tabs) is taken in small and large doses?
"Meth" (methamphetamine) is used in medicine for appetite control, mood elevation, and to raise blood pressure when indicated. The drug is usually ingested in five-milligram tablets one to three times a day. Medical reasons for injecting methamphetamine are specific and few.   1

Tolerance to the amphetamines develops rapidly and increasingly large amounts must be used to achieve the same results. When large amounts are used, blood-pressure may be raised sufficiently high to blow out a blood vessel in the brain, thus causing a stroke.   2

True addiction, as well, seems to occur. Recently, a patient in a drug-abuse clinic stated that it was harder for him to kick the "meth" habit than it was to get off heroin. At the time he was shooting up two hundred milligrams of "crystals" every two hours. He was found dead a few weeks later, apparently from an overdose.   3

An eighteen-year-old boy on methamphetamine climbed out a third-story window in Berkeley not long ago. He is now confined to a neurological institute, completely paralyzed from the effects of a broken back.   4

Both general and student hospitals are seeing increasingly greater numbers of sixteen-to-twenty-five-year-old people who have caught hepatitis from a needle used to inject methamphetamine. Neither boiling water nor soaking in alcohol will necessarily kill the hepatitis virus found in too many spikes.   5

Speed kills.   6

200 words

DISCUSSION | APPLICATION

Dr. Schoenfeld first defines "meth" in terms of its legitimate medical uses, going on to note the normal dosage and usual (ingestion) method of administration. In paragraph 2 he defines the physiological effects of large doses, first noting that the body adjusts rapidly to the drug, necessitating heavier and heavier doses to achieve the original effect. His examples in the third and fourth paragraphs define the dangers inherent in becoming addicted to "speed"

---

* Dr. Schoenfeld's column answers questions sent in by readers of the twelve underground newspapers in which it appears.

and specify the difference between normal dosage (one to three 5-milligram tablets daily) and abnormal dosage (200 milligrams every two hours). A further potential negative effect of injecting methamphetamine is noted in paragraph 5: the difficulty of sterilizing the needle ("spike") to eliminate hepatitis virus. The final paragraph is concise and final. Since he writes for the underground press, the author uses examples from the slang familiar to that audience.

Theme Assignment

One factor motivating individuals to use drugs is believed to be the desire to "escape the limitations of reality." The production of art—literature, music, painting, etc.—is sometimes motivated by a need to escape. Freud, indeed, mused upon the possibility that all art is produced in response to neurosis. Another kind of speed has been described by Ken Purdy in an essay on Grand Prix driver Masten Gregory:

> ... There have been men, sober, intelligent, expert ... who maintained that speed is the penultimate sensuous delight available to humans. ... The race driver can summon 220 miles per hour with his toe, using the power of a herd of 400 horses to move a vehicle weighing a little more than 1,000 pounds. ... The delight of hazard, the sensuous wonder of straight-line sheer speed, the swinging rhythmic pleasure of hills and curves taken flat out, and the conviction of absolute environment control (a professional peculiarity that is always, ultimately, illusory). ...

Select one of the arts or a subject of your own choice; define it in terms of "escape" and develop it with detail, illustration, and example. In addition to speed, other subjects, such as mountain climbing, and other sports or professions, may offer a topic within your range of experience. See, for example, Frank Conroy's "Finally Free" on page 177. Conroy describes his experience mastering a yo-yo: "The yo-yo represented my first organized attempt to control the outside world."

Vocabulary

Paragraph
1. tolerance
2. stroke
3. addiction
5. hepatitis
   virus

MONOGAMY
BRIGID BROPHY

There is a belief, widely held among both sexes, that whereas men are irked by monogamy women are suited to it by nature. 1

Even on the face of it, this seems fishy. After all, monogamy is what we actually have; and the social, religious and legal systems which gave it us were all invented, and until recently run, by men. I can well believe men were masochistic enough to impose monogamy on themselves as a hairshirt, but I find it a touch implausible that the hairshirt designed for the husband just happened to be a comfortable and perfectly fitting garment for the wife. 2

And indeed I suspect that, if you scrutinize the notion that women are naturally monogamous, it turns out to be based on no sounder authority than that rhyme which begins "higamus hogamus, woman is monogamous," and no more cogent evidence than a one-eyed view of biology which is in fact about as good science as 'higamus hogamus' is good Latin. 3

The 'biological' argument goes like this. A man can, if pressed for time, beget a child in twenty-five seconds flat, but a woman can't bring it to birth in less than nine months (seven if it's premature). A woman can therefore, the argument proceeds, be set up in the reproductive business and kept fully occupied at it by the expenditure of only a tiny fraction of a man's time and sexual capacity; he, on the other hand, will have so much of both those to spare that a natural impulse will drive him to distribute them among several other women. Thus, the argument concludes, a woman is so constituted by nature that she can be made happy and 'fulfilled' by the part-time attentions of one man, but if a man is not allowed to pay his attentions to several women he will be frustrated and unhappy. 4

What is one-eyed about this view is that it sees nothing in biology but reproduction. It is also remarkably ignorant of women. In point of fact, biology endows women not only with the ability and an instinct to bear children but also with the ability to experience pleasure and an instinct to seek it. Close the eye which sees nothing but reproduction and open instead the eye which sees the over-riding biological instinct towards pleasure, and you get a very different biological argument. A man is sexually excited on small provocation, satisfied quickly, and often so exhausted by the process that he falls straight asleep. A woman, on the other hand, requires long and skilled wooing if she is to be satisfied at all; when she is, she is often ready to start being wooed again within half a minute. The needs of a man can, therefore, be satisfied to exhaustion point by one woman, but she will still retain capacities and desires which will be frustrated unless she has further men to go on to. Indeed, what her biology really requires is a large number of lovers, from whom she will discard those whose love-making doesn't suit her, and will pick out and keep not one—who would be too quickly exhausted—but three or four permanent husbands. Thus, higamus hogamus, it is man who is monogamous and, hogamus higamus, woman who is, by her biological nature, polygamous.   5

There is of course no reason why we should be bound by nature and biology at all. Much of civilization consists of overcoming them and setting ourselves free to choose. Many people of both sexes choose monogamy, overcoming their biological tendency to polygamy. But it is unreasonable of society to—without good cause—impose monogamy on the ones who have not chosen it. Above all, there is no reason why, human relationships being almost infinitely various, we should impose any one pattern on all marriages—especially when it so often doesn't work.   6

At present, monogamy is the corset into which we try to fit every married couple—a process which has on so many occasions split the seams that we have had to modify the corset. There used to be a social modification which, excused by the erroneous belief that men were naturally more polygamous than women, gave the sort of glancing blow that is really an approving pat to men who broke out of monogamy but seriously and cruelly disapproved of women who did. The injustice of this 'double standard' is now pretty clear to everyone, and in its place we have introduced a legal modification of monogamy. Divorce is a device which makes polygamy permissible, but only nonsimultaneous polygamy. In practice, even this is modified. The law sometimes insists that a divorcée remain a man's wife economically though she is no longer so in name or in bed. The result is that; just as in Mohammedan countries the number of wives a man may legally have simultaneously is often whittled down in practice to the number he can support, so in Europe and the United States, under our modified monogamy, the number of ex-wives a man may legally have simultaneously is often limited to the number of those he can support.   7

Apart from this economic bias against men, divorce is much fairer than the double standard, since it is equally available, on the same grounds, to men and women. Its unfairness starts with the grounds. Divorce is an excellent solution when both married people want to say goodbye. But let them admit that that's what they both want, and English law refuses them a divorce. Often they have to pretend an adultery—which is, legally considered, the best and, rationally considered, the worst conceivable grounds for divorce. Nothing could be more wasteful of that rare and rarely beautiful quality, married love, than that a marriage should break simply because one of the partners would like to enlarge it by co-opting a third.   8

To be sure, the whole business of love and people's behaviour under its stress is irrational in itself; but that is all the more reason to be as rational as we can in coping with our most irrational area. Sexual jealousy is one of the most painful emotions on earth. But in coping with it society licenses us to indulge in a two-year-old's tantrum. To divorce your mate because he has mated with someone else is to cut off your nose to spite the face you suddenly feel holds less attraction for him; it is to act on the principle that no bread is better than half a loaf. In some countries an unwritten law even permits the slighted spouse to kill the adulterous one. Here you may merely make him dead as far as you are concerned, by cutting him out of your life by divorce. This is probably the most perverse approach you could make to what, if you love him, you want, which is to have him living, and with you. 9

The obvious remedy is at least respectabilised and for preference legalised polygamy. No one in his senses could suppose it would be easy or painless to work. But it would give less pain than either of the other courses: to stand on your full monogamous rights and insist that the person you love forgo the company of someone he loves; or to avail yourself of the legal modification to monogamy and insist on yourself forgoing the company of the person you love. 10

1,200 words

DISCUSSION | APPLICATION

1. Is the tone serious? Satirical? Ironic?
2. Do you agree with the author's definition of "monogamy"?
3. The author takes a familiar term and imposes on it a unique set of attitudes that challenge the usual view of monogamy. Are there weaknesses in her position?
4. Does the "biological argument" introduced make logical sense? Why or why not?

Theme Assignments

1. Select a subject about which there is general agreement. Write an extended definition which gives it a unique twist. For example, the laws that require regular attendance of adolescents in high school are widely accepted. They are intended for the adolescents' own good. But do they violate the constitutional rights of these students by taking away their freedom without due process of law?
2. Base your theme on one of the following quotations. Use the quotation as your general statement and clarify it with specific details of your own.

Woman would be more charming if we could fall into her arms without falling into her hands.

Ambrose Bierce

I am glad that I am not a man, for then I should have to marry a woman.

Madame de Stael

Women are shy and shame prevents them from refusing a man.

Irish proverb

Vocabulary

Paragraph

1. irked

2. masochistic
   implausible

3. scrutinize
   authority
   cogent

4. proceeds
   reproductive
   expenditure

capacity

5. exhausted
   wooing
   polygamous

6. infinitely
   various

7. modification
   erroneous
   non-simultaneous
   whittled-down

8. bias
   adultery
   conceivable

9. behavior
   stress
   jealousy
   coping
   unwritten law
   perverse

CATCH-22
JOSEPH HELLER

It was a horrible joke, but Doc Daneeka didn't laugh until Yossarian came to him one mission later and pleaded again, without any real expectation of success, to be grounded. Doc Daneeka snickered once and was soon immersed in problems of his own, which included Chief White Halfoat, who had been challenging him all that morning to Indian wrestle, and Yossarian, who decided right then and there to go crazy.

"You're wasting your time," Doc Daneeka was forced to tell him.

"Can't you ground someone who's crazy?"

"Oh, sure. I have to. There's a rule saying I have to ground anyone who's crazy."

"Then why don't you ground me? I'm crazy. Ask Clevinger."

"Clevinger? Where is Clevinger? You find Clevinger and I'll ask him."

"Then ask any of the others. They'll tell you how crazy I am."

"They're crazy."

"Then why don't you ground them?"

"Why don't they ask me to ground them?"

"Because they're crazy, that's why."

"Of course they're crazy," Doc Daneeka replied. "I just told you they're crazy, didn't I? And you can't let crazy people decide whether you're crazy or not, can you?"

Yossarian looked at him soberly and tried another approach. "Is Orr crazy?"

"He sure is," Doc Daneeka said.

"Can you ground him?"

"I sure can. But first he has to ask me to. That's part of the rule."

"Then why doesn't he ask you to?"

"Because he's crazy," Doc Daneeka said. "He has to be crazy to keep flying combat missions after all the close calls he's had. Sure, I can ground Orr. But first he has to ask me to."

"That's all he has to do to be grounded?"

"That's all. Let him ask me."

"And then you can ground him?" Yossarian asked.

"No. Then I can't ground him."

"You mean there's a catch?"

"Sure there's a catch," Doc Daneeka replied. "Catch-22. Anyone who wants to get out of combat duty isn't really crazy."

There was only one catch and that was Catch-22, which specified that a concern for one's own safety in the face of dangers that were real and immediate was the process of a rational mind. Orr was crazy and could be grounded. All he had to do was ask; and as soon as he did, he would no longer be crazy and would have to fly more missions. Orr would be crazy to fly more missions and sane if he didn't, but if he was sane he had to fly them. If he flew them he was crazy and didn't have to; but if he didn't want to he was sane and had to. Yossarian was moved very deeply by the absolute simplicity of this clause of Catch-22 and let out a respectful whistle.

"That's some catch, that Catch-22," he observed.

"It's the best there is," Doc Daneeka agreed.

Yossarian saw it clearly in all its spinning reasonableness. There was an elliptical precision about its perfect pairs of parts that was graceful and shocking, like good modern art, and at times Yossarian wasn't quite sure that he saw it at all. . . .

550 words

DISCUSSION | APPLICATION

1. Does Heller's definition of "Catch-22" remind you of any comic routines you have seen on television?
2. "Catch-22" is a type of double-talk. Its language is evasive and ambiguous. It is an extension of the gag "Heads I win, tails you lose." Whatever Yossarian does, he loses. Why?
3. What is being satirized in this dialogue?
4. Many popular song lyrics employ a variation of the kind of double-talk or double meaning used by Heller, "Lucy in the sky with diamonds," "everybody's gotta get stoned." Are there any current examples? What is the purpose of lyrics of this kind?

Theme Assignment

Write a nonsense dialogue of your own or three nonsense sentences. They may actually say something cogent, but appear at first glance not to; or they may appear to say something, but upon analysis say nothing. Here are a few examples.

We have met the enemy and they is us.

Walt Kelly

My love is a faded pastel.

Song lyric

Self-knowledge is bad-news.

John Barth

Knowledge keeps like fish.

Lord Whitehead

Given a momentum, numerous angles will develop.
Given an angle, a momentum will develop.

He mistook the exotic wiggle of an erratic woman for the writhe of an erotic wench.

To the inertial all things are overt.

Select a word or phrase in common usage, such as intellectual, generation gap, permissive, longhair, pornography, grunt, and define it in a paragraph or theme.

Vocabulary

rational
reasonableness
elliptical
precision

NOBEL PRIZE AWARD SPEECH
WILLIAM FAULKNER

I feel that this award was not made to me as a man but to my work—a life's work in the agony and sweat of the human spirit, not for glory and least of all for profit, but to create out of the materials of the human spirit something which did not exist before. So this award is only mine in trust. It will not be difficult to find a dedication for the money part of it commensurate with the purpose and significance of its origin. But I would like to do the same with the acclaim too, by using this moment as a pinnacle from which I might be listened to by the young men and women already dedicated to the same anguish and travail, among whom is already that one who will some day stand here where I am standing. 1

Our tragedy today is a general and universal physical fear so long sustained by now that we can even bear it. There are no longer problems of the spirit. There is only the question: When will I be blown up? Because of this, the young man or woman writing today has forgotten the problems of the human heart in conflict with itself which alone can make good writing because only that is worth writing about, worth the agony and the sweat. 2

He must learn them again. He must teach himself that the basest of all things is to be afraid; and, teaching himself that, forget it forever, leaving no room in his workshop for anything but the old verities and truths of the heart, the old universal truths lacking which any story is ephemeral and doomed—love and honor and pity and pride and compassion and sacrifice. Until he does so, he labors under a curse. He writes not of love but of lust, of defeats in which nobody loses anything of value, of victories without hope and, worst of all, without pity or compassion. His griefs grieve on no universal bones, leaving no scars. He writes not of the heart but of the glands. 3

Until he relearns these things, he will write as though he stood alone and watched the end of man. I decline to accept the end of man. It is easy enough to say that man is immortal simply because he will endure; that when the last ding-dong of doom has clanged and faded from the last worthless rock hanging tideless in the last red and dying evening, that even then there will still be one more sound: that of his puny inexhaustible voice, still talking. I refuse to accept this. I believe that man will not merely endure: he will prevail. He is immortal, not because he alone among creatures has an inexhaustible voice but because he has a soul, a spirit capable of compassion and sacrifice and endurance. The poet's, the writer's, duty is to write about these things. It is his privilege to help man endure by lifting his heart, by reminding him of the courage and honor and hope and pride and compassion and pity and sacrifice which have been the glory of his past. The poet's voice need not merely be the record of man, it can be one of the props, the pillars to help him endure and prevail. 4

700 words

DISCUSSION | APPLICATION

Paragraph 2: The only theme worth writing about is the theme of "the human heart in conflict with itself." "Heart" is used as a metaphor. A metaphor is a figure of speech that establishes a direct comparison between one thing and another. What does Faulkner's comparison imply in this context? What does this statement tell you of Faulkner's view of the human condition?

Theme Assignment

Write a definition of one of the following: ". . . courage and honor and pride and compassion and pity and sacrifice which have been the glory of (man's) past." Give an example of a person or an act that specifies your definition.

Vocabulary

Paragraph	ephemeral	lust
1. dedication	verities	4. immortal
commensurate	3. basest	puny
origin	sustained	inexhaustible
pinnacle	2. tragedy	prevail
anguish	doomed	endure
travail	compassion	

ALL Posters 50¢

Any man who hates kids can't be all bad.
W. C. Fields

How does a director shooting a film in New York City identify the locale? He opens the film with a shot of the Statue of Liberty, the New York skyline, the Empire State Building, or shots of all three. In writing, identification is a way of explaining who or what something is. Politicians today seek to identify themselves so the voters will know who they are, what they stand for, and what their name is. It is said that several candidates whose last name happened to be Kennedy won minor posts in Massachusetts simply because many voters identified them with the family of President John F. Kennedy.

In an essay on Ted Williams, John Updike identifies him as "being known to the headlines as TED, KID, SPLINTER, THUMPER, TW, and . . . MISTER WONDERFUL."

Luther "Wimpy" Lassiter has won more major pocket billiard tournaments in the last five years than any other player. He is also one of the more colorful sports figures playing today, as the following identification essay shows. Lassiter had just won a major tournament after shooting steadily from 6 P.M. until 4 A.M.

As the photographers' bulbs popped and the first hint of dawn glinted outside the windows, someone asked the new champion if he were tired.

"Great guns," the silvery-maned Senator Dirksen of pocket billiards remarked, "I was just getting my stroke grooved."

Moments before his winning dawn run, Lassiter had been sprawled in his seat, straddle-legged, tie loosened, looking wilted, exhausted, and an eyelash away from sleep. This is his customary pose when his opponent is shooting.

The instant the opponent misses, the sagging figure slouches out of his chair and arrives sharp-eyed and alert at the table. He shoots at medium tempo and steady pace that seldom vary. As he lines up a shot and grooves his stroke, the shaggy brows move up and down, his eyes going back and forth from cue ball to object ball as many as fifteen times on a crucial shot and seldom less than eight times on a routine shot.

Lassiter, tagged "Wimpy" many years ago because of his fondness for hamburgers, is a true eccentric. With Walt Whitman he might well say, "Do I contradict myself? Very well then, I contradict myself."

"I've got this turrible (sic) gas pain on my stomach," he complains, "and I'm so infected with the sinus that it saps my energy."

"The battle is won in the home stretch," Lassiter blandly explains moments later. "Endurance. That's my long suit. The longer I play the better I get."

Wimpy exudes a friendly "old plantation" air and relates to the audience more as an actor than an athlete. He talks to the fans while he plays, and his sense of timing and drama would warm a script writer's heart. When he arrives within two or three shots of victory, he likes to pause for a moment to focus the attention of his audience.

Then he may give a rebel yell and allow as how he is about to "whomp in that little red and that dirty yellow and that slippery six ball."

Other favored Lassiter expressions are "Goodness gracious," "Lordy," "I do declare," and "My, my."

His between-shot repertoire includes cracking his knuckles, shaking hands with himself, snapping his galluses, smoothing the table in front of a pocket and then shooting a ball in a different pocket, kicking the table lightly, and clearing imaginary debris from the green.

In the following selections Paul Goodman identifies a "useful job." James Reston identifies Joe Namath's dilemma. John Riley writes about a student identified as "The Black Bag." Claude Brown explains the relation between his identity as a man and his ability to use the slang word "baby."

A USEFUL JOB
PAUL GOODMAN

Consider a likely useful job. A youth who is alert and willing but not "verbally intelligent"—perhaps he has quit high school at the eleventh grade (the median), as soon as he legally could—chooses for auto mechanic. That's a good job, familiar to him, he often watched them as a kid. It's careful and dirty at the same time. In a small garage it's sociable; one can talk to the customers (girls). You please people in trouble by fixing their cars, and a man is proud to see rolling out on its own the car that limped in behind the tow truck. The pay is as good as the next fellow's, who is respected.   1

So our young man takes this first-rate job. But what when he then learns that the cars have a built-in obsolescence, that the manufacturers do not want them to be repaired or repairable? They have lobbied a law that requires them to provide spare parts for only five years (it used to be ten). Repairing the new cars is often a matter of cosmetics, not mechanics; and the repairs are pointlessly expensive—a tail fin might cost $150. The insurance rates therefore double and treble on old and new cars both. Gone are the days of keeping the jalopies in good shape, the artist-work of a proud mechanic. But everybody is paying for foolishness, for in fact the new models are only trivially superior; the whole thing is a sell.   2

It is hard for the young man now to maintain his feelings of justification, sociability, serviceability. It is not surprising if he quickly becomes cynical and time-serving, interested in a fast buck. And so, on the notorious *Reader's Digest* test, the investigators (coming in with a disconnected coil wire) found that 63 per cent of mechanics charged for repairs they didn't make, and lucky if they didn't also take out the new fuel pump and replace it with a used one (65 per cent of radio repair shops, but *only* 49 per cent of watch repairmen "lied, overcharged, or gave false diagnoses").   3

There is an hypothesis that an important predisposition to juvenile delinquency is the combination of low verbal intelligence with high manual intelligence, delinquency giving a way of self-expression where other avenues are blocked by lack of schooling. A lad so endowed might well apply himself to the useful trade of mechanic.   4

400 words

DISCUSSION | APPLICATION
1. Goodman begins his essay with a specific example-definition of a useful job. In the second paragraph he demonstrates how dissatisfaction with such a job may develop. How does paragraph 3 relate to the first two paragraphs?
2. Is the point he makes in paragraph 4 valid? Why or why not?

Assignment

Describe in detail a useful job you have held or are familiar with. Note Goodman's definition which specifies the job of auto mechanic and how these specifications become, by implication, the attributes of a useful job. One aspect is that the job itself should give satisfaction over and above the pay one receives for performing it.

Vocabulary

Paragraph
1. sociable
2. obsolescence
   lobbied
   cosmetics

   trivially
3. cynical
   time-serving
   notorious
   diagnosis

4. hypothesis
   predisposition
   verbal intelligence
   manual intelligence

JOE NAMATH, THE NEW ANTI-HERO
JAMES RESTON

One of the most interesting symbols of America today is Joe Namath, the quarterback of the New York football Jets. Joe is not only in tune with the rebellious attitude of the young, but he doubles it. He defies both the people who hate play-boys and the people who hate bully-boys. He is something special: a long-haired hard-hat, the anti-hero of the sports world.   1

In part, he is a familiar American type—the poor boy out of the Pennsylvania hills via the University of Alabama who conquered the big city and was corrupted by it. When he came to New York a few years ago, he was a story straight out of Victorian melodrama. He had the gifts of courage and timing.   2

The Gift of Timing

He could wait until the uttermost split-second, while his receivers were driving and faking for that extra step on the defenders, and then throw with geometric accuracy, long or short, bullet or lob, to the primary or secondary target, just before he was buried by the charging front four of the opposition.   3

This impressed New York; it was Hemingway's definition of courage: grace under pressure. At the start Joe was a character, almost a caricature out of O'Henry's stories about the country yokel who wowed sophisticated Manhattan, but he is now repeating the Thomas Wolfe theme of the Southern boy who takes over the big town and is defeated by success.   4

Ends and Means

He is a significant symbol because he is following the contemporary notion that anything that succeeds is right. It is easy to understand why he does so. Sport is no longer sport but Big Business. The owners of the professional football and baseball teams are selling their wares, primarily to television and the advertisers. They are extending their seasons, and merchandising their stars.   5

Pro football, which is a cool-weather game, now starts in August. Pro baseball, which is a hot-weather game, now starts in the cold and rain of the capricious spring. Pro basketball, which is an indoor winter sport, now runs from late summer to April. Everybody is out for the Big Buck, and the television contracts are king.   6

It is easy to be neutral in the present fight between the sports owners and the sports performers. Both are greedy, and both are caught up in the commercial system, and both may very well be destroyed in the struggle.   7

Joe Namath illustrates the point. To the kids, he is still a hero. He defied all the old-fashioned rules. He didn't work with the "team." He reported late for practice. He was not like the old moral sports heroes—the Reverend Bob Richards arguing on television that sports, religion and the breakfast food for champions were all the same thing. He was not even like Babe Ruth or Walter Hagen, who tried to conceal their alcoholic adventures. He ran his bars and his football on the same track and at the same time, defying all the old assumptions and moralities, and now all he has to prove is that it will work.   8

The guess here is that it won't. Pro football is too tough, too dependent on teamwork. The owners of pro football can be greedy, but the stars like Namath have to prove themselves to their teammates and to their audience in the stands and on television.   9

The Basic Test

The anti-hero has to be even better than the hero. The owners don't have to prove themselves to the fans, but the quarterback does. He is not like a President, who can operate behind the scenes. He has to produce results in the open, and this is Joe Namath's problem.   10

He is now trying to work within the old hero system, and also within the commercial system. He is challenging the greed of the owners but being greedy himself, maybe he can do it. But he will have to be as good as he was at his best, or even better. For he is insisting that he can do what he likes and is better than his teammates and his opposition, and no anti-hero so far has been able to break all the old rules and prove his point.   11

750 words

DISCUSSION | APPLICATION

1. James Reston traces Joe Namath's rise (fall?) to his present identity as a "symbol . . . the new anti-hero" with various tags of identity: ". . . a typical American type—the poor boy," "the country yokel," and "the Southern boy." In paragraph 5 he suggests that Namath ". . . is following the contemporary notion that anything that succeeds is right." Is that a contemporary notion? Can you think of current examples that illustrate the point?
2. Does Reston imply that Namath is the only one in pro football who is "out for the Big Buck"?
3. Does the author weaken his position by noting, in paragraph 8, that athletes in the past (Babe Ruth) violated "the old assumptions and moralities"? Why is Babe Ruth remembered as a lovable clown who could hit the ball a mile rather than as a heavy drinker? Is it because the style and technique of sports reporting have changed or because present day athletes have changed?

Theme Assignment

1. Select a current "hero" and/or "anti-hero" and develop detail, illustration, and example that will identify him as such. Among many possibilities are Norman Rockwell, Frank Lloyd Wright, Rip Torn, George C. Scott, Marilyn Monroe, Ernest Hemingway, Muhammad Ali, Norman Mailer, Elliot Gould, and Dustin Hoffman. Write a 300- to 500-word theme on your subject.
2. Attack Reston's position by writing a 300- to 500-word theme defending Joe Namath in which you identify him as a true hero. Reston notes, for example, that Namath is considered a hero to the young because he "defied all the old-fashioned rules." You might specify instances illustrating Namath's defiance. He obviously never accepted the "humble" role that many pro athletes assume. Before the 1969 Super Bowl game, Namath proclaimed himself the number one quarterback and "guaranteed" to lead his underdog New York Jets team to victory. He did.

Vocabulary

Paragraph
1. anti-hero
2. Victorian melodrama
4. caricature
   sophisticated
8. assumptions

SAGA OF THE BAREFOOT BAG ON CAMPUS
JOHN RILEY

At the beginning of the academic term at Oregon State University this year, the students in a ten-week speech course entitled "Persuasion" noticed right away that one among them was different. He wore a black cotton cloth bag that covered him entirely and he sat, Oriental-style, in the back of the room, well away from his more conventional fellows. When his turn came to introduce himself and explain what he expected from the course, he begged off, saying only "I prefer not to."   1

Professor Charles Goetzinger assured the suspicious class that "The Bag" was indeed a bona fide, full-fledged student who had simply asked to attend the course in that outfit. "I'm enough of a nut," the professor explained, "to try anything once."   2

For the first several weeks The Bag was seldom mentioned in the class, which met three times a week. Then one day a student delivered a required three-minute oration to demonstrate the powers of persuasion that he was supposed to be learning. His theme: The Bag doesn't bother me at all, no siree, not one bit. No, it doesn't bother *me*, he kept saying.   3

In commenting on his speech, the other students agreed that they had been persuaded: The Bag didn't bother him. But then it came out: The Bag bothered the hell out of *them*. One freshman followed The Bag as he walked from the classroom and tried to paste a "Kick Me" label on him. In a later session, The Bag sat opposite the offending freshman and stared at him intently through the black cloth. In horror, the freshman screamed: "Get away from me!"—and probed at The Bag with an umbrella.   4

Word that a black bag was attending the course spread rapidly through the university and various attempts were made to find out who was inside. (The speech department guarded the class roster like a state secret.) The OSU newspaper, the *Daily Barometer*, defended The Bag's right to be a bag. Gawkers began to cluster about the building before and after class. One day two class members followed The Bag on foot across the campus after class. The Bag was alone, and he felt trapped. But he kept his head and slowly walked four blocks to the Chemistry-Physics Building. He entered; went upstairs; they followed. The Bag picked an office at random, hoping it would be unoccupied at the lunch hour. It was. The Bag calmly closed the door after him, and the sleuths, suspecting that The Bag might be a physics professor, gave up and went to lunch.   5

As the weeks went by, department heads, deans and graduate students began dropping in on the speech class. Some professors sniped at Goetzinger in their own classes. One social scientist chided him for not introducing proper "sociological controls" in the "experiment," if indeed it was an experiment, but admitted that he would never allow such an exercise in his own classes, with or without controls. 6

Signs appeared that opinion toward having The Bag in the class was beginning to change. People sounded nicer when they talked to him, and he began to respond. He took to sitting in chairs like the other students. He spoke more. That was a mistake: a silent mystery was all right, but a talking bag required some getting used to. And furthermore, The Bag talked with a New England accent. 7

The class began almost to feel a certain nostalgia for the silent and presumably "safe" bag who had delivered his first three-and-a-half-minute "speech" merely by standing before them without uttering a word. 8

Near the end of the term reporters and television crews descended upon Speech 113. One day the class found itself in a shooting match with no less than three TV crews. The students felt that the invasion was endangering the delicate understanding that had flowered between them and The Bag. Most of them stalked out and reassembled in Goetzinger's office. There a wonderful thing happened to the class—and to The Bag. Later, The Bag explained it to me: 9

"Everybody seemed suddenly to unite in fear of a common thing. It was beautiful. We were just all talking, and I forgot I was inside the bag. It was the first time I forgot. I just shot my mouth off. And after I stopped I said to myself, 'Hey, wait a minute, I'm still in the bag.' And I felt that the rest of the class for a moment had forgotten it too. I can't really see people's facial reactions through the cloth. Maybe it was mental telepathy." 10

At the next class session Goetzinger, The Bag and the rest of the class hashed over the meaning of it all. The students found themselves admitting that their hostility had turned to respect and protectiveness. As for The Bag, he felt humble: "I'm not Jesus Christ or anything. I'm just one of you in a bag." 11

This moved one student to make a confession. In the course of trying to persuade his fraternity brothers that The Bag was no joke, he himself had secretly doubted The Bag's motives. 12

"For some reason he seemed to be in *two bags*," the student explained, as though that explained anything. 13

At this, Professor Goetzinger scooted across the class, shoved his face in front of the student and shouted, "Do you feel any empathy for what this poor man felt six weeks ago?" 14

"If my *mother* tried to take that bag off him," the student replied, "I'd beat the hell out of her." 15

The discussion then turned to whether they really wanted to know who was inside. With a show of hands, all indicated that they did not need to know his identity. The Bag had persuaded them to accept him on his own terms. When the bell rang, they rose and without a word between them formed a phalanx to escort him through a crowd of students who had been hooting at him through a window. 16

Having silently convinced his classmates to accept him, The Bag 17
seemed assured of a passing mark in "Persuasion."

"Everybody's in some kind of a bag," he explains. "I just wear mine 18
on the outside."

1,200 words

DISCUSSION | APPLICATION

1. What motivated the student who gave the speech "The Bag doesn't bother me at all"?
2. What did "The Bag" communicate in his first speech?
3. Would "The Bag" bother you? Would the external appearance of any student bother you? Why or why not?
4. Have you ever reacted in a negative manner to a person you know nothing about except the visual aspects of his dress and appearance? Has anyone ever reacted that way to you?
5. Why did "The Bag" elicit such fear from the umbrella poker? Is the cause of this fear external or internal?

Theme Assignment

1. "Everybody's in some kind of a bag. I just wear mine on the outside." Explain the quotation and identify some of the "bags" you or those you know have been in.
2. Relate the following quotation to "The Bag."

   The question of color . . . operates to hide the graver questions of the self.
   James Baldwin

3. Develop a theme detailing aspects of your own being that would identify you to someone whom you have neither seen nor spoken to.

Vocabulary

Paragraph	8. nostalgia	phalanx
5. gawkers	11. mental telepathy	hooting
sleuths		

The first time I heard the expression "baby" used by one cat to address another was up at Warwick in 1951. Gus Jackson used it. The term had a hip ring to it, a real colored ring. The first time I heard it, I knew right away I had to start using it. It was like saying, "Man, look at me. I've got masculinity to spare." It was saying at the same time to the world, "I'm one of the hippest cats, one of the most uninhibited cats on the scene. I can say 'baby' to another cat, and he can say 'baby' to me, and we can say it with strength in our voices." If you could say it, this meant that you really had to be sure of yourself, sure of your masculinity.   1

It seemed that everybody in my age group was saying it. The next thing I knew, older guys were saying it. Then just about everybody in Harlem was saying it, even the cats who weren't so hip. It became just one of those things.   2

The real hip thing about the "baby" term was that it was something that only colored cats could say the way it was supposed to be said. I'd heard gray boys trying it, but they couldn't really do it. Only colored cats could give it the meaning that we all knew it had without ever mentioning it —the meaning of black masculinity.   3

Before the Muslims, before I'd heard about the Coptic or anything like that, I remember getting high on the corner with a bunch of guys and watching the chicks go by, fine little girls, and saying, "Man, colored people must be somethin' else!"   4

Somebody'd say, "Yeah. How about that? All those years, man, we was down on the plantation in those shacks, eating just potatoes and fatback and chitterlin's and greens, and look at what happened. We had Joe Louises and Jack Johnsons and Sugar Ray Robinsons and Henry Armstrongs, all that sort of thing."   5

Somebody'd say, "Yeah, man. Niggers must be some real strong people who just can't be kept down. When you think about it, that's really something great. Fatback, chitterlin's, greens, and Joe Louis. Negroes are some beautiful people. Uh-huh. Fatback, chitterlin's, greens, and Joe Louis . . . and beautiful black bitches."   6

Cats would come along with this "baby" thing. It was something that went over strong in the fifties with the jazz musicians and the hip set, the boxers, the dancers, the comedians, just about every set in Harlem. I think everybody said it real loud because they liked the way it sounded. It was always, "Hey, baby. How you doin', baby?" in every phase of the Negro hip life. As a matter of fact, I went to a Negro lawyer's office once, and he said, "Hey, baby. How you doin', baby?" I really felt at ease, really felt that we had something in common. I imagine there were many people in Harlem who didn't feel they had too much in common with the Negro professionals, the doctors and lawyers and dentists and ministers. I know I didn't. But to hear one of these people greet you with the street thing, the "Hey, baby"— and he knew how to say it—you felt as though you had something strong in common.

7

I suppose it's the same thing that almost all Negroes have in common, the fatback, chitterlings, and greens background. I suppose that regardless of what any Negro in American might do or how high he might rise in social status, he still has something in common with every other Negro. I doubt that they're many, if any, gray people who could ever say "baby" to a Negro and make him feel that "me and this cat have got something going, something strong going."

8

In the fifties, when "baby" came around, it seemed to be the prelude to a whole new era in Harlem. It was the introduction to the era of black reflection. A fever started spreading. Perhaps the strong rising of the Muslim movement is something that helped to sustain or even usher in this era.

9

I remember that in the early fifties, cats would stand on the corner and talk, just shooting the stuff, all the street-corner philosophers. Sometimes, it was a common topic—cats talking about gray chicks—and somebody might say something like, "Man, what can anybody see in a gray chick, when colored chicks are so fine; they got so much soul." This was the coming of the "soul" thing too.

10

"Soul" had started coming out of the churches and the nightclubs into the streets. Everybody started talking about "soul" as though it were something that they could see on people or a distinct characteristic of colored folks.

11

Cats would say things like, "Man, gray chicks seem so stiff." Many of them would say they couldn't talk to them or would wonder how a cat who was used to being so for real with a chick could see anything in a gray girl. It seemed as though the mood of the day was turning toward the color thing.

12

Everybody was really digging themselves and thinking and saying in their behavior, in every action, "Wow! Man, it's a beautiful thing to be colored." Everybody was saying, "Oh, the beauty of me! Look at me. I'm colored. And look at us. Aren't we beautiful?"

13

1,200 words

DISCUSSION | APPLICATION

1. Who are the "gray people"?
2. Why does Brown associate masculinity with the ability to refer to another as "baby"?
3. The description of the word "baby" in the first two paragraphs is typical of

one kind of change that occurs in language. What are some slang words currently in use on campus? What are some slang words that were popular when you were in high school that have disappeared or taken on new meanings?

4. How do the direct quotations help to characterize the speaker and the scene?

5. Why doesn't the word "nigger" as Brown uses it (paragraph 6) have the derogatory quality and tone it would in other contexts?

6. Paragraph 12. Interpret the meaning of "a cat who was used to being so for real."

Theme Assignments

1. Brown defines his sense of solidarity as a member of a distinct group in terms of the language and experience common to that group. Write an essay in which you identify yourself with a group——a team, club, neighborhood, ethnic group, etc.——in terms of the sense of solidarity and community you feel as part of the group.

2. Use one of the following quotations as a general statement which you then develop in specific detail.

Be not conformed to this world.

Amish precept

To understand and help someone you must first accept him. To accept others you must first accept yourself.

Jung

Everybody's youth is a dream, a form of chemical madness.

F. Scott Fitzgerald

Vocabulary

Paragraph	9. prelude	11. distinct
1. uninhibited	era	characteristic
8. chitterlings	reflection	12. mood
status	sustain	

> I don't care to be associated with a club that would
> have a person like myself as a member.
> Groucho Marx

To recall the most effective teacher in your experience is to recall a teacher who continually clarified his lectures with examples and illustrations. Groucho Marx indicates his rather stringent requirements for an acceptable club by citing an example of the kind of member (himself) he would consider undesirable. The following nonsense verse illustrates the state of mind of the speaker.

> As I was going up the stair
> I saw a man who wasn't there.
> He wasn't there again today,
> I wish to God he'd go away.

The apt illustration or example will be representative of a type, an idea, an approach, or a person. Psychiatrist Robert Coles in his book *Children in Crisis* illustrates the sense of isolation and fear felt by Ruby, six years old and black, as she took part in the integration of a school in New Orleans. He cites examples of drawings made by Ruby in which the figure representing herself is drawn much smaller than figures representing her white classmates. They were, of course, actually about the same size as Ruby. In addition, Ruby's figure in the drawings had very large ears but hardly any mouth at all. What do these details imply about the experience Ruby was living through? Clearly they imply that she listened intently but spoke hardly at all in the presence of her white classmates.

Justin McCarthy's recollection from Studs Terkel's *Hard Times* is itself illustrative of life during the depression of the 1930s. It defines "speed-up" by example and illustrates in its details working conditions and employer-employee relations.

Justin McCarthy quit college in 1933. He was working at a Ford assembly plant in an industrial suburb, near Chicago.

"I sandpapered all the right-hand fenders. I was paid $5 a day. The parts were brought in from the River Rouge plant in Detroit. When I went to work in January, we were turning out 232 cars a day. When I was fired, four months later, we were turning out 535. Without any extra help and no increase in pay. It was the famous Ford Speed-up.

"The gates were locked when you came in at eight o'clock in the morning. They weren't opened again until five o'clock in the evening. People brought their own lunch. No commissary wagons were permitted on the grounds. Nobody bothered to tell me. So I didn't eat that first day. You were supposed to buy your own gloves. Nobody bothered to tell me that, either. Imagine my hands at five o'clock that first day.

"I was aware of men in plain clothes being around the plant, and the constant surveillance. I didn't learn till later these were the men of Ford's service department. Many of them, ex-cons.

"If you wanted to go to the toilet, you had to have permission of the foreman. He had to find a substitute for you on the assembly line, who could sandpaper those two right fenders as they went by. If he couldn't right away, you held it. (Laughs.)

"If you didn't punch that clock at 8:00, if you came in at 8:02, you were docked one hour's pay. There wasn't any excuse. If you did this two or three times, you got fired.

"I made the mistake of telling the foreman I had enrolled at Northwestern University night school. He said, 'Mr. Ford isn't paying people to go to college. You're through.' "

Jeremy Larner illustrates below what it might be like to have the physical attributes and natural talent of a basketball star of the caliber of Lew Alcindor. Donald Barthelme's short story "Game" deals with the games people and nations play. Bruno Bettelheim cites another set of circumstances and responses that might have saved the life of Anne Frank who died in a Nazi concentration camp. Gordon Parks depicts his developing sense of his own mortality as he recalls examples from his childhood confrontations with death.

HECTOR WARMS UP
JEREMY LARNER

None of the others was there, and as he bounced up the iron steps from the lockerroom to the gym floor, the separate clanks echoed lonely metal sounds. He could feel his toes pressing him upward and the arch of his foot.   1

He scooped up a ball and stood there stretching it over his head, whirling it in one hand then another with his arms stiff as semaphores. Leaning over backwards to wake up his back muscles, then bouncing the ball very low and fast off the floor in little figure eights around his feet.   2

He liked to take some shots all alone. He had learned to shoot alone on the darkening California concrete long after the others had gone home to supper, on into the dark, when his red cat's eyes needed no help but the moon's. Silver moonshine—the ghostly silver cords flipping as an invisible ghost ball passed through.   3

He wasn't really warm yet—he was lazy, basically lazy, and needed the press of others to warm him. It was mostly for his fingers that he came up early by himself—his fingers had a special something with the ball and they had to meet each other privately. They had to say hello and feel each other out. When Hector was in a hurry, he knew he was chancing it might be no go.   4

He took a couple of stretchy hook shots, without aiming—one with the right, one with the left hand. The cuffs of the sweatsuit felt tight and sweet on his wrists. But the bandage threw him off balance. *Damn:* he resented it like a defense that hung on his back all night. *A big train pulls so many passengers. . . .*   5

"Chug chug chug chug chug chug chug chug chug chug," he said to himself, as he tried a series of short jump-shots. He let the ball bounce away, and cupping his hands made a locomotive whistle, beautifully shrill & enormous in the high-beamed field house.   6

He stood right under the backboard and tossed up hundreds of lay-ups on both sides of the basket and from the front, hardly ever bored. It was a constant wonderment to him how infinite were the ways and angles of bouncing the ball off the backboard and into the basket. And his fingers were flexing. Occasionally he would spin the ball like a globe on one fingertip, then let it roll down the arm and across his back and out into his other hand. He jumped easily off his feet and stuffed the ball down through the basket, then went back again to lay-ups. Frequently he missed, to his fascination. After about two hundred lay-ups he began bouncing the ball high off the backboard and tapping it back into the basket. There was no noise: he cupped his hand and cushioned each ball on his fingertips as he tapped it through. Everything depended on the feel in his fingertips and the control when his wrist straightened. And his timing: to get the ball at exactly the right time & place.

7

He could see right through the glass backboard and into the vacant stands behind. It looked almost as though the ball were stopped by an invisible hand that took his pass and made the score. But Hector did not indulge that kind of illusion; he had made the play so many times the board was real to him whether he saw it or not, real as the ball which he dribbled and never looked at while dribbling so as to be constantly ready for the shift or the shot or the pass. He saw through the board to the stands and the shadows, but he knew the board was there, and he kept right on working at it and getting better and enjoying getting better.

8

While he was working on his tips his teammates began to drift in and collect at the basket at the opposite end of the floor. It was their custom to stay clear of Hector till he was ready.

9

Suddenly Hector knew that Goose Jefferson was at the bottom of the stairway.

10

He stood waiting with his back to the stairwell for two seconds, then threw the ball over his head so that it took one long bounce into the corner of the gym and would have fallen straight down the stairs had not Goose Jefferson emerged at just that instant, caught the ball without surprise, and dribbled straight over to lay it in the basket.

11

Goose and Hector passed the ball back and forth and took lazy shots at the basket. Goose had the way of the great Negro ballplayers of going up in the air and shooting only after he had stayed in the air a few seconds longer than anyone's nerves would have figured him to. It went like this: Goose in the air and the defensive man right with him, then the defensive man down and Goose still there, finally shooting. He seemed to *hang*, perhaps the result of a couple of centuries of moving with a rope tugging at his neck.

12

Hector stayed up too, in his own way. His was more a bounce than a glide; instead of hanging he seemed simply to keep going up. Often he could grab a rebound off the defensive boards, pivot on his way down, dribble up court while the others were still turning around, and catch maybe only one or two men back on defense. They would cluster near the basket and when he got to the foul line Hector would take off, sailing right up over their heads, either passing off at the last moment to a teammate left unguarded in his wake, or else shifting the ball from one hand to the other and cramming it down through the hoop.

13

There were six boys at the far basket now and six more at one off to the side. They were playing three on three; Hector and Goose stopped to watch them. The boys played basketball white-boss style. There are only two styles of basketball in America, and of the two the white-boss grimly prevails over the Negro. The loose lost Negro style, with its reckless beauty, is the more joyful to watch or play, if you can, but it is the white-boss style that wins. Even the Negroes must play white-boss basketball to win, though fortunately the best ones can't, and end up with both, the Negro coming out despite themselves right on top of the other style. And it is these boss Negro players who are the best in the world, the artists of basketball, the ones every pro team needs two or three or six of if it is to stay beautiful and win. 14

The boys were *hustling* for all they were worth: that's the first essential of white-boss basketball. He who wants to relax and enjoy it is gonna be left behind, or knocked over and his ball ripped away from him. For white bosses play very rough. Unlike Negroes, they will not back off and let a man keep the rebound he has jumped for: they'll tackle him, lean on his back, slap at his hands, tie up his arms, hoping to wrestle away his prize. And even before the rebound, the grim jostling and bumping for position. A good white-boss basketball player is a good football player—deadly, brutal and never satisfied. What keeps him going is the thought that he and no one else must always win, every instant. Let him win twenty games and he will sulk and cry and kick down the referees' lockerroom door because he did not win the twenty-first. So by definition there can be no enjoyment. Can't you hear those bloodcurdling screams from the stands where thousands are tied in by their legs? They scream not for pleasure but revenge. Revenge for a crime that is committed fast as it can be wiped away. Because for every winner there is a loser, and then it is the winner who must pay, sooner or later, and on & on & on, right up to heaven vs. hell. 15

O sweet godgod, thought Hector, *this is my heaven right here!* He swished a blind hook shot from the middle of the floor, and for a moment felt better. *No matter how I feel!* 16

1,400 words

DISCUSSION | APPLICATION

1. What is the implication of each of the following phrases and sentences?
   Paragraph
   7. "It was a constant wonderment to him."
   7. "Frequently he missed, to his fascination."
   8. "Getting better and enjoying getting better."
   12. "Perhaps the result of a couple of centuries of moving with a rope tugging at his neck."
   14. "The boys played basketball white-boss style."

Assignment

1. All of us take pleasure in doing what we do well. Larner shows in his detail the pleasure and satisfaction Hector feels in going through his warm-up drills. Someone not quite so skilled as Hector might become bored with the repetition of an identical routine experienced for the thousandth time. He

finds it ever fascinating. Write a theme on something that you do well or on a person skilled in a trade or profession.

2. Read and write a report, using Larner's essay thesis as your general statement, on "The 80-yard Run" by Irwin Shaw, *Rabbit Run* by John Updike, the film *The Hustler,* or a topic of your own choice.

3. Use this quotation of Friedrich Nietzsche's as your generalization and develop it in terms of a personal experience. "He who has a what to live for needs no why."

Vocabulary

Paragraph
2. semaphores
   illusion

GAME
DONALD BARTHELME

Shotwell keeps the jacks and the rubber ball in his attaché case and will not allow me to play with them. He plays with them, alone, sitting on the floor near the console hour after hour, chanting "Onesies, twosies, three-sies, foursies" in a precise, well-modulated voice, not so loud as to be annoying, not so soft as to allow me to forget. I point out to Shotwell that two can derive more enjoyment from playing jacks than one, but he is not interested. I have asked repeatedly to be allowed to play by myself, but he simply shakes his head. "Why?" I ask. "They're mine," he says. And when he has finished, when he has sated himself, back they go into the attaché case. 1

It is unfair but there is nothing I can do about it. I ache to get my hands on them. 2

Shotwell and I watch the console. Shotwell and I live under the ground and watch the console. If certain events take place upon the console, we are to insert our keys in the appropriate locks and turn our keys. Shotwell has a key and I have a key. If we turn our keys simultaneously the bird flies—certain switches are activated and the bird flies. But the bird never flies. In one hundred thirty-three days the bird has not flown. Meanwhile Shotwell and I watch each other. We each wear a .45 and if Shotwell behaves strangely I am supposed to shoot him. If I behave strangely Shotwell is supposed to shoot me. We watch the console and think about shooting each other and think about the bird. Shotwell's behavior with the jacks is strange. Is it strange? I do not know. Perhaps he is merely a selfish bastard, perhaps his character is flawed, perhaps his childhood was twisted. I do not know. 3

Each of us wears a .45 and each of us is supposed to shoot the other if the other is behaving strangely. What is "strangely"? I do not know. In addition to the .45, I have a .38 that Shotwell does not know about con-cealed in my attaché case, and Shotwell has a .25-calibre Beretta that I do not know about strapped to his right calf. Sometimes instead of watching the console I pointedly watch Shotwell's .45, but this is simply a ruse, simply a maneuver. In reality I am watching his hand when it dangles in the vicinity of his right calf. If he decides I am behaving strangely he will shoot me not with the .45 but with the Beretta. Similarly Shotwell pretends to watch my .45 but he is really watching my hand resting idly atop my attaché case, my hand resting idly atop my attaché case, my hand. My hand resting idly atop my attaché case. 4

In the beginning I took care to behave normally. So did Shotwell. Our behavior was painfully normal. Norms of politeness, consideration, speech, and personal habits were scrupulously observed. But then it became apparent that an error had been made, that our relief was not going to appear. Owing to an oversight. Owing to an oversight we have been here for one hundred thirty-three days. When it became clear that an error had been made, that we were not to be relieved, the norms were relaxed. Definitions of normality were redrawn in the agreement of January 1st, called by us "The Agreement." Uniform regulations were relaxed, mealtimes no longer rigorously scheduled. We eat when we are hungry and sleep when we are tired. Considerations of rank and precedence were temporarily set aside— a handsome concession on the part of Shotwell, who is a captain, whereas I am a first lieutenant. One of us watches the console at all times rather than two of us watching the console at all times, except when we are both on our feet. One of us watches the console at all times and if the console becomes agitated then that one wakes the other and we turn our keys in the locks simultaneously and the bird flies. Our system involves a delay of perhaps twelve seconds but I do not care because I am not well, and Shotwell does not care because he is not himself. After the agreement was signed Shotwell produced the jacks and the rubber ball from his attaché case, and I began to write a series of descriptions of forms occurring in nature, such as a shell, a leaf, a stone, an animal. On the walls.   5

     Shotwell plays jacks and I write descriptions of natural forms on the walls. Aching to get my hands on them, the jacks.   6

     Shotwell is enrolled in a U.S.A.F.I. course leading to a Master's degree in business administration from the University of Wisconsin (although we are not in Wisconsin; we are in Utah, Montana, or Idaho). When we went down it was in either Utah, Montana, or Idaho, I don't remember. We have been here for one hundred thirty-three days owing to an oversight. The pale-green reinforced concrete walls sweat and the air-conditioning zips on and off erratically and Shotwell reads "Introduction to Marketing," by Lassiter and Munk, making notes with a blue ball-point pen. Shotwell is not himself but I do not know it. He presents a calm aspect and reads "Introduction to Marketing" and makes his exemplary notes with a blue ball-point pen, meanwhile controlling the .38 in my attaché case with one-third of his attention. I am not well.   7

     We have been here one hundred thirty-three days owing to an oversight. Although now we are not sure what is oversight, what is plan. Perhaps the plan is for us to stay here permanently, or if not permanently at least for a year, for three hundred sixty-five days. Or if not for a year for some number of days known to them and not known to us, such as two hundred days. Or perhaps they are observing our behavior in some ways— sensors of some kind. Perhaps our behavior determines the number of days. It may be that they are pleased with us, with our behavior, not in every detail but in sum. Perhaps the whole thing is very successful, perhaps the whole thing is an experiment and the experiment is very successful. I do not know. Or perhaps the only way they can persuade sun-loving creatures into their pale-green sweating reinforced concrete rooms under the ground is to say that the system is twelve hours on, twelve hours off. And then lock us below for some number of days known to them and not known to us. Perhaps, perhaps. We eat well, although the frozen enchiladas are damp when defrosted and the frozen devil's food cake is sour and untasty. We sleep uneasily and acrimoniously. I hear Shotwell shouting in his sleep —objecting, denouncing, cursing sometimes, weeping sometimes, in his sleep. When Shotwell sleeps I try to pick the lock on his attaché case, so as to get at the jacks. Thus far I have been unsuccessful. Nor has Shotwell been successful in picking the lock on my attaché case so as to get at the .38. I have seen the marks on the shiny surface. I laughed, in the latrine, pale-green walls sweating and the air-conditioning whispering, in the latrine. I ache to get my hands on them. The jacks.   8

I write descriptions of natural forms on the walls, scratching them on the tile surface with a diamond. The diamond is a two-and-one-half-carat solitaire I had in my attaché case when we went down. It was for Lucy. The south wall of the room containing the console is already covered. I have described a shell, a leaf, a stone, animals, a baseball bat. I am aware that the baseball bat is not a natural form. Yet, I described it. "The baseball bat," I said, "is typically made of wood. It is typically one metre in length or a little longer, fat at one end, tapering to afford a comfortable grip at the other. The end with the handhold typically offers a slight rim, or lip, at the nether extremity, to prevent slippage." My description of the baseball bat ran to forty-five hundred words, all scratched with a diamond on the south wall. Does Shotwell read what I have written? I do not know. I am aware that Shotwell regards my writing-behavior as a little strange. Yet it is no stranger than his jacks-behavior, or than the day he appeared in black bathing trunks with the .25-calibre Beretta strapped to his right calf and stood over the console, trying to span with his two arms outstretched the distance between the locks. He could not do it, I had already tried, standing over the console with my two arms outstreched—the distance is too great. I was moved to comment but did not comment. Comment would have provoked counter-comment, comment would have led God knows where. They had in their infinite patience, in their infinite foresight, in their infinite wisdom already imagined a man standing over the console with his two arms outstretched, trying to span with his two arms outstretched the distance between the locks. Perhaps.   9

Shotwell is not himself. He has made certain overtures. The burden of his message is not clear. It has something to do with the keys, with the locks. Shotwell is strange. He appears to be less affected by our situation than I. He goes about his business stolidly, watching the console, studying "Introduction to Marketing," bouncing his rubber ball on the floor in a steady, rhythmical, conscientious manner. He appears to be less affected by our situation than I. He is stolid. He says nothing. But he has made certain overtures, certain overtures have been made. I am not sure that I understand them. They have something to do with the keys, with the locks. Shotwell has something in mind. Stolidly he shucks the shiny silver paper from the frozen enchiladas, stolidly he stuffs them into the electric oven. But he has something in mind. But there must be a *quid pro quo*. I insist on a *quid pro quo*. I have something in mind.   10

I am not well. I do not know our target. They do not tell us for which city the bird is targeted. I do not know. That is planning. That is not my responsibility. My responsibility is to watch the console and when certain events take place upon the console, to turn my key in the lock. Shotwell bounces the rubber ball on the floor in a steady, stolid, rhythmical manner. I am aching to get my hands on the ball, on the jacks. We have been here one hundred thirty-three days owing to an oversight. I write on the walls. Shotwell chants "Onesies, twosies, threesies, foursies" in a precise, well-modulated voice. Now he cups the jacks and the rubber ball in his hands and rattles them suggestively. I do not know for which city the bird is targeted. Shotwell is not himself.   11

Sometimes I cannot sleep. Sometimes Shotwell cannot sleep. Sometimes when Shotwell cradles me in his arms and rocks me to sleep, singing Brahms' "*Guten Abend, gut' Nacht,*" or when I cradle Shotwell in my arms and rock him to sleep, singing, I understand what it is Shotwell wishes me to do. At such moments we are very close. But only if he will give me the jacks. That is fair. There is something he wants me to do with my key while he does something with his key. But only if he will give me my turn. That is fair. I am not well.   12

1,850 words

DISCUSSION | APPLICATION

"Game" is a short story told in first-person, major point of view. The author invents the "I" of the story, and "I" becomes our "eye" as we peer into his world, his reality. Our task is to determine what is reality, what illusion. When the "I" discusses "normal behavior," the reader tests his evaluation against that of the "I." Thus, there are two stories: the story the "I" recounts and the story which we see in the details of his account.

To deal with "Game," we must become active, not passive, readers. We must bring our own experience and knowledge to bear on the details. We must judge them in the context of our world. When we do this, we reach some conclusions about the narrator, about Shotwell, about the world we inhabit.

1. What do the details in the opening paragraphs imply about the age, sex, and circumstance of "I" and Shotwell? Does the author mislead you? Why? Look up "ambiguous."

2. "We eat well, although the frozen enchiladas are damp when defrosted and the frozen devil's food cake is sour and untasty."
   Do the details confirm or contradict the generalization in this sentence?

Why does the author specify enchiladas and devil's food cake? Why not steak and ice cream?

3. "[The diamond] was for Lucy." Why is this in past tense?

4. Identify the "they" who are constantly referred to.

Theme Assignment

What does the story as a whole say about our world and accepted norms of behavior in it?

Vocabulary

Paragraph

3. console
   simultaneously
   flawed

4. ruse

5. normally
   strange
   precedence

8. sensors
   acrimoniously

10. overtures
    sated
    stolid
    quid pro quo

11. well-modulated

A few words about the world's reaction to the concentration camps: the terrors committed in them were experienced as uncanny by most civilized persons. It came as a shock to their pride that supposedly civilized nations could stoop to such inhuman acts. The implication that modern man has such inadequate control over his cruelty was felt as a threat. Three different psychological mechanisms were most frequently used for dealing with the phenomenon of the concentration camp: (a) its applicability to man in general was denied by asserting (contrary to available evidence) that the acts of torture were committed by a small group of insane or perverted persons; (b) the truth of the reports was denied by ascribing them to deliberate propaganda. This method was favored by the German government which called all reports on terror in the camps horror propaganda (*Greuelpropaganda*); (c) the reports were believed, but the knowledge of the terror was repressed as soon as possible.   1

All three mechanisms could be seen at work after liberation. At first, after the "discovery" of the camps, a wave of extreme outrage swept the Allied nations. It was soon followed by a general repression of the discovery. It may be that this reaction of the general public was due to something more than the shock dealt their narcissism by the fact that cruelty is still rampant among men. It may also be that the memory of the tortures was repressed out of some dim realization that the modern state now has available the means for changing personality. To have to accept that one's personality may be changed against one's will is the greatest threat to one's self respect. It must therefore be dealt with by action, or by repression.   2

The universal success of the *Diary of Anne Frank* suggests how much the tendency to deny is still with us, while her story itself demonstrates how such denial can hasten our own destruction. It is an onerous task to take apart such a humane and moving story, arousing so much compassion for gentle Anne Frank. But I believe that its world-wide acclaim cannot be explained unless we recognize our wish to forget the gas chambers and to glorify attitudes of extreme privatization, of continuing to hold on to attitudes as usual even in a holocaust. Exactly because their going on with private life as usual brought destruction did it have to be glorified, in that way we could overlook the essential fact of how destructive it can be under extreme social circumstances.   3

While the Franks were making their preparations for going passively into hiding, thousands of other Jews in Holland and elsewhere in Europe were trying to escape to the free world, the better to survive or to be able to fight their executioners. Others who could not do so went underground —not simply to hide from the SS, waiting passively, without preparation for fight, for the day when they would be caught—but to fight the Germans, and with it for humanity. All the Franks wanted was to go on with life as nearly as possible in the usual fashion.   4

Little Anne, too, wanted only to go on with life as usual, and nobody can blame her. But hers was certainly not a necessary fate, much less a heroic one; it was a senseless fate. The Franks could have faced the facts and survived, as did many Jews living in Holland. Anne could have had a good chance to survive, as did many Jewish children in Holland. But for that she would have had to be separated from her parents and gone to live with a Dutch family as their own child.   5

Everybody who recognized the obvious knew that the hardest way to go underground was to do it as a family; that to hide as a family made detection by the SS most likely. The Franks, with their excellent connections among gentile Dutch families should have had an easy time hiding out singly, each with a different family. But instead of planning for this, the main principle of their planning was to continue as much as possible with the kind of family life they were accustomed to. Any other course would have meant not merely giving up the beloved family life, but also accepting as reality man's inhumanity to man. Most of all it would have forced them to accept that going on with life as usual was not an absolute value, but can sometimes be the most destructive of all attitudes.   6

There is little doubt that the Franks, who were able to provide themselves with so much, could have provided themselves with a gun or two had they wished. They could have shot down at least one or two of the "green police" who came for them. There was no surplus of such police. The loss of an SS with every Jew arrested would have noticeably hindered the functioning of the police state. The fate of the Franks wouldn't have been any different, because they all died anyway except for Anne's father, though he hardly meant to pay for his survival with the extermination of his whole family. But they could have sold their lives dearly instead of walking to their death.   7

There is good reason why the so successful play ends with Anne stating her belief in the good in all men. What is denied is the importance of accepting the gas chambers as real so that never again will they exist. If all men are basically good, if going on with intimate family living no matter what else is what is to be most admired, then indeed we can all go on with life as usual and forget about Auschwitz. Except that Anne Frank died because her parents could not get themselves to believe in Auschwitz. And her story found wide acclaim because for us too, it denies implicitly that Auschwitz ever existed. If all men are good, there was never an Auschwitz. 8
1,000 words

DISCUSSION | APPLICATION

1. What is the implication of "uncanny" in "the terrors committed in [the concentration camps] were experienced as uncanny by most civilized persons"?
2. How does psychological repression work? Can you find examples in recent news items? In your own experience?
3. Explain in your own words why people could not accept the implications of the concentration camps.
4. Bettelheim's theme is stated in the sentence "If all men are good, there never was an Auschwitz." What does this imply?
5. Does Bettelheim believe that circumstances alter cases?

Assignments

1. Do you "believe in Auschwitz"? Show why you do or do not in terms of your own experience. Note that Bettelheim's statement is not to be taken literally, but as a metaphor.
2. If you have read *The Diary of Anne Frank* or have seen the film of the same title, write a report on one or the other, using Bettelheim's essay as a reference.
3. Use one of the following quotations as a generalization for a theme.

   "He lives by the rules."
   "Does he? Who made the rules?"

   "The truth about human experience is the only purification."

   Tennessee Williams

   The last two sentences in paragraph 2 of Bettelheim's essay.

Vocabulary

Paragraph
1. psychological mechanisms
   repressed
2. narcissism
   rampant

3. privatization
   holocaust
4. passively
5. gentile

6. absolute value
7. surplus
   hindered
8. implicitly

The full meaning of my mother's death had settled over me before they lowered her into the grave. They buried her at two-thirty in the afternoon; now, at nightfall, our big family was starting to break up. Once there had been fifteen of us and, at sixteen, I was the youngest. There was never much money, so now my older brothers and sisters were scraping up enough for my coach ticket north. I would live in St. Paul, Minnesota, with my sister Maggie Lee, as my mother had requested a few minutes before she died.   1

Poppa, a good quiet man, spent the last hours before our parting moving aimlessly about the yard, keeping to himself and avoiding me. A sigh now and then belied his outer calm. Several times I wanted to say that I was sorry to be going, and that I would miss him very much. But the silence that had always lain between us prevented this. Now I realized that probably he hadn't spoken more than a few thousand words to me during my entire childhood. It was always: "Mornin', boy"; "Git your chores done, boy"; "Goodnight, boy." If I asked for a dime or nickel, he would look beyond me for a moment, grunt, then dig through the nuts and bolts in his blue jeans and hand me the money. I loved him in spite of his silence.   2

For his own reasons Poppa didn't go to the depot, but as my sister and I were leaving he came up, a cob pipe jutting from his mouth, and stood sideways, looking over the misty Kansas countryside. I stood awkwardly waiting for him to say something. He just grunted—three short grunts. "Well," Maggie Lee said nervously, "won't you be kissin' your poppa goodbye?" I picked up my cardboard suitcase, turned and kissed his stubbly cheek and started climbing into the taxicab. I was halfway in when his hand touched my shoulder. "Boy, remember your momma's teachin'. You'll be all right. Just you remember her teachin'." I promised, then sat back in the Model T taxi. As we rounded the corner, Poppa was already headed for the hog pens. It was feeding time.   3

Our parents had filled us with love and a staunch Methodist religion. We were poor, though I did not know it at the time; the rich soil surrounding our clapboard house had yielded the food for the family. And the love of this family had eased the burden of being black. But there were segregated schools and warnings to avoid white neighborhoods after dark. I always had to sit in the peanut gallery (the Negro section) at the movies. We weren't allowed to drink a soda in the drugstore in town. I was stoned and beaten and called "nigger," "black boy," "darky," "shine." These indignities came so often I began to accept them as normal. Yet I always fought back. Now I considered myself lucky to be alive; three of my close friends had already died of senseless brutality, and I was lucky that I hadn't killed someone myself. Until the very day that I left Fort Scott on that train for the North, there had been a fair chance of being shot or perhaps beaten to death. I could easily have been the victim of mistaken identity, of a sudden act of terror by hate-filled white men, or, for that matter, I could have been murdered by some violent member of my own race. There had been a lot of killing in the border states of Kansas, Oklahoma and Missouri, more than I cared to remember.   4

I was nine years old when the Tulsa riots took place in 1921. Whites had invaded the Negro neighborhood, which turned out to be an armed camp. Many white Tulsans were killed, and rumors had it that the fight would spread into Kansas and beyond. About this time, a grown cousin of mine decided to go south to work in a mill. My mother, knowing his hot temper, pleaded with him not to go, but he caught a freight going south. Months passed and we had no word of him. Then one day his name flashed across the nation as one of the most-wanted men in the country. He had killed a white millhand who spat in his face and called him "nigger." He killed another man while fleeing the scene and shot another on the viaduct between Kansas City, Missouri, and Kansas City, Kansas.   5

I asked Momma questions she couldn't possibly answer. Would they catch him? Would he be lynched? Where did she think he was hiding? How long did she think he could hold out? She knew what all the rest of us knew, that he would come back to our house if it was possible.   6

He came one night. It was storming, and I lay in the dark of my room, listening to the rain pound the roof. Suddenly, the window next to my bed slid up, and my cousin, wet and cautious, scrambled through the opening. I started to yell as he landed on my bed, but he quickly covered my mouth with his hand, whispered his name, and cautioned me into silence. I got out of bed and followed him. He went straight to Momma's room, kneeled down and shook her awake. "Momma Parks," he whispered, "it's me, it's me. Wake up." And she awoke easily and put her hand on his head. "My Lord, son," she said, "you're in such bad trouble." Then she sat up on the side of the bed and began to pray over him. After she had finished, she tried to persuade him to give himself up. "They'll kill you, son. You can't run forever." But he refused. Then, going to our old icebox, he filled a sack with food and went back out my window into the cornfield.   7

None of us ever saw or heard of him again. And I would lie awake nights wondering if the whites had killed my cousin, praying that they hadn't. I remember the huge sacks of peanut brittle he used to bring me and the rides he gave me on the back of his battered motorcycle. And my days were full of fantasies in which I helped him escape imaginary white mobs.   8

When I was eleven, I became possessed of an exaggerated fear of death. It started one quiet summer afternoon with an explosion in the alley behind our house. I jumped up from under a shade tree and tailed Poppa toward the scene. Black smoke billowed skyward, a large hole gaped in the wall of our barn and several maimed chickens and a headless turkey flopped about on the ground. Then Poppa stopped and muttered, "Good Lord." I clutched his overalls and looked. A man, or what was left of him, was strewn about in three parts. A gas main he had been repairing had somehow ignited and blown everything around it to bits.

9

Then once, with two friends, I had swum along the bottom of the muddy Marmaton River, trying to locate the body of a Negro man. We had been promised fifty cents apiece by the same white policeman who had shot him while he was in the water trying to escape arrest. The dead man had been in a crap game with several others who had managed to get away. My buddy, Johnny Young, was swimming beside me; we swam with ice hooks which we were to use for grappling. The two of us touched the corpse at the same instant. Fear streaked through me and the memory of his bloated body haunted my dreams for nights.

10

One night at the Empress Theater, I sat alone in the peanut gallery watching a motion picture, *The Phantom of the Opera*. When the curious heroine, against Lon Chaney's warning, snatched away his mask, and the skull of death filled the screen, I screamed out loud and ran out of the theater. I didn't stop until I reached home, crying to Momma, "I'm going to die! I'm going to die."

11

Momma, after several months of cajoling, had all but destroyed this fear when another cruel thing happened. A Negro gambler called Captain Tuck was mysteriously killed on the Frisco tracks. Elmer Kinard, a buddy, and I had gone to the Cheney Mortuary out of youthful, and perhaps morbid, curiosity. Two white men, standing at the back door where bodies were received, smiled mischievously and beckoned to us. Elmer was wise and ran, but they caught me. "Come on in, boy. You want to see Captain Tuck, don't you?"

12

"No, no," I pleaded. "No, no, let me go."

13

The two men lifted me through the door and shoved me into a dark room. "Cap'n Tuck's in here, boy. You can say hello to him." The stench of embalming fluid mixed with fright. I started vomiting, screaming and pounding the door. Then a smeared light bulb flicked on and, there before me, his broken body covering the slab, was Captain Tuck. My body froze and I collapsed beside the door.

14

After they revived me and put me on the street, I ran home with the old fear again running the distance beside me. My brother Clem evened the score with his fists the next day, but from then on Poppa proclaimed that no Parks would ever be caught dead in Cheney's. "The Koonantz boys will do all our burying from now on," he told Orlando Cheney.

15

Another time, I saw a woman cut another woman to death. There were men around, but they didn't stop it. They all stood there as if they were watching a horror movie. Months later, I would shudder at the sight of Johnny Young, one of my closest buddies, lying, shot to death, at the feet of his father and the girl he loved. His murderer had been in love with the same girl. And not long after, Emphry Hawkins, who had helped us bear Johnny's coffin, was also shot to death.   16

As the train whistled through the evening, I realized that only hours before, during what seemed like a bottomless night, I had left my bed to sleep on the floor beside my mother's coffin. It was, I knew now, a final attempt to destroy this fear of death.   17

But in spite of the memories I would miss this Kansas land that I was leaving. The great prairies filled with green and cornstalks; the flowering apple trees, the tall elms and oaks bordering the streams that gurgled and the rivers that rolled quiet. The summers of long, sleepy days for fishing, swimming and snatching crawdads from beneath the rocks. The endless tufts of high clouds billowing across the heavens. The butterflies to chase through grass high as the chin. The swallowtails, bobolinks and robins. Nights filled with soft laughter, with fireflies and restless stars, and the winding sound of the cricket rubbing dampness from its wing. The silver of September rain, the orange-red-brown Octobers and Novembers, and the white Decembers with the hungry smells of hams and pork butts curing in the smokehouses. Yet, as the train sped along, the telegraph poles whizzing toward and past us, I had a feeling that I was escaping a doom which had already trapped the relatives and friends I was leaving behind. For, although I was departing from this beautiful land, it would be impossible ever to forget the fear, hatred and violence that Negroes had suffered upon it.   18

It was all behind me now. By the next day, there would be what my mother had called "another kind of world, one with more hope and promising things." She had said, "Make a man of yourself up there. Put something into it, and you'll get something out of it." It was her dream for me. When I stepped onto the chilly streets of St. Paul, Minnesota, two days later, I was determined to fulfill that dream.   19

2,000 words

DISCUSSION | APPLICATION

1. Paragraph 4: Explain the implication of "We were poor, though I did not know it at the time."
2. Paragraph 4: "I began to accept [indignities] as normal." Are they normal? Why does he use the word "indignities" instead of "epithets" or "curses"? What is the opposite of indignity?
3. Paragraph 4: What motivation is implied by "a sudden act of terror by hate-filled white men"?
4. Most people become aware of their own mortality gradually, as did Parks, as the result of several experiences involving the death of others. Have you had any such experiences?

Assignment

1. Parks sleeps beside his mother's coffin in a "final attempt to destroy this fear of death." Show why this destruction is necessary if one is to live a full life. You may use one of the following quotations in the development of your theme.

To gain your life, you must lose it.

Christ

Modern morality has cultivated a sentimental standard by which anything becomes preferable to the thought of dying. Life is thus prolonged in proportion as it is not used. It gains extension at the cost of vitality.

Ortega y Gasset

I want to leave a committed life behind.

Martin Luther King (last sermon)

[Robert Kennedy] loved life completely and lived it intensely.

Edward Kennedy eulogizing his murdered brother

Is there a life after birth?

Alexander King

Vocabulary

Paragraph
3. jutting
4. staunch
    burden
5. pleaded

7. persuade
8. fantasies
9. possessed
    exaggerated
    maimed

10. bloated
12. cajoling
    morbid
18. tufts

I think (onstage nudity) is disgusting, shameful, and damaging to all things American. But if I were twenty-two with a great body, it would be artistic, tasteful, patriotic, and a progressive, religious experience.
Actress Shelley Winters

Comparison and contrast clarify by noting similarities and differences between two persons, situations, ideas, or objects, one of which is familiar to the reader. Our Congress is compared and contrasted to the British Parliament. Present-day film stars, politicians, writers, adolescents, and athletes are compared to and contrasted with those of the past. Political systems, philosophical ideas, and language rules foreign to the United States are clarified by this method.

College students argue about the comparative merits of professors, automobiles, musical groups, and members of the opposite sex. They contrast their experiences with those of their elders, their fellow students, and members of the opposite sex.

The author of the following paragraphs was in Paris, France, when President John F. Kennedy was assassinated. He contrasts the approach of an English and a French newscaster. Both have the same news to report. Both are emotionally moved by the news. Each reacts to the emotion in a fashion that tells us something about the British and the French people.

We tuned in the British Broadcasting Company and immediately heard a calm, English-accented voice say, "Here is a special bulletin. President John F. Kennedy is dead." A long pause followed. Then the same voice, still cool, clipped, precise, but altered nonetheless, said, "We must leave the air for a moment to compose ourselves."

Flicking to a French station we picked up other details, confirming the death of the President, from a French announcer who made no attempt to compose himself. He wept as he read the bulletins. We wept as we listened.

71

Psychiatrist Robert Coles compares and contrasts violence as depicted in literature, films, and comic books with the "real violence in this world" as each affects the mind. He finds the real violence concerns him more.

> I think that the important thing—perhaps in literature, certainly among people, and certainly in societies—is not the *presence* of violence, whether it be in a dream, a fantasy, or for that matter in literature. So, it is no surprise that violence exists. . . . The issue is not the presence of violence. The issue is what is done with it—done with it by the writer, done with it by the society, done with it by people. I think we've gotten over—I hope we've gotten over—the notion we're going to get over violence, analyze violence out of someone, create a nonviolent society in the literal sense of the word. I think that what nonviolence means is that the *deeds* of violence, the social deeds, the violation of people that is built into a social and economic system, will in some way be toned down. . . .
>
> . . . I tell you, I am much more concerned with the effect on the mind, on the minds of all of us—children, grown-ups, whatever—of the real violence in this world, than the violence of any writer, be it Mickey Spillane, or the most cultivated and refined of writers who's suggesting violence to us. All we have to do is look at what we're doing now in Asia; and it seems to me that anything that comes from the typewriter, no matter how brazen and moneygrubbing and all, cannot affect us, all of us, the way what *is going on* in this world affects us, particularly our children as they grow up. And all this talk about violence in books and violence in comic books in particular, and the effect on children—perhaps it's easier for us to worry about that problem than the one of *war*, real war. When we grow up we have to come to terms with sex and violence; and one of the things that happens to all of us, each in his own way, in a beautifully distinctive way, in a human way, and an individual way, is that various *mixtures* of the two, of sex and violence, become uniquely blended with one another. And somehow, today, we're encouraged by the actuality of what's going on in the world, let alone by literature, to undo that balance, that blend. Things are being polarized—and we retreat, go back to these early polarities of sex and violence, which even a seven-year-old child is going to pull together in one way or another.
>
> Certainly we saw it, you know, in Germany—in concentration camps that existed in one of the most civilized nations in the world. Certainly we see it now in the behavior of one of the most advanced nations in the history of the world—technologically advanced. The International Red Cross is chastising us, let alone the Vatican, and the more moderate spectrum of the world. So there seems to be no intellectual or cognitive—use whatever words you want—capacity in us that can prevent us per se from this kind of—again use what words you want—"regression" into the swamplands, where sex and violence do not affect one another; where desire and the fist are in no way blended at all.*

Eric Sevareid's "What really hurts . . ." compares and contrasts his position as a newscaster with the position of congressmen, senators, and

* *The Writer's World*, McGraw-Hill Book Company, 1968.

other elected officials. Martin Weinberger deals with double standards, which usually work to the advantage of the male, but . . . ! "The War Prayer," in its double-tunneled vision, is darkly satiric and semantically as up to date as today's headlines. Nutritionist Jean Mayer suggests the difference between goals sought and results obtained by the destruction of crops in Vietnam. Frances Weismiller, as the length of her title implies, compares and contrasts a multitude of things in "To Ralph Nader with love: History, segregation, manners, and the automobile."

WHAT REALLY HURTS...
ERIC SEVAREID

(Editor's note: The CBS News broadcast published below was evoked by Vice President Spiro Agnew's proposal that television news commentators be publicly examined on their "underlying philosophy.")

What really hurts is the thought that maybe nobody's been listening all this time. If, after some 30 years and thousands of broadcasts, hundreds of articles and a few books, one's general cast of mind, warts and all, remains a mystery, then we're licked and we fail to see how a few more minutes of examination by Government types would solve the supposed riddle.   1

Mr. Agnew wants to know where we stand. We stand—or rather sit—right here, in the full glare, at a disadvantage as against politicans. We can't cast one vote in committee, an opposite vote on the floor; can't say one thing in the North, an opposite thing in the South. We hold no tenure, four years or otherwise, and can be voted out with a twist of the dial.   2

We can't use invective and epithets, can't even dream of impugning the patriotism of leading citizens, can't reduce every complicated issue to yes or no, black or white, and would rather go to jail than do bodily injury to the English language. We can't come down on this side or that side of each disputed public issue because we're trying to explain far more than advocate and because some issues don't have two sides; some have three, four or half a dozen and in these matters we're damned if we know the right answer. This may be why most of us look a bit frazzled while Mr. Agnew looks so serene.   3

Nobody in this business expects for a moment that the full truth of anything will be contained in any one account or commentary, but that through free reporting and discussion, as Mr. Walter Lippmann put it, the truth will emerge. The central point about the free press is not that it be accurate, though it must try to be; not that it even be fair, though it must try to be that; but that it be free. And that means freedom from any and all attempts by the power of Government to coerce it or intimidate it or police it in any way.   4

DISCUSSION | APPLICATION

Eric Sevareid's writing style employs short sentences, short paragraphs, and a precise, essentially simple vocabulary; yet Sevareid succeeds in communicating a series of complicated ideas clearly. Note especially how direct he is in making his statements and how specific he is in developing detail, example, and illustration to clarify the comparsion at the center of his essay.

1. Sevareid makes a series of negative comparisons in paragraphs 2 and 3. With whom is he comparing himself and other commentators?
2. Sevareid says (paragraph 4) that the truth will emerge through free commentary and discussion. Is this a reasonable assumption?
3. Why does he oppose governmental examination of the "underlying philosophy" of commentators? Do you agree or disagree with him? Why?

Theme Assignment

1. Clip from a current periodical a story involving a current controversy that parallels the Agnew-Sevareid dispute either as a freedom-of-the-press issue or an individual-versus-government issue. Defend or attack one side of the issue in a 300- to 500-word theme. Hand in the clipping with your completed paper.
2. Find two articles of opinion which take opposing views of an issue. Write a theme presenting both sides of the issue in an objective and dispassionate style that allows the reader to make up his own mind.

Vocabulary

Paragraph		advocate
2.	tenure	frazzled
3.	invective	serene
	epithets	4. coerce
	impugning	intimidate

THE DOUBLE STANDARDS
MARTIN WEINBERGER

The theme of this short digression is double standards, of which we are all guilty at one time or another. 1

A few days ago, I was witness to an American League baseball game deep in the heart of Orange County—Anaheim, to be exact. The California Angels and the Detroit Tigers were menacing one another, on and off, for some 4 innings when a young lad, perhaps 20 years of age, stripped to the waist and possessor of a beard that looked more like sideburns which had run amuck, marched to the head of an aisle near the Tiger dugout. 2

He sat on the front railing near the Detroit lair, an act which bothered the Tiger manager, a man named Smith who was losing the game. The youth retreated to a seat, presumably his own, then strode again into the aisle, threw his arms around a bit, finally returning once again to his seat. 3

My next view of him was in a different context. Two Orange County policemen, helmeted and in full battle gear, were forcing the young man up an aisle, both his arms twisted at sharp angles behind his body. His head was pushed downward so he could not see easily where he was going and his verbal protests went for naught.

The people near the shirtless lad and the people close to my seat cheered as the police shoved their subject toward an exit. 4

I was reminded of this incident by reading the Monday newspaper. A shapely young lady, in miniskirts, was pictured as running down on the playing field to the side of the third baseman of the Atlanta Braves, kissing him on the cheek, then scampering off while an usher, smiling broadly, gave chase. Good clean fun, this sort of frolicking. 5

The visions tended to merge and blur as I recalled them. The gay young man, meeting some of the qualifications of hippyism, being forced from the grandstand under brute force. The young lady, perhaps the same age, but dressed in acceptable style, being gaily chased by an usher while the Atlanta third baseman drew inspiration and the stadium audience cheered.

Interesting how we react to stereotypes and what people seem to be but probably aren't. 6

375 words

"The Double Standards" compares and contrasts, directly and by implication, life styles as reflected in dress and appearance, group response as reflected in crowd reactions, and the attitude of authority (the police, the usher) as reflected in the response to the youth and to the girl. The essay develops clearly on a straight line: general statement (paragraph

1), episode one specified (paragraphs 2, 3, 4), episode two specified (paragraph 5), summary (paragraph 6), and conclusion (paragraph 7).

DISCUSSION | APPLICATION

1. What is the basis for the stereotyping in this essay?
2. Identify and examine areas in which you tend to stereotype. What is their basis? Sex? Age? Appearance? Attitude? Occupation? Physical attributes? Intellectual attributes? Status? Other?

Theme Assignments

1. Using the same organization employed in "The Double Standards," write a 300- to 500-word comparison/contrast essay on *one* of the following:
   a. Your perception of different experiences within a single context: Navy duty ashore and afloat, a high school class and a college class, dating American style and dating European style, city and small town living, domestic and foreign cars, etc.
   b. A personal experience/observation and a news story.
2. Write an essay about an experience in which you have been the target of stereotyping.

Vocabulary

Paragraph
1. digression
2. amuck
3. lair

presumably
5. frolicking
6. inspiration
7. stereotypes

THE WAR PRAYER
MARK TWAIN

It was a time of great and exalting excitement. The country was up in arms, the war was on, in every breast burned the holy fire of patriotism; the drums were beating, the bands playing, the toy pistols popping, the bunched firecrackers hissing and spluttering; on every hand and far down the receding and fading spread of roofs and balconies a fluttering wilderness of flags flashed in the sun; daily the young volunteers marched down the wide avenue gay and fine in their new uniforms, the proud fathers and mothers and sisters and sweethearts cheering them with voices choked with happy emotion as they swung by; nightly the packed mass meetings listened, panting, to patriot oratory which stirred the deepest deeps of their hearts and which they interrupted at briefest intervals with cyclones of applause, the tears running down their cheeks the while; in the churches the pastors preached devotion to flag and country and invoked the God of Battles, beseeching His aid in our good cause in outpouring of fervid eloquence which moved every listener. It was indeed a glad and gracious time, and the half-dozen rash spirits that ventured to disapprove of the war and cast a doubt upon its righteousness straightway got such a stern and angry warning that for their personal safety's sake they quickly shrank out of sight and offended no more in that way.   1

Sunday morning came—next day the battalions would leave for the front; the church was filled; the volunteers were there, their young faces alight with martial dreams—visions of the stern advance, the gathering momentum, the rushing charge, the flashing sabers, the flight of the foe, the tumult, the enveloping smoke, the fierce pursuit, the surrender!—then home from the war, bronzed heroes, welcomed, adored, submerged in golden seas of glory! With the volunteers sat their dear ones, proud, happy, and envied by the neighbors and friends who had no sons and brothers to send forth to the field of honor, there to win for the flag or, failing, die the noblest of noble deaths. The service proceeded; a war chapter from the Old Testament was read; the first prayer was said; it was followed by an organ burst that shook the building, and with one impulse the house rose, with glowing eyes and beating hearts, and poured out that tremendous invocation—

> "God the all-terrible! Thou who ordainest,
> Thunder thy clarion and lightning thy sword!"

Then came the "long" prayer. None could remember the like of it for passionate pleading and moving and beautiful language. The burden of its supplication was that an ever-merciful and benignant Father of us all would watch over our noble young soldiers and aid, comfort, and encourage them in their patriotic work; bless them, shield them in the day of battle and the hour of peril, bear them in His mighty hand, make them strong and confident, invincible in the bloody onset; help them to crush the foe, grant to them and to their flag and country imperishable honor and glory— 2

An aged stranger entered and moved with slow and noiseless step up the main aisle, his eyes fixed upon the minister, his long body clothed in a robe that reached to his feet, his head bare, his white hair descending in a frothy cataract to his shoulders, his seamy face unnaturally pale, pale even to ghastliness. With all eyes following him and wondering, he made his silent way; without pausing, he ascended to the preacher's side and stood there, waiting. With shut lids the preacher, unconscious of his presence, continued his moving prayer, and at last finished it with the words, uttered in fervent appeal, "Bless our arms, grant us the victory, O Lord our God, Father and Protector of our land and flag!" 3

The stranger touched his arm, motioned him to step aside—which the startled minister did—and took his place. During some moments he surveyed the spellbound audience with solemn eyes in which burned an uncanny light; then in a deep voice he said: 4

"I come from the Throne—bearing a message from Almighty God!" The words smote the house with a shock; if the stranger perceived it he gave no attention. "He has heard the prayer of His servant your shepherd and will grant it if such shall be your desire after I, His messenger, shall have explained to you its import—that is to say, its full import. For it is like unto many of the prayers of men, in that it asks for more than he who utters it is aware of—except he pause and think. 5

"God's servant and yours has prayed his prayer. Has he paused and taken thought? Is it one prayer? No, it is two—one uttered, the other not. Both have reached the ear of Him Who heareth all supplications, the spoken and the unspoken. Ponder this—keep it in mind. If you would beseech a blessing upon yourself, beware! lest without intent you invoke a curse upon a neighbor at the same time. If you pray for the blessing of rain upon your crop which needs it, by that act you are possibly praying for a curse upon some neighbor's crop which may not need rain and can be injured by it. 6

"You have heard your servant's prayer—the uttered part of it. I am commissioned of God to put into words the other part of it—that part which the pastor, and also you in your hearts, fervently prayed silently. And ignorantly and unthinkingly? God grant that it was so! You heard these words: 'Grant us the victory, O Lord our God!' That is sufficient. The whole of the uttered prayer is compact into those pregnant words. Elaborations were not necessary. When you have prayed for victory you have prayed for many unmentioned results which follow victory—must follow it, cannot help but follow it. Upon the listening spirit of God the Father fell also the unspoken part of the prayer. He commandeth me to put it into words. Listen! 7

"O Lord our Father, our young patriots, idols of our hearts, go forth to battle——be Thou near them! With them, in spirit, we also go forth from the sweet peace of our beloved firesides to smite the foe. O Lord our God, help us to tear their soldiers to bloody shreds with our shells; help us to cover their smiling fields with the pale forms of their patriot dead; help us to drown the thunder of the guns with the shrieks of their wounded, writhing in pain; help us to lay waste their humble homes with a hurricane of fire; help us to wring the hearts of their unoffending widows with unavailing grief; help us to turn them out roofless with their little children to wander unfriended the wastes of their desolated land in rags and hunger and thirst, sports of the sun flames of summer and the icy winds of winter, broken in spirit, worn with travail, imploring Thee for the refuge of the grave and denied it——for our sakes who adore Thee Lord, blast their hopes, blight their lives, protract their bitter pilgrimage, make heavy their steps, water their way with their tears, stain the white snow with the blood of their wounded feet! We ask it, in the spirit of love, of Him Who is the Source of Love, and Who is the ever-faithful refuge and friend of all that are sore beset and seek His aid with humble and contrite hearts. Amen.   8

(*After a pause*) "Ye have prayed it; if ye still desire it, speak! The messenger of the Most High waits."   9

It was believed afterward that the man was a lunatic, because there was no sense in what he said.   10

1200 words

War is Peace, Peace is War.

George Orwell: 1984

> The most shocking concealment of military assistance funds in terms of rhetorical techniques concerns the Food for Peace Program. According to the budget document, "This program . . . combats hunger and malnutrition, promotes economic growth in developing countries, and develops and expands export markets for U.S. commodities." That is a direct quotation from the Act. Yet . . . in the past six years nearly $700 million of Food for Peace funds have been channeled into military assistance programs. . . . To continue using Food for Peace funds for military purposes is, to say the least, a corruption of the English language.
>
> *Senator William Proxmire*
> *Joint Economic Committee (1/4/71)*

Referring to the current Soviet practice of dealing with dissenters by confining them in mental institutions on the grounds they are insane, Russia's greatest living novelist, Alexander Solzhenitsyn, said (*Time* magazine: 6/29/71): "The incarceration of free-thinking, healthy people in madhouses is spiritual murder. It is a variant of the gas chamber, but it is an even more cruel variation, for the tortures of those being held are more vicious and prolonged. (It) . . . is a devious method of reprisal without determining guilt when the real cause is too shameful to be stated."

DISCUSSION | APPLICATION

1. Twain compares and contrasts two perceptions of an identical experience. He sets the scene and defines the atmosphere in the opening paragraph. He tells *about* the minister's prayer, summarizing "... the burden of its supplication," but he gives the stranger's prayer in direct discourse. Why?

2. Specify some of the words in the first two paragraphs that set the tone of the essay and the mood of the society.

3. Why is the visitor not identified except as "the stranger"?

4. How does the final sentence emphasize the ironic tone of the essay? Is there "any sense" in what the stranger said?

5. Bring in some examples from the advertising media of man's tendency to use language to force experience into preferred patterns ("giant size quart").

6. In his autobiography, Twain suggests that "... all lies are acts and speech has no part in them. ... I am speaking of the law of silent assertion. ... For instance, it would not be possible for a humane and intelligent person to invent a rational excuse for slavery; yet you will remember that in the early days of the emancipation agitation in the North, the agitators got small help ... from anyone. Argue ... as they might, they could not break the universal stillness that reigned, from pulpit and press all the way down to the bottom of society—the clammy stillness created and maintained by the lie of silent assertion—the silent assertion that there wasn't anything going on in which humane and intelligent people were interested."

   A contemporary poet and novelist, Wendell Berry, echoes Twain: "... consider the moral predicament of the master who sat in church with his slaves, thus attesting his belief in the immortality of the souls of people whose bodies he owned and used. ... How could he presume to own the body of a man whose soul he considered as worthy of salvation as his own? To keep this question from articulating itself in his thoughts and demanding an answer, he had to perfect an empty space in his mind, a silence, between heavenly concerns, between body and spirit."*

   Are there contemporary examples of Twain's "silent assertion" from recent history and/or experience?

Theme Assignments

1. Many popular songs and ballads by Bob Dylan, John Lennon, Paul Mc-Cartney, Paul Simon, etc. employ an approach and tone similar to those used in "The War Prayer." Other songs and ballads tend to emphasize unreal and romantic ideals. Choosing an example from one of these two types, write a 300- to 500-word theme summarizing "the burden of (a

---

* Wendell Berry, *The Hidden Wound*, p. 19.

song's) supplication'' and detailing the contrasting ideas which remain
unspoken in the lyrics.
2. Write a 300- to 500-word theme comparing and contrasting Twain's ideas in
number 6 above with a contemporary situation.

Vocabulary

Paragraph
1. invoked
   fervid
   eloquence
   rash
   righteousness
2. noble
   invocation
   supplication
   benignant

   invincible
3. cataract
4. spellbound
   uncanny
6. ponder
8. writhing
   desolated
   blight
   protract
   contrite

In wartime, the ethics of means always pose difficult problems. Having spent five years of war as a forward artillery observer and as commander of artillery units, I know all too well that my contribution to the demise of the Wehrmacht was accompanied by the demolition of houses, churches, and works of art and by the killing and wounding of children, women, and civilian men in Africa, Italy, France, and Germany. 1

Still, while knowledge that this was so forced me—and all Allied officers in similar positions—to extreme care so as to minimize such casualties, some such casualties were in the last analysis unavoidable if we were to conduct successful operations and eliminate the Nazi nightmare. 2

The situation seems to me entirely different when we consider the crop and stores destruction program in South Vietnam. The aim of the program is to starve the Viet Cong by destroying those fields that provide the rice for their rest—and field-rations. This aim is, in essence, similar to that which every food blockade (such as the one imposed against the central powers in World War I) has attempted. 3

As a nutritionist who has seen famines on three continents, one of them Asia, and as a historian of public health with an interest in famines, I can say flatly that there has never been a famine or a food shortage—whether created by lack of water (droughts, often followed by dust storms and loss of seeds, being the most frequent), by plant disease (such as fungous blights), by large-scale natural disturbances affecting both crops and farmers (such as floods and earthquakes), by disrupting of farming operations due to wars and civil disorders, or by blockade or other war measures directly aimed at the food supply—which has not first and overwhelmingly affected the small children. 4

In fact, it is very clear that death from starvation occurs first of all in young children and in the elderly, with adults and adolescents surviving better (pregnant women often abort; lactating mothers cease to have milk and the babies die). Children under 5, who in many parts of the world—including Vietnam—are often on the verge of kwashiorkor (a protein-deficiency syndrome which often hits children after weaning and until they are old enough to eat "adult" food) and of marasmus (a combination of deficiency of calories and of protein), are the most vulnerable. 5

In addition, a general consequence of famine is a state of social disruption (including panic). People who are starving at home tend to leave, if they can, and march toward the area where it is rumored that food is available. This increases the prevailing chaos. Families are separated and children are lost—and in all likelihood die. Adolescents are particularly threatened by tuberculosis; however, finding themselves on their own, they often band together in foraging gangs, which avoid starvation but create additional disruption. The prolonged and successful practice of banditry makes it difficult to rehabilitate members of these gangs. 6

I have already said that adults, and particularly adult men, survive usually much better than the rest of the population. Bands of armed men do not starve and—particularly if not indigenous to the population and therefore unhampered by direct family ties with their victims—find themselves entirely justified in seizing what little food is available so as to be able to continue to fight. 7

Destruction of food thus never seems to hamper enemy military operations but always victimizes large numbers of children. During World War I, the blockade had no effect on the nutrition and fighting performance of the German and Austrian armies, but—for the first time since the 18th century—starvation, vitamin-A deficiency, and protein deficiency destroyed the health, the sight, and even the lives of thousands of children in Western Europe. 8

We obviously do not want to take war measures that are primarily, if not exclusively, directed at children, the elderly, and pregnant and lactating women. 9

To state it in other words, my point is not that innocent bystanders will be hurt by such measures, but that only bystanders will be hurt. Our primary aim—to disable the Viet Cong—will not be achieved, and our proclaimed secondary aim—to win over the civilian population—is made a hollow mockery. 10

900 words

DISCUSSION | APPLICATION

1. Why is the author qualified to write on the aspect of the Vietnam war he deals with here?
2. Why does he introduce the material in paragraph 1 on his experience as an artillery officer in World War II?
3. Why does famine first and overwhelmingly affect small children?
4. Who is apt to survive famine in Vietnam? Why?
5. The author specifies several reasons why famine causes a general state of social disruption. What are those reasons?
6. What ecological impact is the type of military operation described apt to have?

Theme Assignments

1. Attack or defend the following *ironic* statement:

All wars are boyish.

Herman Melville

2. Develop an essay around an experience (not limited to any specific field) you have lived through in which an attempt to solve one problem brought unanticipated problems once it was solved.

Vocabulary

Paragraph
1. demise
   Wehrmacht
   demolition
2. minimize
   casualties

eliminate
4. nutritionist
   famines
   droughts
5. calories

protein
6. disruption
   rehabilitate
7. indigenous
10. mockery

Once upon a time, in this country, people of various ages saw a great deal of one another, as did people of various classes and colors. "Tom Sawyer" taught you that when you were 12.

1

A gigantic shift away from this condition began with the bicycle and the trolley-car; but it began very gradually. The trolley-car and the bike made it possible for people to go some distance to work, which meant that in cities people did not have to live over stores, or near factories, or in servants' quarters. In parts of the South the little houses of negroes still line the alleys behind the houses of the well-to-do, but this is going fast; and everywhere else there is considerable separation between rich districts and poor.

2

The Model T took the gradualness out of the shift. The trolley-car had not gone everywhere, and bicycles were not as good then as they are now. Walking distance still had to be considered. But as the automobile proliferated, the necessity to walk shrank away.

3

People have always shown the inclination to stick to their "own kind" as much as possible. Kids like to get off with other kids. Educated people like to talk to one another. "Birds of a feather flock together." When walking-distance ruled humanity, the proper behavior of different kinds of people was carefully taught: how servants and other employes treated the people above them in the class hierarchy; how children behaved toward grown-ups; how children behaved toward grown-ups of different classes; what the obligations of masters to servants were; and so on. Shakespeare, Cervantes and Jane Austen are full of examples. These proper behaviors were called "manners" and also "morals." Their usefulness was (and to some extent still is) in minimizing the discomfort and anxiety of mixing and dealing with "the others," people who are not "one's own kind," people whose lives one does not quite understand because those people are older or younger or richer or poorer or differently educated than oneself. Under walking-distance conditions there was no escaping contact with such people. One met them everywhere, or else hid in one's room. The main protection one had from their "differentness" was "good manners" and the chance to flee to one's own kind—to "flock together."

4

These "good manners" and arrangements for "flocking together" were among the mechanisms of class and caste structure, which should be distinguished from the geographic class and caste segregation we see today. Tom Sawyer's and William Faulkner's South was not a "segregated" society, though it was structured in its customs by the manners and morals considered proper to its classes and castes. That South was a mixed society, in which old and young and black and white saw a great deal of one another and perforce knew a great deal about what one another's lives were like. Our society is a segregated society; and it has been made so by the automobile.   5

Booker T. Washington's *Up From Slavery* describes mixing of black and white and rich and poor during and after slavery, and into the period before World War I, which has no parallel today. White country gentry who imported governesses and tutors for their children had the children's black playmates taught at the same time. Class and caste lines were maintained, but personal respect could and did cut across those lines along with affection and protectiveness in both directions. The opportunity for a black youngster to "better himself" was probably, in reality, greater in that custom-structured society than it is in our geographically segregated world, despite the official lifting of limitations on opportunities for blacks. For he knew the people who could teach him and help him. He saw them often because they had to walk, just as he did. By making himself agreeable and useful to them, he could get something from them. This had its price in insult and humiliation; but it is more than a ghetto youngster is likely to get today through his concentration-camp school.   6

The automobile has enabled the (apparently basic) tendency to cling to "one's own kind" and avoid the mysteries and menaces of "the others," to turn a mixed society into a segregated society. The rich no longer have to see the poor in their misery. The well-educated no longer have to explain their remarks to the ill-educated. The old and the young no longer have to put up with one another. They live in Leisure World and Isla Vista.   7

A walking-distance society can be compared to fresh milk, in which all the tiny globules of cream-fat are dispersed in a colloidal solution with the proteins and vitamins and enzymes and sugars and water and whatever else there is in fresh milk. Our society can be compared to that milk if it were allowed to sour and then heated. The cream forms buttery solid lumps which mostly lie on top of greenish-white curds in yellow whey. Many of the subtler nutrients have been destroyed.   8

And most of the souring and heating have been done by the automobile. (Labor-saving devices which allow the well-to-do to function without servants have done a little too.)   9

It is not necessary to remind anyone that the automobile is poisoning our air, which we have to breathe; that the land we have paved for it is lost to us and no longer available to soak up rain, so that rain runs off and destroys more land by flooding and erosion; that by giving sexual privacy outside the home the automobile has revolutionized our sexual morals; that every automobile a family owns costs it as much as, or more than, an added person; that cars are dangerous to dogs and little children, which and who must therefore be imprisoned in yards except when they are being carefully escorted on walks by their keepers. There are probably several more charges of this kind to be brought against our beautiful and luxurious contractions.   10

But most people do not recognize the destructive action on human society. It is my opinion that even if cars did not pollute and poison at all, they would still, over a period of time, so alienate different kinds of people from one another that no nation of any size could survive. I think we are curdling and congealing into enclaves, dividing by "kind," and will soon live in more or less walled villages, guarded by armed hirelings (if we are not asphyxiated first) unless we grind up and melt down our private automobiles, and restrict the use of little electric cars to semi-invalids.   11

Mass transit mixes people a little. Walking mixes them more. Bicycling, in terms of mixing people, is not much better than driving, but at least you can see a cyclist's face and exchange a few words with him. Motorcycles are as bad as cars.   12

Why do we love these obnoxious vehicles so much that we poison and pauperize ourselves for them? What do they give us?   13

A sense of ease, primarily. We do not need to plan the timing of our expeditions for groceries and the movies and the laundry and the Cub Scout meeting so accurately as we would have to otherwise. Distance limits us less—far less.   14

The sense of ease also comes from another feature of the contraption: it gives privacy. This must account for the fact that commuters do not cut their costs by carpooling, but instead travel in lonely state, each controlling the buttons on his radio, thinking his own thoughts. Most people have no other solitude, no other time to let their minds comb out the tangles of experience. Adding a room or two to the house would be a cheaper way to get this; but no one who is supporting cars feels he can afford to build.   15

People who wanted solitude used to go for solitary walks, explaining that they "needed the exercise." Old novels give us another hint of how privacy used to be gained when they tell us that someone stood a long time at a closed door before he found the temerity to knock. This implies one of the many items of good manners which maintained separation from "the others" when the physical equipment of the automobile did not provide it. There was a taboo against disturbing anyone who had indicated that he wanted to be alone by closing his door. There was a taboo against interrupting people at their work. There were specified times of day when it was permissible to visit: ladies made "calls" between 3 and 4 in the afternoon. Even interrupting someone who was speaking was considered very rude; today we find it only a bit objectionable.   16

In our world of the brutally interrupting telephone and the automobile-given freedom from "the others" all these manners are undermined, and so the automobile becomes the protector of the psyche. This is a vicious circle. The automobile gives us the insulation from others which we continue to need, while it reduces the necessity to instruct children and remind adults to avoid intruding and annoying. So "manners" become so sketchy that the peace and privacy of the tiny, cushioned armored room moving obediently along the highway seems essential to sanity. (This suggests that commuter busses, equipped inside with something like the old curtained Pullman berths, might meet with less commuter-resistance than the busses with rows of seats which we are used to.)   17

Another component of the sense of ease which the automobile gives us is what might be called the "feeling of space." This is a rather special thing. Most parents have learned that a violently crying, raging child will become quiet if he is taken outdoors. This behavior is particularly striking in babies; they will stop in the middle of a wail, look up and around; and seem to recognize that the sky is going straight up forever above them, that the ceiling and walls are gone. Probably they detect a change in noise: the racket they are making is no longer bouncing back into their ears.   18

But the matter of reverberating sound is not all of it. Next time you walk out of your house, notice a kind of sense of relief which is not entirely caused by your having left whatever constraints exist for you indoors. It may have to do with the fact that your eyes are re-focusing for distance; but your whole body, in a way, re-focuses for distance. You do not have to pay unconscious attention to the possibility of bumping into a wall or a table. The air smells and feels different. All these things are involved in the "feeling of space," and it is one of the gifts of the automobile which can also be enjoyed on a bicycle in decent weather. (It is also an indication that the Pullman commuter needs clean windows.)   19

We must get rid of the automobile if we are to survive as living beings and as members of "the larger society"; and though the second part of this statement is an unfamiliar thought to most people, the first is not.   20

Why, then, are we doing so little toward saving our own lives? Why are we not using what mass transportation we have, and organizing delivery services and setting people up in little businesses like the old vegetable-peddlers and fish-peddlers and so on, who walked their horse-drawn wagons around the neighborhoods? Why are housewives who could ride big delivery tricycles to their local shopping centers and back, trailing a child on a little bicycle, making no move toward any such thing? The financial saving would be tremendous, and the errand pleasant enough. All over Europe women drag children and shopping bags to market in all kinds of weather. The human animal is perfectly capable of doing things like that. Why, when such things will soon be a matter of life and death, are we not even trying to get the hang of them?   21

There are 3 obvious answers. The damned cars are so convenient. We hesitate to make ourselves conspicuous by doing things which have not been customary. We do not quite believe that the automobile is getting ready to threaten not just our health, but our lives.   22

There are two less obvious answers, of a practical nature. Some of us have lost so much in health to bad air and lack of exercise that we haven't the physical energy to change our habits. Stores are not selling the equipment which would make the change attractive—the adult tricycles, the well-sprung big red hand-wagons, the shopping-bags on good wheels like the golf-club carriers you pull around the links.

23

But behind all these lie vaguer and deeper reasons. The automobile satisfies psychological needs of which we are only half aware. It fills our hungers for escape and the consciousness of power. It gives us the pleasures of solitude, of being for an hour or even just a few minutes left in peace, as well as the pleasure of calling on friends and the sense of space and speed.

24

It will be difficult for us to unhook ourselves from our addiction to the abominable thing unless we pay close attention to all the pleasures it gives us, and figure out how to replace most of them. It will be quite a trick to recreate some of the manners people once used to protect themselves and one another from discomfort and intrusion when they were at home, and to maintain enough separation from "the others" to protect whatever "the others" endanger when they went out, without recreating some of the disagreeable distinctions of class we have managed to mute.

25

The whole job is really overwhelming. It is going to take hard and subtle thinking, and experiment and pioneering. Sociologists and city planners and supermarkets and the rest of us are confronted by puzzling new dilemmas. How to make all these transitions? If manufacturers design and make the good equipment we need they will have trouble selling it at first, though they may eventually become rich. Turning cars into bicycles, and gas stations into bike shops and bus stations, is like beating swords into plowshares only in principle. It is far slower and more complicated. Still, it is easier than figuring out what to do with Boeing.

26

We are now in a time of apparent standstill, a time of latency, when things must change but we do not know yet how to change them. But even now clever people we know nothing about are cracking some of the problems. Very soon the first faint signs of adaptation should appear: better bus schedules, more middle-aged men and women on bicycles, less waiting for automobile repairs, slightly cleaner air. (And, unfortunately, tales of grave financial trouble in all the automotive industries.)

27

With these must come some dissolving of our many segregations, and it will feel strange. We are not used to it. But perhaps it will not be very difficult. Even in the first strangeness it may feel rather natural, like something we were made for, and know in our bones how to do. Though we naturally "cling to our own kind," especially when we are tired or frightened, walking out to see the world is natural too.

28

2,600 words

DISCUSSION | APPLICATION

1. The central comparison/contrast in Frances Weismiller's "To Ralph Nader. . ." is between past and present. This technique allows her to suggest future changes that may require a return to the manners of the past to minimize

"the discomfort and anxiety of mixing and dealing" with people who are not "one's own kind." We are used to seeing the word "segregation" used in a narrow sense related to civil rights for blacks. Weismiller uses it in a broader sense. Define "segregation" as she uses it in her essay.

2. In addition to comparison/contrast, Weismiller makes use of definition (paragraph 4 defining "manners" and "morals" in terms of their usefulness), historical analysis of the development and impact of the automobile in and on our society, cause-effect analysis (paragraphs 13–15), example drawn from personal observation (paragraph 18), rhetorical questions (paragraph 21), and classification by cause (paragraph 22). Find examples of specific uses of comparison/contrast in the following paragraphs: 5, 6, 7, 8, 12, and 16.

3. Their tendency to pollute the atmosphere aside, Weismiller suggests that automobiles "would still, over a period of time, so alienate different kinds of people from one another that no nation of any size could survive." (Paragraph 11) Do you agree? What reasons does she give to specify and clarify this generalization?

4. German sociologist Helmut Schelsky's studies seem to bear out Weismiller's conjecture in question 3. He suggests that the car is "depersonalizing" because ". . . drivers no longer meet each other on a person-to-person basis, but remain anonymous behind the mask of an . . . automobile. People who would be very polite to one another . . . face to face . . . turn into aggressive idiots behind the wheel." Do you feel that your personality changes when you slip behind the wheel of your car?

5. Is it realistic or practical to contemplate the elimination of the automobile in industrialized societies? Was it realistic in 1900 to contemplate the elimination of the horse and buggy? How do these situations differ?

6. The society Weismiller envisions in which people walk rather than drive their cars thus "confronting one another" exists in microcosm on many college campuses. If this is true of your campus, do you feel a greater sense of community because of this confrontation as you walk across campus than you feel when you're driving your car to college?

7. What symbolic role does the automobile play in our society? The motorcycle?

Theme Assignments

1. In a 300- to 500-word essay, compare and contrast your automobile or motorcycle (if you drive one) in terms of its practical value as a means of transportation and its symbolic value to you. Be candid!

2. Paragraph 14: Our vehicles give us ". . . a sense of ease." Compare and contrast your own experiences, feelings, and/or ideas with any of the examples below that are relevant to them.

   a. In a recent novel, *Play It as It Lays*, Joan Didion's actress-heroine attempts to calm her jittery nerves and escape the depression that threatens to overwhelm her by driving aimlessly at high speed, back and forth along the freeways of Los Angeles.

b. In the film *Easy Rider* the two cyclists set out to drive the country without any particular goal or plan.

c. Thom Gunn prefaces his poem "On the Move" with the quotation, "Man, you gotta go." It captures in its details the use of the motorcycle as a form of tension release and a way to ward off anxiety by creating the illusion of doing something, of going somewhere:

> At worst, one is in motion; and at best,
> Reaching no absolute, in which to rest,
> One is always nearer by not keeping still.

Vocabulary

Paragraph
3. proliferated
   shrank
4. hierarchy
   minimizing
5. caste
6. gentry
   humiliation
7. tendency
8. colloidal
   proteins
   enzymes
   nutrients
10. erosion
    contraptions
11. pollute
    enclaves
    asphyxiated
13. obnoxious
    pauperize
16. solitude
    temerity
    taboo
17. insulation
    intruding
    sketchy
    obediently
19. reverberating
22. conspicuous
25. abominable
    intrusion
    endanger
    mute
26. transitions
27. latency
    adaptation
28. dissolving

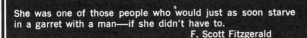

She was one of those people who would just as soon starve
in a garret with a man—if she didn't have to.
F. Scott Fitzgerald

Classification clarifies by grouping ideas, people, or things according
to significant characteristics common to each member of the class.
The classifications of man are infinite. People may be classified as
male or female; elderly, middle-aged, adolescent, or infantile; tall,
wide, short, thin, or pudgy; rich or poor. Cars are classified by their
price and body style. Teams are classified by the league they play in,
major/minor, or the individual skill of the members joined together
into first team, second team, third team. In a lifetime a human being
enjoys or endures a myriad of classifications: baby, grade schooler,
adolescent, adult, bride, soldier, housewife, consumer, homeowner,
father, grandmother, senior citizen, patient, loved one—the last
being a euphemism used by the funeral industry meaning corpse!

In his famous letter "Advice to a Young Man," Benjamin Franklin urges the young man "that in all your amours you should prefer
older women to young ones."

Franklin then goes on to clarify his reasons for classifying older
women as superior in this instance.

1. They have more knowledge of the world.
2. Because when women cease to be handsome they study to be good.
   To maintain their influence over men, they supply the diminution of
   beauty by an augmentation of utility.
3. Because there is no hazard of children, which irregularly produced
   may be attended with much inconvenience.
4. They are more prudent and discreet.
5. As in the dark all cats are grey, the pleasure . . . with an old woman
   is at least equal and frequently superior; every knack being by practice capable of improvement.

6. Because the sin is less.
7. Having made a young girl miserable may give you frequent bitter reflections; none of which can attend making an old woman happy.
8. They [old women] are so grateful!

William V. Shannon, writing in the *New York Times*,* classifies in precise detail a man he calls a "dedicated radical."

> He is inflexible in his aims and relentless in his determination. Like a true revolutionary, he has sacrificed the pleasures of society and the comforts of family life. He lives in a furnished room. He keeps his telephone unlisted and changes the number every few months. He meets his contacts in public places and in modest restaurants. He is determined to change America, and his work is his life.
> This is not a portrait of a Black Panther or a Weatherman or an underground disciple of Che Guevara. This dedicated radical is Ralph Nader, the meticulous, self-disciplined young Ivy League lawyer who has become the leader of the safety and consumer movements. He has shown that the way to beat "the system" is not to drop out of it or take up arms against it but to master its techniques and make use of its opportunities.

Shirley Chisholm's essay, the introduction to her book *Unbought and Unbossed,* shows how she qualifies for the wry classification, "celebrity." Katherine Whitehorn classifies the times we live in and shows with detail, example, and illustration why she likes them. *Newsweek* and *Time* magazines delve into the difficulties of classifying two types of mass killer in this century, Nazi Adolph Eichmann and Austin tower slayer Charles Whitman.

* "The Man Who Beat the System," (8/23/70).

There are 435 members of the House of Representatives and 417 are white males. Ten of the others are women and nine are black. I belong to both of these minorities, which makes it add up right. That makes me a celebrity, a kind of side show attraction. I was the first American citizen to be elected to Congress in spite of the double drawbacks of being female and having skin darkened by melanin.

1

When you put it that way, it sounds like a foolish reason for fame. In a just and free society it would be foolish. That I am a national figure because I was the first person in 192 years to be at once a congressman, black, and a woman proves, I would think, that our society is not yet either just or free.

2

Sometimes the media make me feel like a monkey in a cage. As soon as I was elected, the newspapers and networks started to besiege me. The first question was almost always, "How does it feel?" Naturally, it feels good. I am proud and honored that the people of my district believed in me enough to choose me to represent them. My Twelfth Congressional District of Brooklyn is mostly composed of poor neighborhoods with all the problems of poverty in an aggravated form: slum housing, high unemployment, too few medical services, high crime rate, neglected schools—the whole list. About 69 percent of my people are black and Puerto Rican. The rest are Jewish, Polish, Ukranian, and Italian. Speaking for them at this moment in history is a great responsibility because they have been unrepresented and ignored for so long and their needs are so many and so urgent.

3

But I hope if I am remembered it will finally be for what I have done, not for what I happen to be. And I hope that my having made it, the hard way, can be some kind of inspiration, particularly to women. The number of women in politics has never been large, but now it is getting even smaller.

4

Women are a majority of the population, but they are treated like a minority group. The prejudice against them is so widespread that, paradoxically, most persons do not yet realize it exists. Indeed, most women do not realize it. They even accept being paid less for doing the same work as a man. They are as quick as any male to condemn a woman who ventures outside the limits of the role men have assigned to females: that of toy and drudge.

5

Of my two "handicaps," being female put many more obstacles in my path than being black. Sometimes I have trouble, myself, believing that I made it this far against the odds. No one, not even my father, whose hopes for me were extravagant, would ever have dared to predict it.

6

420 words

1. The title of Shirley Chisholm's autobiography, *Unbought and Unbossed,* classifies her in terms of what she is not. Her introduction classifies her in terms of what she is and hopes to become. What additional elements are classified in paragraph 3?
2. Chisholm categorizes the members of the House of Representatives by number, by sex, and by color. What further categories are possible for members of the House?
3. Classify an organization of whch you have been a member into a minimum of four categories.
4. Paragraph 5: "The prejudice against (women) is so widespread that . . . most persons do not yet realize it exists." Do you? Why?
5. Paragraph 6: "Of my two 'handicaps,' being female put many more obstacles in my path than being black." This statement is the most widely quoted sentence in Chisholm's book. Why do you suppose this is so?

Theme Assignments

1. Using Shirley Chisholm's essay as your guide, write a 300- to 500-word essay in which you classify yourself.
2. Select one of the ideas from the following quotations which appear in the chapter titled "Youth and America's Future" in *Unbought and Unbossed* and develop it in a 300- to 500-word essay.
   a. "Most young people are not yet revolutionary, but politicians and police and other persons in power almost seem to be conspiring to turn them into revolutionaries."
   b. "The main thing I have in common with the kids is that we are tired of being lied to. What we want is for people to mean what they say."
   c. "The most tragic error into which older people can fall is one that is common among educators and politicians. It is to use youth as scapegoats for the sins of their elders. Is the nation wasting its young men and its honor in an unjust war? Never mind—direct your frustration at the long-haired young people who are shouting in the streets that the war must end. Curse them as hippies and immoral, dirty fanatics; after all, we older Americans cannot have been wrong about anything important, because our hearts are all in the right place and God is always on our side, so anyone who opposes us must be insane, and probably in the pay of the godless Communists."

Vocabulary

Paragraph
1. melanin
3. media
   aggravated
5. paradoxically
   drudge
6. extravagant

A FINE TIME TO BE ALIVE
KATHERINE WHITEHORN

Now that it has more central heating and fewer mouldering gibbets, the countryside is more pleasant than it was. But it is still agreeable to get back to town after a country Christmas, simply because so many people in the country seem positively to detest the times we live in. The sixties, to them, mean nothing but pylons and noise and overcrowding, tradespeople failing to call and charwomen being wasted in factories; the country is going to the dogs, and even the dogs aren't what they were.   1

It is an attitude ably summed up by the headmaster of Harrow, I am told, when he looked out of his train window between Slough and London, shuddered, and said: "Not our century, is it?" I must say it is very much mine, and maybe the New Year is as good a time as any to stand up for it. 2

We may as well start the argument in the usual place—with those technical and scientific achievements usually dismissed in one scornful half-sentence about moon rockets and electric shoe polishers. But I think one should spare a better word for them. Dirty nappies* are dirty nappies in any age—but more people have washing machines or Paddi Pads than ever had skivvies to wash for them—and, anyway, what about the skivvies?† 3

Modern medicine I am not inclined to pooh-pooh, having survived acute appendicitis; and I cannot help wondering whether the people who long for the peace and poetry of the eighteenth century have considered what dying in childbirth without anaesthetics must have been like. Nor is it all utilitarian, either—how many people (except friends of blind violinists) made love to music before this century?   4

Youth is supposed to be bored and aimless; yet the figures for every hobby you can name are on the increase, and any of the young that one meets seem to be full of confidence and zip. But even if all these things were true, I am still not sure it would not be outweighed by the vast increase in the freedom of choice enjoyed by the lower orders—by which I mean working people, young people and, above all, women. You hear people asking at dinner parties what real benefits the liberation of women has, after all, brought: the poor things, they say, were a good deal more serene when they knew their role in society and stuck to it. For the majority who enjoy above all things talking and working with men the benefits are obvious: nuns, no doubt, were always allowed to work and tarts to talk, but doing both and being respectably married as well is quite an innovation.   5

But in arguing about this people often forget that the biggest advance is in women's legal strength *as* women—freedom to hang on to their own

* Diapers.
† Washerwomen.

children, for example, to have some sort of legal share in a disbanded home. . . . 6

It is women, too, who have mainly benefited from the let-up in family tyranny. I knew a woman, now dead, who spent her whole life as a dependent spinster because her Congregationalist father refused to let her marry her beloved Anglican. Beatrix Potter's parents were still balking at her choice of mate when she was 40, and Florence Nightingale wasted 15 years picking up her mother's hairpins in the cause of family duty. It was she, too, who coined the phrase "busy idleness" for the awful genteel boredom that went with the "age of leisure." That the servants were downtrodden we all accept, but a lady's existence must have been pretty restricted too: think of the number of things a nice woman simply did not do—including all the activities covered by that story of the Victorian bride who was sternly told on her wedding night that "ladies do not move." 7

And while we are on the subject of marriage, it is worth pointing out that for all the high proportion of failures, our *ideal* of marriage must be one of the highest the world has ever had. The notion of a complete sharing at every level; of fathers taking as much interest in the children's upbringing as mothers, of mothers really understanding a man's working life: this can hardly have been possible when the man's world and the woman's world were so separate that they overlapped only at bed and table. We talk about problems of communication; but a hundred years ago people operated in such separate grooves that they didn't *have* to communicate. 8

The most serious charge against the time, I suppose, is the decline in morals. But even here there may be something on the credit side. For one thing, you no longer have a situation where the respectable paterfamiliae keep one prostitute in business for every two of them; and although I realize that we keep to our current proportion of one per 4,000 only by the profusion of our private arrangements, I still think there is something fundamentally more honest about what Willy Stone called "Fellers sleeping with other fellers' sisters." 9

And there is another dimension to morality since socialism: nobody now supposes that you can be a good Christian slumming in ermine and pearls. The most horrifying thing about Cecil Woodham Smith's book about the Irish famine ("The Great Hunger"), it seems to me, was not the sufferings of the starving or even the callousness of the evicting landlords, but the fact that no one seemed to think the famine their responsibility. Whatever disasters happen nowadays, we do assume that somebody ought to do something; that at any rate it is our business. I don't think you can rate our morals without considering the increase in the social conscience, which is the bit this century has added to the available ideology. 10

In the regrettable absence of a time machine, it may seem pretty futile to ask whether these are good times to live in at all. But the point is that the things that are badly wrong with our times—the ugliness, the remaining social injustice, the sluggishness of the national tripes—are not to be put right by nostalgically looking back to a golden age that never was. Social justice is not to be had by deploring the Welfare State as a piece of modern nonsense, but by repairing the holes in its fabric. It is not the preservation of rural England, but more exciting suburban architecture which is going to make the place look better.   11

The Royal Dukes may be as rich as Clore, but they can no longer command a policeman to arrest me. Widows' pensions are not what they might be—but at least the poor don't receive the scraps of Blenheim Palace mixed indiscriminately like pigswill, as they did till an American put a stop to it. We may not have the serene certainty that God is on the side of the British Empire—but at least He isn't on the side of father, either. And even if we have to make up our own minds how we should behave as women, at least we don't have to behave like ladies. It may be worth living in the sixties for that alone.   12

1,000 words

DISCUSSION | APPLICATION

1. Is Katherine Whitehorn persuasive in her defense of the present? Cite additional details for or against her position, especially as they relate to our society.
2. Paragraph 7: Explain the expression "family tyranny."
3. Does she seem to emphasize the woman's view?

Theme Assignments

1. Attack or defend the final sentences, "At least we don't have to behave like ladies. It may be worth living in the sixties for that alone."
2. Optimist: "This is the best of all possible worlds." Pessimist: "That's what I'm afraid of!" Write a theme from the optimist's or the pessimist's point of view, making specific reference to Katherine Whitehorn's essay.
3. The author obviously believes that women have been emancipated and that it's a good thing. Is it? For men too? Classify the advantages for men or the disadvantages.

Vocabulary

Paragraph
1. gibbets
   detest
4. acute
   anaesthetics
   utilitarian
5. serene

   innovation
6. disbanded
7. benefited
   tyranny
   genteel
   boredom
   downtrodden

9. paterfamiliae
   profusion
10. dimension
    callousness
    evicting
    social conscience
11. futile

Although he was hanged on May 31, 1962, his body cremated and his ashes scattered in the Mediterranean beyond the borders of Israel, Adolf Eichmann, the Nazi head of the Department of Jewish Affairs in Hitler's government, is still causing unrest and misery among the people whose terrifying nemesis he was. A new book, "Eichmann in Jerusalem" *(275 pages. Viking. $5.50),* by the profound and brilliant political philosopher Hannah Arendt, raises many more questions than it succeeds in answering, but it demonstrates once more that the destruction of 6 million European Jews by the bureaucracy of Nazi Germany is still an event which the Western world is desperately trying to digest and understand.

1

The misery and agony which the dead Eichmann is still creating comes from the inevitable reaction by most of world Jewry to Miss Arendt's subtle attempt to analyze a phenomenon which, at bottom, defies analysis. Miss Arendt has the kind of courage which only first-rate intelligences have —the courage not only of her convictions, but also of the power of her thinking processes. It is here that she runs tragically afoul of her fellow Jews, who like most of mankind, have merely the courage of their convictions. They *know* what has happened to the Jews in recent history; Miss Arendt is constantly struggling to find out, to break through what appears to be the congealed surface of events to the life below. On her side, the difficulty is that she sometimes dives too deep and not only loses contact with the surface, but also with the human oxygen that makes common-sense breathing and thinking possible.

2

Miss Arendt's book first appeared as a series of five articles in The New Yorker magazine. Almost immediately, there was a startled reaction on the part of most Jews as her thesis developed. That thesis consisted basically of two elements. One was that Eichmann, far from being the perverted monster and anti-Semitic sadist that the Israeli prosecution had charged, was, in fact, exactly what he presented himself as being—a minor cog in a vast impersonal machine, the quintessence of human mediocrity caught up in a gigantic operation of destruction.

3

Dark Chapter

The second element in her thesis was even harder for many Jews to swallow. Miss Arendt contended that the Jews of Europe, in the persons of leaders of various organizations, had in effect abetted their own destruction by cooperation with and appeasement of the mass murderers. "To a Jew," she writes, "this role of the Jewish leaders in the destruction of their own people is undoubtedly the darkest chapter of the whole dark story . . . Jewish officials could be trusted to compile lists of persons and of their property, to secure money from the deportees to defray the expenses of their deportation and extermination, to keep track of vacated apartments, to supply police forces to help seize Jews and get them on trains, until, as a last gesture, they handed over the assets of the Jewish community in good order for final confiscation." 4

As soon as Miss Arendt's articles started to appear in the pages of The New Yorker, most Israeli correspondents in the United States cabled back detailed extracts and reported that American Jews were deeply disturbed. Three of the installments appeared in full in Tel Aviv's newspaper Ha'aretz. In America, even before the series came to an end, Jewish organizations bitterly protested what they considered to be slander and defamation. The Council of Jews From Germany issued an angry statement: "Hannah Arendt considers herself entitled to state that Jewish leaders had had a part in the annihilation of their own people . . . She misinterprets the attitude of men about whose integrity and self-sacrifice there can be no possible doubt . . . Bitter injustice is done to the leaders and officials of those organizations by . . . attaching a moral stigma to their efforts to mitigate the lot of the Jews . . ." And a headline in a Midwestern Jewish weekly proclaimed: SELF-HATING JEWESS WRITES PRO-EICHMANN SERIES FOR NEW YORKER MAGAZINE. In Israel, columnist Shlomo Grodsensky suggested that Hannah Arendt's views were understandable since she has a "Jewish Prussian soul." 5

Hannah Arendt, born in 1906, did indeed grow up in Königsberg, eastern Prussia. She studied with the existentialist philosophers Martin Heidegger and Karl Jaspers at Heidelberg, where she received her doctorate in philosophy. Escaping from Germany to Paris in 1933, she worked for the Jewish Agency until the country was overrun by the Germans in 1940. After five weeks in a concentration camp, she managed to escape and reached America, where she has taught at several universities, including Princeton. Her book "The Origins of Totalitarianism" is probably the most penetrating and important analysis of the subject in the English language. 6

Marionettes

In that book, one can find the best reply to Dr. Arendt's own accusation of Jewish passivity. Writing of the Nazi purpose, she says: "It is . . . significant that . . . there were scarcely any serious revolts . . . For to destroy individuality is to destroy spontaneity . . . Nothing then remains but ghastly marionettes . . . which all react with perfect reliability even when going to their own death . . . This is the real triumph of the system." 7

In "Eichmann in Jerusalem," on the other hand, she can write that Eichmann "did not expect the Jews to share the general enthusiasm over their destruction, but he did expect more than compliance, he expected—and received, to a truly extraordinary degree—their cooperation." But how can these "destroyed individualities" be accused of complying "to a truly extraordinary degree" with their destroyers? Perhaps part of the answer to this question lies in Dr. Arendt's statement, in the Eichmann book, that "the deliberate attempt at the trial to tell only the Jewish side of the story distorted the truth, even the Jewish truth." Dr. Arendt vehemently wants to know the "whole" truth.

8

The "whole" truth can never be known, but the basic truth is tragically simple: one nation, Nazi Germany, erected a vast political and technical apparatus solely to rid Europe of this "biological material"—the Jews. The subtitle of Dr Arendt's book is "A Report on the Banality of Evil." And Eichmann was its incarnation. "The trouble with Eichmann," she states, "was precisely that so many were like him, and that the many were neither perverted nor sadistic, that they were, and still are, terribly and terrifyingly normal . . . this normality was much more terrifying than all the atrocities put together, for it implied . . . that this new type of criminal . . . commits his crimes under circumstances that make it . . . impossible for him to know or feel he is doing wrong."

9

Victims

There is thus an apparent imbalance between the book's two most important and controversial points. It is almost as if all Dr. Arendt's analytical juices are set flowing by the "predicament" of the executioner, and not by that of the victim. Norman Podhoretz, editor of the influential periodical Commentary, published by the American Jewish Committee, said: "If Hannah Arendt had exercised the same degree of imagination about the victims as she did about Eichmann, she would have written a great book."

10

On vacation in Rome last week, Dr. Arendt spoke to Newsweek about the storm that she has stirred up: "Eichmann in his police testimony, and later in court, makes the cooperation of the Jewish leaders very important. Without them there would not have been the know-how and manpower to round up the Jews. Hitler would have taken victims—but . . . 6 million would not have been possible . . . The Jewish leaders could have said to their communities, 'A terrible disaster has happened. We can no longer help you. We can only share your fate.' " Dr. Arendt, asked if that would not have been an invitation to anarchy, replied: "Yes! and that's better—the Nazis numbered hundreds of thousands while millions of Jews would have gone underground."

11

Self-styled Nobody

This thinking is not worthy of Dr. Arendt. To ask anarchy of the least anarchic of people is unreasonable enough, but to picture a Nazi-dominated Europe with "millions of Jews" underground is to cosmeticize the ravaged face of twentieth-century Europe. And it is strange that Dr. Arendt should use Eichmann as an authority on Jewish collaboration. As Harold Rosenberg said in a brilliant essay on the Eichmann trial in Commentary: "Why should this self-styled nobody who had hurled into silence so many of the subtlest and most human intellects of Europe have been permitted to elaborate on each trait of his character, his opinions on all sorts of matters, including Kant's categorical imperative, and his conception of himself as Pontius Pilate and as a 'romantic,' his reaction to his wife's reading the Bible, his drinking of mare's milk and schnapps? One question would have sufficed to complete the formation of his culpability: 'Weren't you the head of Sec. IV B4 of RSHA charged with the extermination of the Jews of Europe, and did you not carry out the function assigned to you to the best of your ability?' "   12

In the end it is the failure or unwillingness of Dr. Arendt to keep this ethical simplicity of the Eichmann case front and center that is the weakness of her book. She wants no kind or degree of culpability to escape her analytic net, but it is perhaps the great moral crime of the Nazis that they *forced* culpability in their own victims—they tricked, cajoled, and terrorized millions into aiding, often shamefully, their own destruction. Adolf Eichmann will never die if he is permitted, as a "helpless" executioner, to become half of a weird Dance of Death with his "helpful" victims.   13

1,650 words

DISCUSSION | APPLICATION

The crux of the controversy over Hannah Arendt's book involves the classification of Adolph Eichmann. At his trial in Jerusalem he was depicted as a perverse monster. This appears to be the most widely held view. Hannah Arendt, however, classifies Eichmann as quite ordinary. He had a function to perform, a job to do. It was legal and socially acceptable in his society. It involved killing millions of human beings because they were Jews.

In reviewing Hannah Arendt's book, Bruno Bettelheim agreed with her view. "By all scientific standards," Bettelheim writes, "Eichmann was a 'normal' person. Half a dozen psychiatrists had certified him as 'normal.' " The minister who visited him in prison, according to Arendt, "reassured everybody by declaring Eichmann to be 'a man with very positive ideas.' "

Contemplating Eichmann, Bettelheim notes, "Obviously our standards of normality do not apply to behavior in totalitarian societies."

Why is there such shock and repugnance at the idea that Eichmann is, after all, human? Is it easier for us to deal with the idea of the kind of mass murders he was involved in if we label him "monster" rather than "normal"? If Eichmann is not a monster, he becomes as you or I. And we, of course, are "normal"?

Hannah Arendt's book also deals with the "language rules" the Nazis used when writing or talking about the extermination of the Jews. These rules operated by special code. The rule for communicating about "exterminating the Jews" was to use the phrase "the final solution of the Jewish problem," or to speak of "special treatment," or "resettlement." All of these meant one thing to those who knew the code: the transportation of all Jews to death camps and final destruction.

"Language rules" were made fun of by George Orwell ("All are equal, but some are more equal than others."), and their use has been examined by semanticists. They help people to hide from themselves, as well as from others, exactly what they are doing.

1. How do you classify Eichmann? Why?
2. How do you classify Brig. Gen. Paul W. Tibbets, who piloted the B-29 bomber *Enola Gay* on the 1945 bomb run over Hiroshima where 70,000 were killed and 70,000 injured? "I was acting under orders at the time," General Tibbets is quoted as saying, "and would do it again if called upon to do so. . . . Do I have pangs of conscience for it? I can assure you that I don't, since I never took it personally, but as a military operation."
3. Should Eichmann have challenged the system? Should General Tibbets? Would you?
4. Paragraph 11: Is there ever a situation where anarchy is acceptable? Is there any relationship between ghetto riots in United States cities and Arendt's statement in this paragraph?

Theme Assignments

1. Attack or defend Hannah Arendt's classification of Eichmann.
2. Distinguish between and classify the difference between one who advocates "law and order" and one who advocates "law and justice."
3. "The ideal of the good life has faded from the educational process, leaving only miscellaneous prospects of jobs and joyless hedonism," according to former Yale President Robert Goheen. Write a classification theme on "my ideal of the good life."

Vocabulary

Paragraph
1. nemesis
2. subtle
   congealed
3. perverted
   sadist
   quintessence
   mediocrity

4. abetted
   appeasement
   defray
   confiscation
5. slander
   defamation
   annihilation
   integrity

stigma
6. existentialist
7. spontaneity
8. vehemently
9. banality
11. anarchy
13. culpability

THE MADMAN IN THE TOWER
TIME

In the forenoon of a blazing August day, a blond, husky young man strolled into a hardware store in Austin, Texas, and asked for several boxes of rifle ammunition. As he calmly wrote a check in payment, the clerk inquired with friendly curiosity what all the ammunition was for. "To shoot some pigs," he replied. At the time, the answer seemed innocent enough, for wild pigs still abound not far from the capital. The horror of its intent only became obvious a few hours later, when the customer, Charles Joseph Whitman, 25, a student of architectural engineering at the University of Texas, seized his grisly fame as the perpetrator of the worst mass murder in recent U.S. history.   1

That morning, Charles Whitman entered two more stores to buy guns before ascending, with a veritable arsenal, to the observation deck of the limestone tower that soars 307 feet above the University of Texas campus. There, from Austin's tallest edifice, the visitor commands an extraordinary view of the 232-acre campus, with its green mall and red tile roofs, of the capital, ringed by lush farm lands, and, off to the west, of the mist-mantled hills whose purple hue prompted Storyteller O. Henry to christen Austin the "City of a Violet Crown." Whitman had visited the tower ten days before in the company of a brother, and had taken it all in. Today, though, he had no time for the view; he was too intent upon his deadly work.   2

Methodically, he began shooting everyone in sight. Ranging around the tower's walk at will, he sent his bullets burning and rasping through the flesh and bone of those on the campus below, then of those who walked or stood or rode as far as three blocks away. Somewhat like the travelers in Thornton Wilder's *The Bridge of San Luis Rey,* who were drawn by an inexorable fate to their crucial place in time and space, his victims fell as they went about their various tasks and pleasures. By lingering perhaps a moment too long in a classroom or leaving a moment too soon for lunch, they had unwittingly placed themselves within Whitman's lethal reach. Before he was himself perforated by police bullets, Charles Whitman killed 13 people and wounded 31—a staggering total of 44 casualties. As a prelude to his senseless rampage, it was later discovered, he had also slain his wife and mother, bringing the total dead to 15.   3

In a nation that opened its frontiers by violence and the gun, Whitman's sanguinary spree had an unsettling number of precedents, both in fiction and in fact. The imaginary parallels are grisly—and suggestive—enough: from *The Sniper,* a 1952 movie about a youth who shoots blondes, to *The Open Square,* a 1962 novel by Ford Clarke, whose protagonist climbs a tower on a Midwestern campus and begins picking people off. (So far as police know, Whitman had neither seen the movie nor read the book.) Even the fiction, however, pales before the fact. There was Scripture-reading Howard Unruh's 20-minute orgy that brought death to 13 people in Camden, N.J., in 1949, and bandy-legged Charles Starkweather's slaying of ten during a three-day odyssey through Nebraska and Wyoming in 1958. There were the two murderers of the Clutter family, Richard Hickock and Perry Smith, now enshrined in Truman Capote's *In Cold Blood,* the year's most talked-about bestseller. Only last month, when eight student nurses were slain in a Chicago town house, and Richard Speck was charged with the crime, an official there called the murders "the crime of the century." Sadly, Austin Police Chief Robert A. Miles observed last week: "It isn't any more." 4

Unusual Undercurrents

Like many mass murderers, Charles Whitman had been an exemplary boy, the kind that neighborhood mothers hold up as a model to their own recalcitrant youngsters. He was a Roman Catholic altar boy and a newspaper delivery boy, a pitcher on his parochial school's baseball team and manager of its football team. At twelve years and three months, he became an Eagle Scout, one of the youngest on record. To all outward appearances, the family in which he grew up in Lake Worth, Fla.—including two younger brothers besides his mother and father, a moderately successful plumbing contractor—was a typical American family. Charlie joined the Marines in 1959 when he was 18, later signed up at the University of Texas, where he was a B student. 5

Yet beneath the easy, tranquil surface of both family and boy there flowed some unusual undercurrents. Charlie was trained to use guns as soon as he was old enough to hold them—and so were his brothers. "I'm a fanatic about guns," says his father, Charles A., 47. "I raised my boys to know how to handle guns." Charlie could plug a squirrel in the eye by the time he was 16, and in the Marine Corps he scored 215 points out of a possible 250, winning a rating as a sharpshooter, second only to expert. In the Marines, though, he also got busted from corporal to private and sentenced to 30 days' hard labor for illegal possession of a pistol, was reprimanded for telling a fellow Marine that he was going "to knock your teeth out." He rated his favorite sports as hunting, scuba diving and karate. 6

A tense situation also prevailed behind the family façade. His father was—and is—an authoritarian, a perfectionist and an unyielding disciplinarian who demanded much of his sons and admitted last week that he was accustomed to beating his wife. In March, Margaret Whitman walked out on him, summoning Charlie from Austin to help her make the break. While his mother was packing her belongings, a Lake Worth police car sat outside the house, called by Charlie presumably because he feared that his father would resort to violence. To be near Charlie, Mrs. Whitman moved to

Austin. The youngest son, John, 17, left home last spring. When he was arrested for pitching a rock through a storefront glass, the judge gave him a choice of a $25 fine or moving back in with his father; he paid the fine. Patrick, 21, who works for his father, is the only son who lives with him.   7

His parents' separation troubled Charlie deeply, and last March 29, he finally went to Dr. Maurice Heatly, the University of Texas' staff psychiatrist. In a two-hour interview, he told Heatly that, like his father, he had beaten his wife a few times. He was making "intense efforts" to control his temper, he said, but he was worried that he might explode. In notes jotted down at the time, Heatly described Whitman as a "massive, muscular youth" who "seemed to be oozing with hostility." Heatly took down only one direct quote of Whitman's—that he was "thinking about going up on the tower with a deer rifle and start shooting people." That did not particularly upset Heatly; it was, he said, "a common experience for students who came to the clinic to think of the tower as the site for some desperate action."[1] Nonetheless, Heatly urged Whitman to return the next week to talk some more. Charlie Whitman never went back. Instead, some time in the next few months, he decided to act.   8

"I Love My Mother"

The evening before his trip to the tower, Whitman sat at a battered portable in his modest brick cottage. Kathy, his wife of four years (they had no children), was at work. "I don't quite understand what is compelling me to type this note," he began. "I've been having fears and violent impulses. I've had some tremendous headaches. I am prepared to die. After my death, I wish an autopsy on me to be performed to see if there's any mental disorders." He also wrote: "I intend to kill my wife after I pick her up from work. I don't want her to have to face the embarrassment that my actions will surely cause her."   9

At one point he had to break off when a fellow architecture student, Larry Fuess, and his wife dropped by to chat. Fuess found him looking "particularly relieved about something—you know, as if he had solved a problem." After the couple left, Whitman drove off in his black '66 Chevrolet to pick up Kathy at her summer job as a telephone information operator. He apparently decided not to kill her immediately, instead dropped her off at their house and sped across the Colorado River to his mother's fifth-floor flat in Austin's Penthouse Apartments. There he stabbed Margaret Whitman in the chest and shot her in the back of the head, somehow also breaking several bones in her left hand with such force that the band of her diamond engagement ring was driven into her finger and the stone broken loose. "I have just killed my mother," Charlie wrote in a hand-printed note addressed

---

[1] Three persons have jumped from the tower to their deaths since its completion in 1937. Two others have died in accidental falls.

"To whom it may concern." "If there's a heaven, she is going there. If there is not a heaven, she is out of her pain and misery. I love my mother with all my heart."

10

Tragic Timetable

Back home—it was now after midnight—Whitman stabbed his wife three times in the chest, apparently as she lay sleeping, and drew the bed sheet over her nude body. Then he returned to the note—partially typewritten, partially handwritten, partially printed—that was to be his valedictory. Included was a tragic timetable: "12:30 a.m.—Mother already dead. 3 o'clock —both dead." He hated his father "with a mortal passion," he wrote, and regretted that his mother had given "the best 25 years of her life to that man." Clearly, the erratic orbit of his mind had already carried him off to some remote aphelion of despair. "Life is not worth living," he wrote. He had apparently concluded that if it were not worth living for him, it need not be for the others, either. With the special lucidity of the mad, Whitman meticulously prepared to take as many people with him to the grave as he possibly could.

11

Into a green duffel bag and a green foot locker that bore the stenciled words, "Lance Cpl. C. J. Whitman," he stuffed provisions to sustain him during a long siege and to cover every contingency: Spam, Planters peanuts, fruit cocktail, sandwiches and boxes of raisins, jerricans containing water and gasoline, rope, toilet paper, and, in a bizarre allegiance to the cult of cleanliness, a plastic bottle of Mennen spray deodorant. He also stowed away a private armory that seemed sufficient to hold off an army: machete, Bowie knife, hatchet, a 6-mm. Remington bolt-action rifle with a 4-power Leupold telescopic sight (with which, experts say, a halfway decent shot can consistently hit a 6½-in. circle from 300 yds.), a 35-mm. Remington rifle, a 9-mm. Luger pistol, a Galesi-Brescia pistol and a .357 Smith & Wesson Magnum revolver. At home, he left three more rifles, two derringers.

12

Whether Whitman slept at all during the following few hours is not known. He was next seen at 7:15 a.m. when he rented a mover's dolly from an Austin firm. Then, deciding that he needed even more firepower, he went to Sears, Roebuck and bought a 12-gauge shotgun on credit, sawed off both barrel and stock. He visited Davis Hardware to buy a .30-cal. carbine. And at Chuck's Gun Shop, he bought some 30-shot magazines for the new carbine. All told, he had perhaps 700 rounds.

13

Left to Die

Around 11 a.m., Whitman boldly breezed into a parking spot reserved for university officials, near the main administration and library building at the base of the tower. Dressed in tennis sneakers, blue jeans and a pale polo shirt, he wheeled the loaded dolly toward an elevator, gave passersby the impression that he was a maintenance man. The elevator stops at the 27th floor; Whitman lugged his bizarre cargo up three flights of steps to the 30th floor. There, at a desk next to the glass-paneled door that opens onto the observation deck, he encountered Receptionist Edna Townsley, 47, a spirited divorcee and mother of two young sons. Whitman bashed her head in, probably with a rifle butt, with such force that part of her skull was torn away, also shot her in the head. Then he left her behind a sofa to die. 14

As Whitman began assembling his equipment on the deck, six sight-seers arrived, led by Mark and Mike Gabour, the 16- and 19-year-old sons of M. J. Gabour, a service-station owner in Texarkana, Texas. "Mark opened the door to the observation deck and a gun went off," said Gabour. "Mike screamed." Then his sons, his wife and his sister, Mrs. Marguerite Lamport, "came rolling down the stairs. Whoever did the shooting slammed the door." Gabour turned his younger son over, saw he had been shot in the head. He was dead. So was Gabour's sister. Critically injured, his wife and his older son were bleeding profusely. Gabour and his brother-in-law dragged their dead and wounded to the 27th floor, sought help but could find none. 15

Splashed with Blood

Outside, on the six-foot-wide walkway that runs around all four sides of the tower, Whitman positioned himself under the "VI" of the gold-edged clock's south face. Looking toward the mall, a large paved rectangle, he could see scores of students below him. Had Mrs. Townsley and the Gabours not held him up, he might have had another thousand students as targets when classes changed at 11:30 a.m. Now, at 11:48 a.m., Charles Whitman opened fire. The 17-chime carillon above him was to ring the quarter-hour six times before his guns were silenced. 16

For a moment, nobody could make out what the odd explosions from atop the tower meant. Then men and women began crumpling to the ground, and others ran for cover. On the fourth floor of the tower building, Ph.D. Candidate Norma Barger, 23, heard the noises, looked out and saw six bodies sprawled grotesquely on the mall. At first she thought it was just a tasteless joke. "I expected the six to get up and walk away laughing." Then she saw the pavement splashed with blood, and more people falling. In the first 20 minutes relying chiefly on the 6-mm. rifle with the scope but switching occasionally to the carbine and the .357 revolver, Whitman picked off most of his victims. 17

On the sun-dappled mall, Mrs. Claire Wilson, 18, eight months pregnant, was walking from an anthropology class when a bullet crashed into her abdomen; she survived, but later gave birth to a stillborn child whose skull had been crushed by the shot. A horrified classmate, Freshman Thomas Eckman, 19, knelt beside her to help, was shot dead himself. Mathematician Robert Boyer, 33, en route to a teaching job in Liverpool, England, where his pregnant wife and two children were awaiting him, stepped out onto the mall to head for lunch, was shot fatally in the back. More fortunate was Secretary Charlotte Darehshori, who rushed out to help when the first victims dropped, suddenly realized she was under fire and spent the next hour-and-a-half crouched behind the concrete base of a flag-pole—one of the few persons to venture onto the mall and survive the siege uninjured.   18

At the south end of the mall, Austin Patrolman Billy Speed, 23, one of the first policemen on the scene, took cover behind the heavy, columnar stone railing, but a bullet zinged between the columns and killed him. Still farther south, 500 yds. from the tower, Electrical Repairman Roy Dell Schmidt, 29, walked toward his truck after making a call, was killed by a bullet in the stomach. To the east, Iran-bound Peace Corps Trainee Thomas Ashton, 22, was strolling on the roof of the Computation Center when Whitman shot him dead.   19

Directing his fire west, Whitman found shop-lined Guadalupe Street, the main thoroughfare off campus—known locally as "The Drag"—astir with shoppers and strollers. Paul Sonntag, 18, lifeguard at an Austin pool and grandson of Paul Bolton, longtime friend of Lyndon Johnson and news editor of the Johnsons' Austin television station, was accompanying Claudia Rutt, 18, for a polio shot she needed before entering Texas Christian University. Claudia suddenly sank to the ground. Paul bent over her, then pitched to the sidewalk himself. Both were dead. A block north, Political Scientist Harry Walchuk, 39, a father of six and a teacher at Michigan's Alpena Community College, browsed in the doorway of a newsstand after working all morning in the college library. He was shot dead on the spot. A few steps farther up the street, Senior Thomas Karr, 24, was walking sleepily toward his apartment after staying up almost all night for a 10 a.m. exam when he dropped to the pavement, dying.   20

Impossible to Hit

Four minutes after Whitman opened fire, Austin police received a report about "some shooting at the University Tower." In seconds, a "10-50" trouble signal went out, directing all units in the vicinity to head for the university. In a din of wailing sirens, more than 100 city cops, reinforced by some 30 highway patrolmen, Texas Rangers and U.S. Secret Service men from Lyndon Johnson's Austin office, converged on the campus.   21

The lawmen sent hundreds of rounds of small-arms fire crackling toward the tower deck. A few smashed into the faces of the clocks above Whitman, and most pinked ineffectually into the four-foot-high wall in front of him, kicking up puffs of dust. Ducking below the wall, Whitman began using narrow drainage slits in the wall as gunports. He proved almost impossible to hit, but he kept finding targets—to the north, where he wounded two students on their way to the Biology Building; to the east, where he nicked a girl sitting at a window in the Business Economics Building; but particularly to the south, where the mall looked like a no man's land strewn with bodies that could not safely be recovered, and to the west, where The Drag was littered with four dead, eleven wounded.   22

Riding along The Drag, Newsboy Aleck Hernandez was practically catapulted off his bicycle when a bullet slammed into its seat—and his, inflicting a painful wound. Three blocks up The Drag, Basketball Coach Billy Snowden of the Texas School for the Deaf stepped into the doorway of the barbershop where he was having his hair cut and was wounded in the shoulder. Outside the Rae Ann dress shop on The Drag, Iraqi Chemistry Student Abdul Khashab, 26, his fiancée Janet Paulos, 20, whom he was to have married next week, and Student-Store Clerk Lana Phillips, 21, fell wounded within seconds of each other. At Sheftall's jewelers, Manager Homer Kelley saw three youths fall wounded outside, was helping to haul them inside when Whitman zeroed in on the shop. Fragments from two bullets tore into Kelley's leg. Windows shattered. Bullets tore huge gashes in the carpeting inside. North of the tower, Associated Press Reporter Robert Heard, 36, was hit in the shoulder while he was running full tilt. "What a shot!" he marveled through his pain.   23

Green Flag

Unable to get at Whitman from the ground, the police chartered a light plane, sent sharpshooting Lieut. Marion Lee aloft in it. The sniper's fire drove it away. Finally four men, who had made their way separately to the tower building through subterranean passages or by zigzagging from building to building, decided to storm the observation deck. Three were Austin patrolmen who had never been in a gunfight: Houston McCoy, Jerry Day and Ramiro Martinez, who was off duty when he heard of the sniper, got into uniform and rushed to the campus. The fourth was Civilian Allen Crum, 40, a retired Air Force tailgunner, who had "never fired a shot" in combat. 24

The four rode to the 27th floor, headed single file up the last three flights, carefully removed a barricade of furniture that Whitman had set at the top of the stairs. While cops on the ground intensified their fire to divert Whitman's attention, Martinez slowly pushed away the dolly propped against the door leading to the walkway around the tower, crawled out onto its south side and began moving stealthily to the east. Crum followed through the door and turned toward the west. Hearing footsteps, Crum fired into the southwest corner to keep Whitman from bursting around the corner and shooting him. Martinez, meanwhile, rounded one corner, then, more slowly, turned onto the north side of the walkway. 25

Fifty feet away from him, in the northwest corner, crouched Whitman, his eyes riveted on the corner that Crum was about to turn. Martinez poured six pistol shots into Whitman's left side, arms and legs. McCoy moved up, blasted Whitman with a shotgun. Martinez, noting that the sniper's gun "was still flopping," grabbed the shotgun and blasted Whitman again. As an autopsy showed, the shotgun pellets did it: one pierced Whitman's heart, another his brain. Crum grabbed a green towel from Whitman's foot locker, waved it above the railing to signal cease-fire. At 1:24 p.m., 96 murderous minutes after his first fusillade from the tower, Charlie Whitman was dead. 26

Tumors & Goofballs

Whitman's bloody stand profoundly shocked a nation not yet recovered from the Chicago nurses' murders. One effect was to prompt a re-examination of U.S. arms laws and methods of handling suspected psychotics. There was a spate of ideas, some hasty and ill conceived. Texas Governor John Connally, who broke off a Latin American tour and hurried home after the shootings, demanded legislation requiring that any individual freed on the ground of insanity in murder and kidnaping cases be institutionalized for life. New York's Senator Robert Kennedy proposed that persons acquitted of all federal crimes on the ground of insanity be committed for psychiatric treatment. Had Whitman lived to face trial, said Kennedy, he would "undoubtedly" have been acquitted because "he was so clearly insane." 27

An autopsy showed that Whitman had a pecan-size brain tumor, or astrocytoma, in the hypothalamus region, but Pathologist Coleman de Chenar said that it was "certainly not the cause of the headaches" and "could not have had any influence on his psychic behavior." A number of Dexedrine tablets—stimulants known as "goofballs"—were found in Whitman's possession, but physicians were not able to detect signs that he had taken any before he died. 28

Half-staff

Precisely what triggered Whitman's outburst is a mystery. And it is likely to remain so, though psychiatrists will undoubtedly debate the causes for years. The role of Whitman's father in shaping—or misshaping—his son's personality has already come under intense scrutiny, but other psychiatrists feel that the cause of his illness must be sought in his relationship with his mother. Whatever its cause, Charlie Whitman's psychosis was poured out in detail in his farewell notes, which, a grand jury said, will be released only to "authorized investigating agencies, since they contain unverified statements of an insane killer concerning an innocent individual." 29

In the end, Charlie Whitman and his mother returned together to Florida, he in a grey metal casket, she in a green-and-white one. With hundreds of curiosity seekers gawking and jostling in a rolling, palm-fringed cemetery in West Palm Beach, mother and son were buried with Catholic rites. Charlie had obviously been deranged, said the Whitman's priest, and was not responsible for the sin of murder and therefore eligible for burial in hallowed ground. 30

In Austin, where two of those wounded by Whitman remain in critical condition and three in serious condition, most flags flew at half-staff through the week. This week the flags go back to full staff as the university and the capital attempt to return to normal. That may take a while. The 17 chimes in the tower from which Charlie Whitman shot peal each quarter-hour, resounding over the tree-shaded campus and the mist-mantled hills beyond. 31

3,600 words

DISCUSSION | APPLICATION

"Each year in this country guns are involved in more than 6,500 murders. This compares with 30 in England, 99 in Canada, 68 in West Germany and 37 in Japan."

President Lyndon Johnson
June, 1968

"The private arsenal in U.S. homes now totals 90 million weapons, according to an estimate by the FBI. Family gun racks in the 63 million U.S. households boast 35 million rifles and 31 million shotguns. Add to that 24 million hand guns. The small-arms inventory for the U.S. armed forces: 4.8 million guns, including those in Vietnam."

Newsweek (8/17/70)

1. Why does *Time* magazine title the story of Charles Whitman "The Madman in the Tower"? What evidence is there that he was "mad"? What is the definition of "madness"?

2. Note the listings in this essay—previous mass murders and their consequences are listed, the number and types of weapons Whitman had with him on the tower are noted, the other items he took up with him are cataloged, and the number of victims is ticked off in chronological order. What

effect do these listings have on the reader's understanding of Whitman's actions? On the impact the story makes?

3. In this essay the effect—15 dead, 31 wounded—is quite clear. Is the cause clear? What do you think caused Whitman to kill?

4. Paragraph 1, sentence 1: Why is the verb "strolled" apt in the context? What does it imply?

5. Might a line such as "Whitman . . . seized his grisly fame as the perpetrator of the worst mass murder in recent U.S. history" motivate others to emulate Whitman?

6. Paragraph 9: What does this sentence indicate as to Whitman's value system? It is the motive he gives for killing his wife: "I don't want her to have to face the embarrassment that my actions will surely cause her." Does Whitman consider embarrassment as being worse than death?

Theme Assignments

1. "Guns don't kill people. People kill people." Attack or defend this statement.

2. "There are some problems that can't be solved. The greatest problem is life, not death."

Carl Rogers

"I am prepared to die."

Charles Whitman

Using or disregarding Rogers' and/or Whitman's quotation, write a theme on the subject: "I am prepared to live."

3. "Anyone at any time, may equally find himself victim or executioner."

Sartre

"Love thy neighbor as thyself." (Unless you hate yourself?)

"What takes nerve is to face, not hardship, but the real and existing possibilities of living up to one's best."

Jeremy Larner

"Support mental health or I'll kill you!"

Using one of the quotations above as the theme, develop an essay through classification of such words as "victim," "executioner," "love," "self," "living up to one's best."

Vocabulary

Paragraph
1. grisly
2. veritable
3. inexorable
   lethal
4. sanguinary

spree
fiction
fact
7. authoritarian
   disciplinarian
8. oozing

I don't see any harm in sex, so I like it.
Bertrand Russell

Analysis clarifies and develops a topic by breaking it into its component parts. When John Gunther began to do research for his book *Inside U.S.A.*, he decided immediately to approach this monumental task on a state-by-state basis. Newspaper columnists use analysis to probe and predict the outcome of future elections. Psychology texts feature the analysis of human experience. History texts analyze the impact of battles, treaties, and statesmen.

Analysis often deals with cause/effect. A medical scientist seeks a cure by searching for the cause of the effect known as cancer. The President speaks to the nation on the causes of increased taxes—an effect which typically needs a good deal of explanation! Analysis often involves the ordering of detail and data to persuade the reader that a certain cause/effect relationship exists. Do comic books cause crime? What are the causes of juvenile delinquency? Does living in smog cause damage to the heart and lungs over a long period? Why did our candidate win/lose the election?

Who commits murder? Susan Edmiston, writing in *New York* magazine, cites statistical analyses:

> Murder is almost exclusively a lower-class crime, the middle and upper classes preferring to work out their problems through suicide. In a landmark study of criminal homicide in Philadelphia, conducted by Dr. Marvin Wolfgang of the University of Pennsylvania, all 588 murders during a five year period were committed by "representatives from the lower social and economic classes, especially the unskilled working group."... replications of Dr. Wolfgang's study in Chicago, St. Louis and Washington, D.C., have borne out the same conclusions, further confirmed by a study of

crimes of violence in seventeen major American cities conducted by the National Commission on the Causes of Prevention and Violence.*

Interviewed by *Newsweek*, psychoanalyst Erik Erikson gave this analysis of permissiveness and delegated authority in youth-adult relationships.

> ... authoritativeness and permissiveness are two sides of the same cloth, the same frame of mind. For the permissive as well as the authoritarian adult makes decisions for the young without considering what reasonability and responsibility they may be ready for themselves. The ability to confer delegated authority, in contrast, would require that one learn to sense that readiness and, more, become ready, deep down, to share that responsibility. Only thus can one gauge how far the young of today can learn to participate in decisions—if with some tumult on their part and some anxiety on ours.†

In the first essay below, Tom Wolfe explains how the demolition derby came into being as a sport and analyzes its appeal to both spectator and participant. Marshall McLuhan conjectures on the meaning and impact of Jack Ruby's murder of Lee Harvey Oswald as millions watched on television. *Newsweek* considers the importance of Marshall McLuhan's "electronic age" culture. Gloria Steinem tells of how it will be if women win.

---

* "Murder, New York Style: A Crime of Class," *New York*, (8/17/70).
† "Erik Erikson: The Quest for Identity," *Newsweek*, (12/21/70).

CLEAN FUN AT RIVERHEAD
TOM WOLFE

The inspiration for the demolition deby came to Lawrence Mendelsohn one night in 1958 when he was nothing but a spare-ribbed twenty-eight-year-old stock-car driver halfway through his 10th lap around the Islip, L.I., Speedway and taking a curve too wide. A lubberly young man with a Chicago boxcar haircut came up on the inside in a 1949 Ford and caromed him 12 rows up into the grandstand, but Lawrence Mendelsohn and his entire car did not hit one spectator.   1

"That was what got me," he said, "I remember I was hanging upside down from my seat belt like a side of Jersey bacon and wondering why no one was sitting where I hit. 'Lousy promotion,' I said to myself."   2

"Not only that, but everybody who was in the stands forgot about the race and came running over to look at me gift-wrapped upside down in a fresh pile of junk."   3

At that moment occurred the transformation of Lawrence Mendelsohn, racing driver, into Lawrence Mendelsohn, promoter, and, a few transactions later, owner of the Islip Speedway, where he kept seeing more of this same underside of stock car racing that everyone in the industry avoids putting into words. Namely, that for every purist who comes to see the fine points of the race, such as who is going to win, there are probably five waiting for the wrecks to which stock car racing is so gloriously prone.   4

The pack will be going into a curve when suddenly two cars, three cars, four cars tangle, spinning and splattering all over each other and the retaining walls, upside down, right side up, inside out and in pieces, with the seams bursting open and discs, rods, wires and gasoline spewing out and yards of sheet metal shearing off like Reynolds Wrap and crumpling into the most baroque shapes, after which an ash-blue smoke starts seeping up from the ruins and a thrill begins to spread over the stands like Newburg sauce.   5

So why put up with the monotony between crashes?   6

Such, in brief, is the early history of what is culturally the most important sport ever originated in the United States, a sport that ranks with the gladiatorial games of Rome as a piece of national symbolism. Lawrence Mendelsohn had a vision of an automobile sport that would be all crashes. Not two cars, not three cars, not four cars, but 100 cars would be out in an area doing nothing but smashing each other into shrapnel. The car that outrammed and outdodged all the rest, the last car that could still move amid the smoking heap, would take the prize money.   7

So at 8:15 at night at the Riverhead Raceway, just west of Riverhead, L.I., on Route 25, amid the quaint tranquility of the duck and turkey farm flatlands of eastern Long Island, Lawrence Mendelsohn stood up on the back of a flat truck in his red neon warmup jacket and lectured his 100 drivers on the rules and niceties of the new game, the "demolition derby." And so at 8:30 the first 25 cars moved out onto the raceway's quarter-mile stock car track. There was not enough room for 100 cars to mangle each other. Lawrence Mendelsohn's dream would require four heats. Now the 25 cars were placed at intervals all about the circumference of the track, making flatulent revving noises, all headed not around the track but toward a point in the center of the infield.   8

Then the entire crowd, about 4,000, started chanting a countdown, "Ten, nine, eight, seven, six, five, four, three, two," but it was impossible to hear the rest, because right after "two" half the crowd went into a strange whinnying wail. The starter's flag went up, and the 25 cars took off, roaring into second gear with no mufflers, all headed toward that same point in the center of the infield, converging nose on nose.   9

The effect was exactly what one expects that many simultaneous crashes to produce: the unmistakable tympany of automobiles colliding and cheap-gauge sheet metal buckling; front ends folding together at the same cockeyed angles police photographs of night-time wreck scenes capture so well on grainy paper; smoke pouring from under the hoods and hanging over the infield like a howitzer cloud; a few of the surviving cars lurching eccentrically on bent axles. At last, after four heats, there were only two cars moving through the junk, a 1953 Chrysler and a 1958 Cadillac. In the Chrysler a small fascia of muscles named Spider Ligon, who smoked a cigar while he drove, had the Cadillac cornered up against a guard rail in front of the main grandstand. He dispatched it by swinging around and backing full throttle through the left side of its grille and radiator.   10

By now the crowd was quite beside itself. Spectators broke through a gate in the retaining screen. Some rushed to Spider Ligon's car, hoisted him to their shoulders and marched off the field, howling. Others clambered over the stricken cars of the defeated, enjoying the details of their ruin, and howling. The good, full cry of triumph and annihilation rose from Riverhead Raceway, and the demolition derby was over.   11

That was the 154th demolition derby in two years. Since Lawrence Mendelsohn staged the first one at Islip Speedway in 1961, they have been held throughout the United States at the rate of one every five days, resulting in the destruction of about 15,000 cars. The figures alone indicate a gluttonous appetite for the sport. Sports writers, of course, have managed to ignore demolition derbies even more successfully than they have ignored stock car racing and drag racing. All in all, the new automobile sports have shown that the sports pages, which on the surface appear to hum with life and earthiness, are at bottom pillars of gentility. This drag racing and demolition derbies and things, well, there are too many kids in it with sideburns, tight Levis and winkle-picker boots.   12

Yet the demolition derbies keep growing on word-of-mouth publicity. The "nationals" were held last month at Langhorne, Pa., with 50 cars in the finals, and demolition derby fans everywhere know that Don McTavish, of Dover, Mass., is the new world's champion. About 1,250,000 spectators have come to the 154 contests held so far. More than 75 per cent of the derbies have drawn full houses. 13

The nature of their appeal is clear enough. Since the onset of the Christian era, i.e., since about 500 A.D., no game has come along to fill the gap left by the abolition of the purest of all sports, gladiatorial combat. As late as 300 A.D. these bloody duels, usually between men but sometimes between women and dwarfs, were enormously popular not only in Rome but throughout the Roman Empire. Since then no game, not even boxing, has successfully acted out the underlying motifs of most sport, that is, aggression and destruction. 14

Boxing, of course, is an aggressive sport, but one contestant has actually destroyed the other in a relatively small percentage of matches. Other games are progressively more sublimated forms of sport. Often, as in the case of football, they are encrusted with oddments of passive theology and metaphysics to the effect that the real purpose of the game is to foster character, teamwork, stamina, physical fitness and the ability to "give-and-take." 15

But not even those wonderful clergymen who pray in behalf of Congress, expressway ribbon-cuttings, urban renewal projects and testimonial dinners for ethnic aldermen would pray for a demolition derby. The demolition derby is, pure and simple, a form of gladiatorial combat for our times. 16

As hand-to-hand combat has gradually disappeared from our civilization, even in wartime, and competition has become more and more sophisticated and abstract, Americans have turned to the automobile to satisfy their love of direct aggression. The mild-mannered man who turns into a bear behind the wheel of a car—i.e., who finds in the power of the automobile a vehicle for the release of his inhibitions—is part of American folklore. Among teen-agers the automobile has become the symbol, and in part the physical means, of triumph over family and community restrictions. Seventy-five per cent of all car thefts in the United States are by teen-agers out for "joy rides." 17

The symbolic meaning of the automobile tones down but by no means vanishes in adulthood. Police traffic investigators have long been convinced that far more accidents are purposeful crashes by belligerent drivers than they could ever prove. One of the heroes of the era was the Middle Eastern diplomat who rammed a magazine writer's car from behind in the Kalorama embassy district of Washington two years ago. When the American bellowed out the window at him, he backed up and smashed his car again. When the fellow leaped out of his car to pick a fight, he backed up and smashed his car a third time, then drove off. He was recalled home for having "gone native." 18

The unabashed, undisguised, quite purposeful sense of destruction of the demolition derby is its unique contribution. The aggression, the battering, the ruination are there to be enjoyed. The crowd at a demolition derby seldom gasps and often laughs. It enjoys the same full-throated participation as Romans at the Colosseum. After each trial or heat at a demolition derby, two drivers go into the finals. One is the driver whose car was still going at the end. The other is the driver the crowd selects from among the 24 vanquished on the basis of his courage, showmanship or simply the awesomeness of his crashes. The numbers of the cars are read over loudspeakers, and the crowd chooses one with its cheers. By the same token, the crowd may force a driver out of competition if he appears cowardly or merely cunning. This is the sort of driver who drifts around the edge of the battle avoiding crashes with the hope that the other cars will eliminate one another. The umpire waves a yellow flag at him and he must crash into someone within 30 seconds or run the risk of being booed off the field in dishonor and disgrace. 19

The frank relish of the crowd is nothing, however, compared to the kick the contestants get out of the game. It costs a man an average of $50 to retrieve a car from a junk yard and get it running for a derby. He will only get his money back—$50—for winning a heat. The chance of being smashed up in the madhouse first 30 seconds of a round are so great, even the best of drivers faces long odds in his shot at the $500 first prize. None of that matters to them. 20

Tommy Fox, who is nineteen, said he entered the demolition derby because, "You know, it's fun. I like it. You know what I mean?" What was fun about it? Tommy Fox had a way of speaking that was much like the early Marlon Brando. Much of what he had to say came from the trapezii, which he rolled quite a bit, and the forehead, which he cocked, and the eye-brows, which he could bring together expressively from time to time. "Well," he said, "you know, like when you hit 'em, and all that. It's fun." 21

Tommy Fox had a lot of fun in the first heat. Nobody was bashing around quite like he was in his old green Hudson. He did not win, chiefly because he took too many chances, but the crowd voted him into the finals as the best showman. 22

"I got my brother," said Tommy. "I came in from the side and he didn't even see me." 23

His brother is Don Fox, thirty-two, who owns the junk yard where they both got their cars. Don likes to hit them, too, only he likes it almost too much. Don drives with such abandon, smashing into the first car he can get a shot at and leaving himself wide open, he does not stand much chance of finishing the first three minutes. 24

For years now sociologists have been calling upon one another to undertake a serious study of America's "car culture." No small part of it is the way the automobile has, for one very large segment of the population, become the focus of the same sort of quasi-religious dedication as art is currently for another large segment of a higher social order. Tommy Fox is unemployed, Don Fox runs a junk yard, Spider Ligon is a maintenance man for Brookhaven Naval Laboratory, but to categorize them as such is getting no closer to the truth than to have categorized William Faulkner in 1926 as a clerk at Lord & Taylor, although he was.   25

Tommy Fox, Don Fox and Spider Ligon are acolytes of the car culture, an often esoteric world of arts and sciences that came into its own after World War II and now has believers of two generations. Charlie Turbush, thirty-five, and his son, Buddy, seventeen, were two more contestants, and by no stretch of the imagination can they be characterized as bizarre figures or cultists of the death wish. As for the dangers of driving in a demolition derby, they are quite real by all physical laws. The drivers are protected only by crash helmets, seat belts and the fact that all glass, interior handles, knobs and fixtures have been removed. Yet Lawrence Mendelsohn claims that there have been no serious injuries in 154 demolition derbies and now gets his insurance at a rate below that of stock car racing.   26

The sport's future may depend in part on word getting around about its relative safety. Already it is beginning to draw contestants here and there from social levels that could give the demolition derby the cachet of respectability. In eastern derbies so far two doctors and three young men of more than passable connections in eastern society have entered under whimsical *noms de combat* and emerged neither scarred nor victorious. Bull fighting had to win the same social combat.   27

All of which brings to mind that fine afternoon when some highborn Roman women were out in Nero's box at the Colosseum watching this sexy Thracian carve an ugly little Samnite up into prime cuts, and one said, darling, she had an inspiration, and Nero, needless to say, was all for it. Thus began the new vogue of Roman socialites fighting as gladiators themselves, for kicks. By the second century A.D. even the Emperor Commodus was out there with a tiger's head as a helmet hacking away at some poor dazed fall guy. He did a lot for the sport. Arenas sprang up all over the empire like shopping center bowling alleys.   28

The future of the demolition derby, then, stretches out over the face of America. The sport draws no lines of gender, and post-debs may reach Lawrence Mendelsohn at his office in Deer Park.   29

2,600 words

DISCUSSION | APPLICATION

1. "Clean Fun at Riverhead" appears in Tom Wolfe's book *The Kandy-kolored Tangerine-flake Streamline Baby* in a section headed "The New Culture-makers." He approaches the demolition derby as an art critic might approach a new painting. How does this approach affect the tone of the essay?
2. Does he give the subject more weight than it deserves?

3. What caused Lawrence Mendelsohn to innovate the demolition derby?
4. Explain the statement in paragraph 25: "For one very large segment of the population, [the car has] become the focus of the same sort of quasi-religious dedication as art is currently for another large segment of a higher social order."

Theme Assignments

1. Write a cause/effect analysis of a crowd's reactions to an event you have witnessed—a horse show, a daredevil car driving team, a school or professional stage play, a horror film, a track meet, a circus or carnival act, etc. Use paragraph 19 as your guide, but be specific in furnishing your own details.
2. Write a cause/effect theme on one of the following: Paragraph 17: "Americans have turned to the automobile to satisfy their love of direct aggression." Paragraph 17: "The automobile has become the symbol . . . of triumph over family and community restrictions."

You have to reach the conclusion that . . . customized cars are art objects. . . . I don't have to dwell on the point that cars mean more to these kids than architecture did in Europe's great formal century. . . . They [customized cars] are freedom, style, sex, power, motion, color—everything is right there.

Tom Wolfe
The Kandy-kolored Tangerine-flake Streamline Baby

Vocabulary

Paragraph
3. transformation
   purist
   prone
4. baroque
6. monotony
7. culturally
   symbolism
8. quaint
   tranquility
9. wail
10. simultaneous

tympany
howitzer
lurching
eccentrically
12. gluttonous
15. passive
   metaphysics
17. inhibitions
19. unabashed
26. acolytes
   esoteric

McLuhan, right or wrong?   1

The Oracle of Toronto thinks big—his theory of communications offers nothing less than an explanation of all human culture, past, present and future. And he excites large passions. "McLuhan's teaching is radical, new, animated by high intelligence, and capable of moving people to social action," writes the novelist George P. Elliott. "If he is wrong, it matters." "He's swinging, switched on, with it and NOW," says Amherst Prof. Benjamin DeMott. "And wrong." "He makes us question all the shibboleths of Western culture," counters critic Gerald Stearn. "He can only be considered a stimulating thinker on a scale quite similar to Freud and Einstein." 2

Freud, Einstein—Marshall McLuhan?   3

On first inspection, there are some rough similarities. Freud and Einstein, each in his turn, offered propositions about the psyche and the universe that were plainly contradicted by the senses of all right-thinking men (Sex drives in infants? Space is curved?). And now McLuhan proclaims equally barmy notions to contradict the eye and bend and boggle the mind. He firmly avows for instance, that watching television is a tactile rather than a visual experience; that man goes through life looking through the rearview mirror, aware of his environment only after he has left it, and that what is communicated doesn't count as much as how it is communicated. This last, of course, is expressed in the aphorism that is McLuhan's trademark: "The Medium Is the Message."   4

If these propositions are correct, the implications of McLuhanism are staggering. In his world view, wars are obsolete and so are political dogmas, the assembly line and white supremacy; the age of the individual is over, and a new man is emerging.   5

"I explore, I don't explain," McLuhan explains. Yet he offers himself to the world as a kind of Dr. Spock of pop culture. Are the children alienated? McLuhan has the answer there—somewhere. From Marshall's McClues, Camp Followers supposedly can tell which fashions will sell, and politicians which candidates will go over big. A girl can even read McLuhan's notion of why she makes herself more provocative when she wears dark glasses and fishnet stockings.   6

McLuhan in short-course form goes like this:

The basic premise is that there have been three Ages of Man—the Pre-literate or Tribal, the Gutenberg or Individual and the present Electric or Retribalized. Each age, says McLuhan, is shaped by the form of the information available. And by information McLuhan means not only the standard media such as print and TV, but also clothes, clocks, money and any artifact that conveys meaning.   7

Triple Play

McLuhan's claim is that these information modes or media alter our sensory life—that is, what we see, hear, feel, taste and smell, and, therefore, know. For example, the development of such "media" as tools and language among the low-browed hominids led to the explosive development of the brain and to man's differentiation from other species—and not the other way around. McLuhan sees each medium as a similar extension and modifier of man; just as the caveman's ax is an extension of the hand, so the book is an extension of the eye, and so electric circuitry—the telegraph, telephone and television—is an extension of the central nervous system. Each such extension, McLuhan maintains, changes the balance among the five senses—making one sense dominant and altering the way man feels, thinks and acts toward information. As a result, a new environment is created, spatial relations are re-conceptualized. It is a triple play: new media to new sensory balance to new environment. This, he says, is why the medium is the message, why the effect is important, why the fact that the TV image is composed of phosphor dots is more important than whether the dots are carrying the Smothers Brothers or Uncle Vanya.   8

Bomb

Thus in the pre-alphabet age, the ear was dominant; "hearing was believing." Man lived in acoustic space—a world of tribes, emotion, mystery and communal participation. Beginning with the Greeks, the new medium of the phonetic alphabet forced the magic world of the ear to yield to a new sensory balance centered on the neutral world of the eye. Later, Gutenberg's invention of movable type forced man to comprehend in a linear, uniform, connected, continuous fashion. A whole new environment—the Gutenberg Galaxy—emerged. The portable book was like a hydrogen bomb dropped on the tribal world; for the first time, man could read and think in isolation. Individualism was born, and it became possible to separate thought from action (vide Hamlet). Politically, the newly discovered privacy of the reader made a point of view possible; economically, linear thought produced the assembly line and industrial society; in physics, it led to the Newtonian and Cartesian views of the universe as a mechanism in which it is possible to locate a physical event in space and time; in art, linearity produced perspective; in literature, the chronological narrative.   9

   Then, in the nineteenth century man entered the Electric Age with the invention of a new medium, the telegraph. The Gutenberg galactic explosion that had shattered the old tribal unity of the ancients gave way to a huge implosion; electric circuitry bound up the world in a web of instant awareness and brought all the fragmentary pieces back together. The old, linear visual connections were severed, and the aural and tactile senses emerged once again. With Telstar and other high-speed communications annihilating space and time, an "all-at-once" environment has taken shape. Tribal man has returned and the world has contracted into a global village in which everyone is involved with everyone else—the haves with the have-nots (foreign aid, war on poverty), Negroes with whites (sit-ins and rights marches) adults with teen-agers (Sunset Strip riots). 10

'Hot' and 'Cool'

Thus, to McLuhan, the key word in the new Electric Age is "involvement." His second major insight (or outrage, if one disagrees) is that the old print medium involves one sense (the visual) while the new electric media, particularly television, involve all the senses simultaneously. This is why he says that some media are "hot" and some "cool." Print, McLuhan insists, is a hot medium: the printed page projects plenty of information; it comes in as high definition for one sense—but does not involve all the senses. By contrast, he says, TV is a cool, low-definition medium; that is, it provides a minimum of information—but involves all the senses all at once. This means there is high participation and involvement. 11

To the man who has stared for hours on end at the little black box this simply doesn't make sense—to him, quite naturally, TV seems visual. McLuhan would reply: that's eye thinking. In reality, he says, with television *you* are the screen; the TV image is not a still photo but a ceaselessly forming contour of mosaic projecting all those little Seurat-like dots onto you, the screen, at the rate of 3 million impulses a second. You have to fill in the mosaic, connect all the dots. "You have to be 'with it,'" McLuhan admonishes, adding Delphically that "the phrase 'with it' came in since TV." 12

McLuhan also holds that the same messages come over differently via different media. As a prime example, he cites the 1960 debates between Nixon and Kennedy. To those who simply concluded that Kennedy looked and spoke better, McLuhan's theory seems absurd. The public Richard Nixon, he says, was a hot, forceful, high-definition type, while the public Kennedy was a cool, nonchalant low-definition figure. During the later debates, Nixon became more forceful—hot and definite in McLuhan's terms—and many of the political sages thought he was catching Kennedy. But for McLuhan it was the end of Nixon. In a newspaper interview which appeared on Oct. 15, 1960, McLuhan gave the nod to Kennedy. (Yet when McLuhan watched Nixon in another context on TV—talking in a relaxed manner on the "Jack Paar Show"—he knew that *that* Nixon could have won the Presidency.) 13

Television brings not only the voting booth into the living room but also the civil-rights march along Alabama's U.S. 80 and the bulldozing of a village in Vietnam—and involves the audience intimately. "Without television, there would be no civil-rights legislation," McLuhan declares, sweepingly. Moreover, "a hot war like Vietnam over a cool medium like TV is doomed. The young oppose the war not out of pacifism but out of their pain of involvement."

14

Ending—eventually—the war in Vietnam is only one of the effects McLuhan claims for television. McLuhan holds that the changes in the environment "since TV" are so pervasive that he despairs of presenting them. All he is able to offer is an "inventory" of effects that includes:

Sex. Among the first victims of television that McLuhan counts are his own views in "The Mechanical Bride" emphasizing the visual nature of advertising, particularly the sexual come-on. "There has been a dimming down of the visual," he says. "We are now in the all-involving tactile mode." That's why discothèques are loud and dark. It is also why a girl is sexier in cool media like dark glasses and fishnet stockings: these things invite involvement.

15

Morals. There will be more sleeping around among single young people, McLuhan says, but married couples will be models of rectitude—because that's how it is in tribal culture.

16

Fashions. The shift from the visual to the tactile also is signaled by boys and girls who dress alike and cut their hair alike—gender differentiation now comes with touch. Miniskirts, topless waitresses and the trend toward nudity on beaches and in films are also signs of the TV times: as the visual becomes less important no one minds a show of skin.

17

Sports. Baseball is linear, individual—the pitcher stands on the mound, the batter waits. By contrast football is like the TV mosaic itself—action occurs simultaneously, with the entire team involved and scattering all over the screen. So football has supplanted baseball as the most popular U.S. sport.

18

The politics of consensus. McLuhan claims TV is killing off the voting bloc and elevating the leader who tries to be the all-inclusive image; instead of offering a political viewpoint, politicians now will take inclusive political postures.

19

The generation gap. The young TV generation has a completely different sensory life than the adult generation which grew up on hot radio and hot print. Hence, young people today reject jobs and goals—that's linear thinking. They reject the consumer life—that's fragmented and specialist. They want roles, that is, involvement.

20

Business reorganizations. The mosaic mesh of TV is driving out lineality in industry. Since TV, McLuhan declares, the assembly line has disappeared and staff and line structures have dissolved in management. In fact, all lines are disappearing: stag lines, receiving lines and pencil lines from the backs of nylons.

21

Some of this looks—sounds, feels—plausible; some, preposterous. Pencil lines have disappeared from nylons, but have assembly lines disappeared from Detroit? Certainly they have, McLuhan would reply. What then are the automakers doing in those plants? Beginning to make custom cars, McLuhan says, like the "basic" Mustang which comes with a score of optional accessories. Why then don't we all realize this? The trouble, says McLuhan, is that people are still looking through the rear-view mirror.   22

The idea of rear-view mirrorism is the newest McLuhanism. When faced with a new situation, McLuhan writes in "The Medium is the Massage," "we always tend to attach ourselves to the objects, to the flavor of the most recent past." Contemporary society is like a driver who sees neither ahead to the future nor outside his side window to the present but looks only at the past in the rear-view mirror. U.S. adult society, he says, exists imaginatively among the Cartwrights of Bonanzaland, closing off its life—like so many wagons drawn in a circle—unaware of what's happening outside.   23

DEW-liner

But a few people are alert. Mostly they are the avant-garde poets, artists and sleuths—McLuhan includes himself in these categories—who have consciously sharpened their perceptions, realized the phoniness of the rear-view mirror and forced themselves to look ahead and see the environment as it really is. The artist, McLuhan says, serves like Canada's Distant Early Warning (DEW) Line; his job is to alert society.   24

From this short—and considerably glossed over—course on McLuhan, several judgments can be drawn.   25

First, none of his basic ideas is in itself startling or even original. Discussions about form as content date to Aristotle; Buckminster Fuller, and Henri Bergson before him, explained how tools of man can become extensions of man, and sociologists long ago gave the designation "cultural lag" to situations in which social organization falls behind technological development. Even the aphorism about the medium and the message is not wholly new; the late Canadian economic historian Harold Innis pointed out the role of print in the transformation of culture more than a decade ago—a priority McLuhan has graciously acknowledged.   26

Reply

Second, McLuhan is a synthesizer. He has gathered amorphous and scattered ideas, thought them through with force and vivacity, and opened up new areas of awareness. "He has joyously enriched the scope of what is relevant," says the English critic George Steiner. "He has made the jungle of the world more interesting." And Harvard's David Riesman lauds McLuhan as "a reply to the solemn commentators who look with alarm on the rise of pop culture."   27

Third, McLuhan himself isn't a very good DEW Line. The essence of a DEW Line is to discriminate between the radar scope blips of real incoming enemy planes and the patterns caused by flights of geese and the northern lights. But in his books and in his conversations, McLuhan lets everything through, no matter how outrageous or exaggerated or contradictory. He often takes the good insights that he has hit upon and pushes them too far. The U.S. may still be largely a visual culture just emerging from the nineteenth century. The Soviet Union may be an aural-tactile culture, just emerging from the Middle Ages. But is that why the CIA sends U-2 reconnaissance planes over the Soviet Union while the KGB plants bugs in U.S. embassies? Everything becomes grist for his mad, mod mill. Is the subject the youthful Red Guards? That's easy. China is still a tribal environment, says McLuhan, and, of course, this permits participation of children in adult affairs. 28

Fourth, the leaky DEW Line and the impossibly broad argument are the inevitable consequences of McLuhan's own beliefs. He is delivering his message via a medium—the printed page—which he has stated is no longer adequate to command the attention and involvement of modern electric man. McLuhan's solution in "Galaxy" and "Media" is to invent a "mosaic writing" that attempts to simulate the disconnected, low-definition coolness of television—and thus capture the reader. The result is deliberately repetitious, confused and dogmatic. In McLuhans new picture book, "The Medium Is the Massage," he attempts to go further toward mosaic presentation but in shorter, less repetitive takes. 29

Tailor-made

Despite his dilemma, McLuhan doesn't plan to abandon the book form. He and Toronto Prof. Richard Schoeck are collaborating on a series of volumes of poetry and prose for high-school seniors and college freshmen (written non-mosaically but with accompanying tapes); there is "Culture Is Our Business" as well as "Space in Poetry and Painting," with Harley Parker and "A Message to the Fish," with management-consultant Ralph Baldwin. "The Fish," explains McLuhan, "are the corporation heads moving about in media they know nothing about." Finally, he is writing "The Future of the Book," with William Jovanovich, the president of Harcourt, Brace & World. The *future* of the book? Yes, thanks to photocopying and computers, McLuhan allows that books have a future; they will no longer be assembly-line products, they will be services, tailor-made (like the car of the future) to meet specific demands phoned to the information retrieval center. 30

But neither does McLuhan plan to abandon his methods of presentation. "Unless a statement is startling," he says candidly, "no one will pay any attention; they will put it down as a point of view." He considers statements in his books and his speeches as tentative probes—disposable as Kleenex. "I don't necessarily agree with everything I say," he adds. 31

"Most of my work in the media is like that of a safecracker," McLuhan says in the introduction to Gerald Stearn's "McLuhan, Hot and Cool." "In the beginning I don't know what's inside. I just set myself down in front of the problem and begin to work. I grope, I probe, I listen, I test —until the tumblers fall and I'm in." 32

Jokes

But does he really want to get in—or stay out? His attitude about the media is a little like the punch line in one of his after-dinner jokes: a man went out on a date with Siamese twins and the next day a friend asked if he had a good time; his answer: "Well, yes and no."   33

Sometimes he seems to be saying the media threaten man. Education, he says, must serve as civil defense against the media fallout; the Ivory Tower must become the control tower. And he likens modern man to the mariner in Edgar Allan Poe's story, "A Descent into the Maelstrom." The mariner is caught in a whirlpool; but he figures out the relative velocities of currents and saves himself. The sailor's strategy, McLuhan suggests, is his own: understand our predicament, our electrically configured whirl, and save ourselves from drowning.   34

On the other hand, McLuhan describes, with obvious approval, cool men in a tribal world of full sensory involvement and group participation. It is a situation that the Catholic McLuhan finds not unlike the rich liturgical services of his church. Further, the scholar McLuhan acknowledges that a world where the Ivory Tower is so important can't be too bad.   35

McLuhan isn't specific about his future strategy of social action; he speaks instead in science-fiction terms about learning how to control the thermostat of the environment in order to shape the new world to come. The thought of just such a thermostat, manipulated by technicians or hidden persuaders, chills many of McLuhan's readers. But he says, optimistically, that the futurists will use their thermostats rationally, for "who would want to turn up the heat to 150?"   36

McLuhan, right or wrong?   37

Well, yes and no.   38

3,000 words

DISCUSSION | APPLICATION

Marshall McLuhan's theories deal with the impact of the *means* used to communicate information. Your generation is the first to be exposed from childhood to television, which involves all the senses simultaneously. If McLuhan is right, your exposure to television has had a crucial impact in shaping the way you view reality.

1. Give an example of the use of the telephone as "an extension of the central nervous system." (paragraph 8)
2. "The Medium Is the Message," McLuhan says. What does he mean? One example in *Understanding Media* concerns American films in the Orient. For American viewers a film might convey a plot involving, perhaps, a detective in New York City. For the Orient "a Hollywood movie [became] . . . a world in which *ordinary people* had cars and electric stoves and refrigerators."* The message the Orient received then was that Orientals who

* Marshall McLuhan, *Understanding Media*, McGraw-Hill, N.Y., 1964, p. 294.

were "ordinary people" had been deprived of the ordinary man's birthright. Can you think of other examples—in the field of rock music, perhaps? Comic strips which use drawings based on the way we perceive film—from different angles, close up, far away, etc.?

3. Paragraph 7: How does clothing become a medium of communication? What is the message? Cite some examples currently in the news or being discussed on campus.

4. Paragraph 8 implies that "reality" exists only as a conception of man and as a result of the way he organizes how and what he perceives. Can you cite examples of this or explain it in your own words?

5. Paragraph 10: Cite an example of the way electric circuitry has brought "instant awareness" by contrasting a recent news item on television with a similar item and its communication before radio and television.

6. Paragraph 13: Do you agree or disagree that "the same messages come over differently via different media"? Can you think of an example other than those mentioned in the essay?

7. Paragraph 15: Is a girl sexier in dark glasses and fishnet stockings? Why, according to McLuhan? Why not, according to you, if you disagree?

8. Paragraph 17: Do you accept McLuhan's reasoning in the matter of boys and girls dressing and cutting their hair alike?

9. Do you take McLuhan to be an optimist or a pessimist about the future of Western civilization in the electronic age? Why?

Assignments

1. McLuhan has developed a number of unique and provocative ideas and perceptions. Take one of these of your own choice or from the citations that follow and develop its implications in a cause/effect analysis. You may agree or disagree with the idea you choose and should develop it accordingly.

   a. Paragraph 4: "The Medium Is the Message." McLuhan has a pun on this in paragraph 23: "The Medium Is the Massage." Use one or both in your theme.

   b. Paragraph 7: "Each age is shaped by the form of the information available."

   c. Paragraph 9: "The portable book was like a hydrogen bomb . . . for the first time, man could read and think in isolation."

   d. Paragraph 20: "[Young people] reject the consumer life—that's fragmented and specialist. They want roles, that is, involvement."

Vocabulary

Paragraph	3. psyche	6. alienated
2. shibboleths	avows	provocative
radical	tactile	8. modes
animated	aphorism	sensory

differentiation
extension
modifier
environment
spatial
re-conceptualized
9. acoustic
linear
perspective
chronological
10. implosion

fragmentary
12. mosaic
Delphic (ally)
13. nonchalant
16. rectitude
24. avant-garde
26. cultural lag
priority
27. synthesize
amorphous
vivacity

29. consequence
dogmatic
30. retrieval
31. tentative
probes
34. velocities
predicament
configured
35. liturgical
36. futurists

MURDER BY TELEVISION
MARSHALL McLUHAN

Jack Ruby shot Lee Oswald while tightly surrounded by guards who were paralyzed by television cameras. The fascinating and involving power of television scarcely needed this additional proof of its peculiar operation upon human perceptions. The Kennedy assassination gave people an immediate sense of the television power to create depth involvement, on the one hand, and a numbing effect as deep as grief, itself, on the other hand. Most people were amazed at the depth of meaning which the event communicated to them. Many more were surprised by the coolness and calm of the mass reaction. The same event, handled by press or radio (in the absence of television), would have provided a totally different experience. The national "lid" would have "blown off." Excitement would have been enormously greater and depth participation in a common awareness very much less.

As explained earlier, Kennedy was an excellent TV image. He had used the medium with the same effectiveness that Roosevelt had learned to achieve by radio. With TV, Kennedy found it natural to involve the nation in the office of the Presidency, both as an operation and as an image. TV reaches out for the corporate attributes of office. Potentially, it can transform the Presidency into a monarchic dynasty. A merely elective Presidency scarcely affords the depth of dedication and commitment demanded by the TV form. Even teachers on TV seem to be endowed by the student audiences with a charismatic or mystic character that much exceeds the feelings developed in the classroom or lecture hall. In the course of many studies of audience reactions to TV teaching, there recurs this puzzling fact. The viewers feel that the teacher has a dimension almost of sacredness. This feeling does not have its basis in concepts or ideas, but seems to creep in uninvited and unexplained. It baffles both the students and the analysts of their reactions. Surely, there could be no more telling touch to tip us off to the character of TV. This is not so much a visual as a tactual-auditory medium that involves all of our senses in depth interplay. For people long accustomed to the merely visual experience of the typographic and photographic varieties, it would seem to be the *synesthesia,* or tactual depth of TV experience, that dislocates them from their usual attitudes of passivity and detachment.

The banal and ritual remark of the conventionally literate, that TV presents an experience for passive viewers, is wide of the mark. TV is above all a medium that demands a creatively participant response. The guards who failed to protect Lee Oswald were not passive. They were so involved by the mere sight of the TV cameras that they lost their sense of their merely practical and specialist task. 3

Perhaps it was the Kennedy funeral that most strongly impressed the audience with the power of TV to invest an occasion with the character of corporate participation. No national event except in sports has ever had such coverage or such an audience. It revealed the unrivaled power of TV to achieve the involvement of the audience in a complex *process*. The funeral as a corporate process caused even the image of sport to pale and dwindle into puny proportions. The Kennedy funeral, in short, manifested the power of TV to involve an entire population in a ritual process. By comparison, press, movie and even radio are mere packaging devices for consumers. 4

Most of all, the Kennedy event provides an opportunity for noting a paradoxical feature of the "cool" TV medium. It involves us in moving depth, but it does not excite, agitate or arouse. Presumably, this is a feature of all depth experience. 5

600 words

DISCUSSION | APPLICATION

1. What has been the influence of television on your life?
2. Why were Oswald's guards "paralyzed by television cameras"?
3. Why is television "cool" while the press and radio are "hot" media? What do "cool" and "hot" mean as McLuhan uses them?
4. Does McLuhan's description of the way people experience television fit your experience of television viewing?

Assignment

Write a one-paragraph explanation of one of the following:

1. "[Television] demands a creatively participant response."
2. "[Television has the power] to involve an entire population in a ritual process."

Any change is fearful, especially one affecting both politics and sex roles, so let me begin these utopian speculations with a fact. To break the ice. 1

Women don't want to exchange places with men. Male chauvinists, science-fiction writers and comedians may favor that idea for its shock value, but psychologists say it is a fantasy based on ruling-class ego and guilt. Men assume that women want to imitate them, which is just what white people assumed about blacks. An assumption so strong that it may convince the second-class group of the need to imitate, but for both women and blacks that stage has passed. Guilt produces the question: What if they could treat us as we have treated them? 2

That is not our goal. But we do want to change the economic system to one more based on merit. In Women's Lib Utopia, there will be free access to good jobs—and decent pay for the bad ones women have been performing all along, including housework. Increased skilled labor might lead to a four-hour workday, and higher wages would encourage further mechanization of repetitive jobs now kept alive by cheap labor. 3

With women as half the country's elected representatives, and a woman President once in a while, the country's *machismo* problems would be greatly reduced. The old-fashioned idea that manhood depends on violence and victory is, after all, an important part of our troubles in the streets, and in Viet Nam. I'm not saying that women leaders would eliminate violence. We are not more moral than men; we are only uncorrupted by power so far. When we do acquire power, we might turn out to have an equal impulse toward aggression. Even now, Margaret Mead believes that women fight less often but more fiercely than men, because women are not taught the rules of the war game and fight only when cornered. But for the next 50 years or so, women in politics will be very valuable by tempering the idea of manhood into something less aggressive and better suited to this crowded, post-atomic planet. Consumer protection and children's rights, for instance, might get more legislative attention. 4

Men will have to give up ruling-class privileges, but in return they will no longer be the only ones to support the family, get drafted, bear the strain of power and responsibility. Freud to the contrary, anatomy is not destiny, at least not for more than nine months at a time. In Israel, women are drafted, and some have gone to war. In England, more men type and run switchboards. In India and Israel, a woman rules. In Sweden, both parents take care of the children. In this country, come Utopia, men and women won't reverse roles; they will be free to choose according to individual talents and preferences. 5

If role reform sounds sexually unsettling, think how it will change the sexual hypocrisy we have now. No more sex arranged on the barter system, with women pretending interest, and men never sure whether they are loved for themselves or for the security few women can get any other way. (Married or not, for sexual reasons or social ones, most women still find it second nature to Uncle-Tom.) No more men who are encouraged to spend a lifetime living with inferiors; with housekeepers, or dependent creatures who are still children. No more domineering wives, emasculating women, and "Jewish mothers," all of whom are simply human beings with all their normal ambition and drive confined to the home. No more unequal partnerships that eventually doom love and sex.   6

In order to produce that kind of confidence and individuality, child rearing will train according to talent. Little girls will no longer be surrounded by air-tight, self-fulfilling prophecies of natural passivity, lack of ambition and objectivity, inability to exercise power, and dexterity (so long as special aptitude for jobs requiring patience and dexterity is confined to poorly paid jobs; brain surgery is for males).   7

Schools and universities will help to break down traditional sex roles, even when parents will not. Half the teachers will be men, a rarity now at preschool and elementary levels; girls will not necessarily serve cookies or boys hoist up the flag. Athletic teams will be picked only by strength and skill. Sexually segregated courses like auto mechanics and home economics will be taken by boys and girls together. New courses in sexual politics will explore female subjugation as the model for political oppression, and women's history will be an academic staple, along with black history, at least until the white-male-oriented textbooks are integrated and rewritten. 8

As for the American child's classic problem—too much mother, too little father—that would be cured by an equalization of parental responsibility. Free nurseries, school lunches, family cafeterias built into every housing complex, service companies that will do household cleaning chores in a regular, businesslike way, and more responsibility by the entire community for the children: all these will make it possible for both mother and father to work, and to have equal leisure time with the children at home. For parents of very young children, however, a special job category, created by Government and unions, would allow such parents a shorter work day. 9

The revolution would not take away the option of being a housewife. A woman who prefers to be her husband's housekeeper and/or hostess would receive a percentage of his pay determined by the domestic relations courts. If divorced, she might be eligible for a pension fund, and for a job-training allowance. Or a divorce could be treated the same way that the dissolution of a business partnership is now.   10

If these proposals seem farfetched, consider Sweden, where most of them are already in effect. Sweden is not yet a working Women's Lib model; most of the role-reform programs began less than a decade ago, and are just beginning to take hold. But that country is so far ahead of us in recognizing the problem that Swedish statements on sex and equality sound like bulletins from the moon. 11

Our marriage laws, for instance, are so reactionary that Women's Lib groups want couples to take a compulsory written exam on the law, as for a driver's license, before going through with the wedding. A man has alimony and wifely debts to worry about, but a woman may lose so many of her civil rights that in the U.S. now, in important legal ways, she becomes a child again. In some states, she cannot sign credit agreements, use her maiden name, incorporate a business, or establish a legal residence of her own. Being a wife, according to most social and legal definitions, is still a 19th century thing. 12

Assuming, however, that these blatantly sexist laws are abolished or reformed, that job discrimination is forbidden, that parents share financial responsibility for each other and the children, and that sexual relationships become partnerships of equal adults (some pretty big assumptions), then marriage will probably go right on. Men and Women are, after all, physically complementary. When society stops encouraging men to be exploiters and women to be parasites, they may turn out to be more complementary in emotion as well. Women's Lib is not trying to destroy the American family. A look at the statistics on divorce—plus the way in which old people are farmed out with strangers and young people flee the home—shows the destruction that has already been done. Liberated women are just trying to point out the disaster, and build compassionate and practical alternatives from the ruins. 13

What will exist is a variety of alternative life-styles. Since the population explosion dictates that childbearing be kept to a minimum, parents-and-children will be only one of many "families": couples, age groups, working groups, mixed communes, blood-related clans, class groups, creative groups. Single women will have the right to stay single without ridicule, without the attitudes now betrayed by "spinster" and "bachelor." Lesbians or homosexuals will no longer be denied legally binding marriages, complete with mutual-support agreements and inheritance rights. Paradoxically, the number of homosexuals may get smaller. With fewer overpossessive mothers and fewer fathers who hold up an impossibly cruel or perfectionist idea of manhood, boys will be less likely to be denied or reject their identity as males. 14

Changes that now seem small may get bigger:

Men's Lib

Men now suffer from more diseases due to stress, heart attacks, ulcers, a higher suicide rate, greater difficulty living alone, less adaptability to change and, in general, a shorter life span than women. There is some scientific evidence that what produces physical problems is not work itself, but the inability to choose which work, and how much. With women bearing half the financial responsibility, and with the idea of "masculine" jobs gone, men might well feel freer and live longer. 15

Religion

Protestant women are already becoming ordained ministers; radical nuns are carrying out liturgical functions that were once the exclusive property of priests; Jewish women are rewriting prayers—particularly those that Orthodox Jews recite every morning thanking God they are not female. In the future, the church will become an area of equal participation by women. This means, of course, that organized religion will have to give up one of its great historical weapons: sexual repression. In most structured faiths, from Hinduism through Roman Catholicism, the status of women went down as the position of priests ascended. Male clergy implied, if they did not teach, that women were unclean, unworthy and sources of ungodly temptation, in order to remove them as rivals for the emotional forces of men. Full participation of women in ecclesiastical life might involve certain changes in theology, such as, for instance, a radical redefinition of sin. 16

Literary Problems

Revised sex roles will outdate more children's books than civil rights ever did. Only a few children had the problem of a *Little Black Sambo,* but most have the male-female stereotypes of "Dick and Jane." A boomlet of children's books about mothers who work has already begun, and liberated parents and editors are beginning to pressure for change in the textbook industry. Fiction writing will change more gradually, but romantic novels with wilting heroines and swashbuckling heroes will be reduced to historical value. Or perhaps to the sado-masochist trade. (*Marjorie Morningstar,* a romantic novel that took the '50s by storm, has already begun to seem as unreal as its '20s predecessor, *The Sheik.*) As for the literary plots that turn on forced marriages or horrific abortions, they will seem as dated as Prohibition stories. Free legal abortions and free birth control will force writers to give up pregnancy as the *deus ex machina.* 17

Manners and Fashion

Dress will be more androgynous, with class symbols becoming more important than sexual ones. Pro- or anti-Establishment styles may already be more vital than who is wearing them. Hardhats are just as likely to rough up antiwar girls as antiwar men in the street, and police understand that women are just as likely to be pushers or bombers. Dances haven't required that one partner lead the other for years, anyway. Chivalry will transfer itself to those who need it, or deserve respect: old people, admired people, anyone with an armload of packages. Women with normal work identities will be less likely to attach their whole sense of self to youth and appearance; thus there will be fewer nervous breakdowns when the first wrinkles appear. Lighting cigarettes and other treasured niceties will become gestures of mutual affection. "I like to be helped on with my coat," says one Women's Lib worker, "but not if it costs me $2,000 a year in salary."

18

For those with nostalgia for a simpler past, here is a word of comfort. Anthropologist Geoffrey Gorer studied the few peaceful human tribes and discovered one common characteristic: sex roles were not polarized. Differences of dress and occupation were at a minimum. Society, in other words, was not using sexual blackmail as a way of getting women to do cheap labor, or men to be aggressive.

19

Thus Women's Lib may achieve a more peaceful society on the way toward its other goals. That is why the Swedish government considers reform to bring about greater equality in the sex roles one of its most important concerns. As Prime Minister Olof Palme explained in a widely ignored speech delivered in Washington this spring: "It is *human beings* we shall emancipate. In Sweden today, if a politician should declare that the woman ought to have a different role from man's, he would be regarded as something from the Stone Age." In other words, the most radical goal of the movement is egalitarianism.

20

If Women's Lib wins, perhaps we all do.

21

2,000 words

DISCUSSION | APPLICATION

The title indicates that the emphasis in this essay will be on a possible effect. The cause, women's liberation at some future date, is implied in the effects specified.

1. The modern phase of the women's lib movement began in 1957 with the publication in the United States of Simone de Beauvoir's *The Second Sex*, a monumental history of woman's place in a man's world. The source of de Beauvoir's title indicates where women have been and how far they have come:

> ... women remain children their whole life long; never seeing anything but what is quite close to them, cleaving to the present moment, taking appearance for reality, and preferring trifles to matters of first importance. ... The weakness of their reasoning faculty also explains why it is that ... they are inferior to men in point of justice, and less honorable and conscientious. ...
>
> *They form the sexus sequoir*—the second sex, inferior in every respect to the first; their infirmities should be treated with consideration; but to show them great reverence is ... ridiculous, and lowers us in their eyes.
>
> Arthur Schopenhauer
> *Nineteenth-century philosopher*

Bring to class a periodical article that indicates how far women still have to go to achieve equality with men.

2. Paragraph 2: What is implied by the question: "Guilt produces the question: What if they could treat us as we have treated them?"

3. Paragraph 4: Can you specify some of the "*machismo* problems" referred to? What is "consumer protection"? Should protecting the consumer be a function of government or should "let the buyer beware" be the rule?

4. Paragraph 6: *Do* "most women find it second nature to Uncle-Tom"? Can you cite some examples that prove or disprove Steinem's statement?

5. Paragraph 16: What reasons does Steinem give for stating that sexual repression is one of organized religion's great historical weapons? It is sometimes suggested that sexual repression is a weapon necessary to highly industrialized societies. Do you agree? Why?

6. Paragraph 21: "If Women's Lib wins, perhaps we all do." Why?

Theme Assignments

Write a 300- to 500-word analysis of an idea drawn from Steinem's essay or based on one of the following quotations.

A. . . . most women will have to exercise their much denied but very much alive instincts for power through men for awhile yet.

Gloria Steinem

"Women and Power"

B. This women's liberation is an effort by the system to separate black men from black women. Historically black women have been mother, father, everything. Now it's time for the black man to be god, and we follow his leadership.

black activist Saundra Henry

C. Being a liberated woman isn't the same as being liberated from being a woman.

Novelist Doris Lessing

D. A woman's place is in the wrong.

James Thurber

E. . . . Judy Stein, 16, pays her own way on dates. "Otherwise," she says, "it's like the guy is renting you for the evening."

Newsweek (3/23/70)

F. "Many (women) have been sisters in a family where the brother got the better of it—the brother got to go to college, though the girl was brighter. Is she neurotic or justifiably angry?"

psychiatrist Judd Marmor

G. Sexual emancipation is not the natural way for women.

psychiatrist Melvin Anchell

H. These chicks (women's lib) are our natural enemy. . . . (They are) unalterably opposed to the romantic boy-girl society that *Playboy* promotes.

Hugh Hefner

Playboy publisher

PEOPLE,

It is not what people know that hurts them, it's what they know that isn't so.
Mark Twain

PROVOCATIONS,

It became necessary to destroy the town to save it.
a U.S. Army Major (Vietnam: 2/7/68)

PERCEPTIONS,

A child learns what he experiences. You yell, "Stop that." He learns to yell.

PRECONCEPTIONS,

I have not committed nor ever could commit a violent act—except in self-defense.

IDEAS,

A leader must take an absolute position in order for his followers to
take a reasonable position.
Martin Luther King, Jr.

AND IRRITATIONS

You can tell the ideals of a nation by its advertisements.
Norman Douglas

The challenge today is to make the consumer raise his level of demand.
ad agency bulletin

Exuberance is beauty.
William Blake

They're having all sorts of illicit relations there—living a happy normal life.
Paul Goodman

Is the space program "the noblest expression of the Twentieth Century
or the quintessential statement of our fundamental insanity"? Both.
Norman Mailer

We do not want churches. They will teach us to quarrel about God. We
may quarrel with men sometimes about things on this earth, but we never
quarrel about God.
Chief Joseph of the Nez Percés

I HAVE A DREAM
MARTIN LUTHER KING, JR.

Five score years ago, a great American, in whose symbolic shadow we stand, signed the Emancipation Proclamation. This momentous decree came as a great beacon light of hope to millions of Negro slaves who had been seared in the flames of withering injustice. It came as a joyous day-break to end the long night of captivity.   1

But one hundred years later, we must face the tragic fact that the Negro is still not free. One hundred years later, the life of the Negro is still sadly crippled by the manacles of segregation and the chains of discrimina-tion. One hundred years later, the Negro lives on a lonely island of poverty in the midst of a vast ocean of material prosperity. One hundred years later, the Negro is still languished in the corners of American society and finds himself an exile in his own land. So we have come here today to dramatize an appalling condition.   2

In a sense we have come to our nation's Capital to cash a check. When the architects of our republic wrote the magnificent words of the Constitution and the Declaration of Independence, they were signing a promissory note to which every American was to fall heir. This note was a promise that all men would be guaranteed the unalienable rights of life, liberty, and the pursuit of happiness.   3

It is obvious today that America has defaulted on this promissory note insofar as her citizens of color are concerned. Instead of honoring this sacred obligation, America has given the Negro people a bad check; a check which has come back marked "insufficient funds." But we refuse to believe that the bank of justice is bankrupt. We refuse to believe that there are in-sufficient funds in the great vaults of opportunity of this nation. So we have come to cash this check—a check that will give us upon demand the riches of freedom and the security of justice. We have also come to this hallowed spot to remind America of the fierce urgency of *now*. This is no time to engage in the luxury of cooling off or to take the tranquilizing drug of gradualism. *Now* is the time to make real the promises of Democracy. *Now* is the time to rise from the dark and desolate valley of segregation to the sunlit path of racial justice. *Now* is the time to open the doors of op-portunity to all of God's children. *Now* is the time to lift our nation from the quicksands of racial injustice to the solid rock of brotherhood.   4

It would be fatal for the nation to overlook the urgency of the moment and to underestimate the determination of the Negro. This sweltering sum-mer of the Negro's legitimate discontent will not pass until there is an invigorating autumn of freedom and equality. 1963 is not an end, but a beginning. Those who hope that the Negro needed to blow off steam and will now be content will have a rude awakening if the nation returns to business as usual. There will be neither rest nor tranquility in America until the Negro is granted his citizenship rights. The whirlwinds of revolt will continue to shake the foundations of our nation until the bright day of justice emerges.   5

But there is something that I must say to my people who stand on the warm threshold which leads into the palace of justice. In the process of gaining our rightful place we must not be guilty of wrongful deeds. Let us not seek to satisfy our thirst for freedom by drinking from the cup of bitterness and hatred. We must forever conduct our struggle on the high plane of dignity and discipline. We must not allow our creative protest to degenerate into physical violence. Again and again we must rise to the majestic heights of meeting physical force with soul force. The marvelous new militancy which has engulfed the Negro community must not lead us to a distrust of all white people, for many of our white brothers, as evidenced by their presence here today, have come to realize that their destiny is tied up with our destiny and their freedom is inextricably bound to our freedom. We cannot walk alone.   6

And as we walk, we must make the pledge that we shall march ahead. We cannot turn back. There are those who are asking the devotees of civil rights, "When will you be satisfied?" We can never be satisfied as long as the Negro is the victim of the unspeakable horrors of police brutality. We can never be satisfied as long as our bodies, heavy with the fatigue of travel, cannot gain lodging in the motels of the highways and the hotels of the cities. We cannot be satisfied as long as the Negro's basic mobility is from a smaller ghetto to a larger one. We can never be satisfied as long as a Negro in Mississippi cannot vote and a Negro in New York believes he has nothing for which to vote. No, no, we are not satisfied, and we will not be satisfied until justice rolls down like waters and righteousness like a mighty stream.   7

I am not unmindful that some of you have come here out of great trials and tribulations. Some of you have come fresh from narrow jail cells. Some of you have come from areas where your quest for freedom left you battered by the storms of persecution and staggered by the winds of police brutality. You have been the veterans of creative suffering. Continue to work with the faith that unearned suffering is redemptive.   8

Go back to Mississippi, go back to Alabama, go back to South Carolina, go back to Georgia, go back to Louisiana, go back to the slums and the ghettos of our northern cities, knowing that somehow this situation can and will be changed. Let us not wallow in the valley of despair.   9

I say to you today, my friends, that in spite of the difficulties and frustrations of the moment I still have a dream. It is a dream deeply rooted in the American dream.   10

I have a dream that one day this nation will rise up and live out the true meaning of its creed: "We hold these truths to be self-evident; that all men are created equal."   11

I have a dream that one day on the red hills of Georgia the sons of former slaves and the sons of former slaveowners will be able to sit down together at the table of brotherhood.   12

I have a dream that one day even the state of Mississippi, a desert state sweltering with the heat of injustice and oppression, will be transformed into an oasis of freedom and justice.   13

I have a dream that my four little children will one day live in a nation where they will not be judged by the color of their skin but by the content of their character.   14

I have a dream today.   15

I have a dream that one day the state of Alabama, whose governor's lips are presently dripping with the words of interposition and nullification, will be transformed into a situation where little black boys and black girls will be able to join hands with little white boys and white girls and walk together as sisters and brothers.   16

I have a dream today.   17

I have a dream that one day every valley shall be exalted, every hill and mountain shall be made low, the rough places will be made plains, and the crooked places will be made straight, and the glory of the Lord shall be revealed, and all flesh shall see it together.   18

This is our hope. This is the faith with which I return to the South. With this faith we will be able to hew out of the mountain of despair a stone of hope. With this faith we will be able to transform the jangling discords of our nation into a beautiful symphony of brotherhood. With this faith we will be able to work together, to pray together, to struggle together, to go to jail together, to stand up for freedom together, knowing that we will be free one day.   19

This will be the day when all of God's children will be able to sing with new meaning

> My country, 'tis of thee,
> Sweet land of liberty,
>   Of thee I sing:
> Land where my fathers died,
> Land of the pilgrims' pride,
> From every mountain-side
>   Let freedom ring.   20

And if America is to be a great nation this must become true. So let freedom ring from the prodigious hilltops of New Hampshire. Let freedom ring from the mighty mountains of New York. Let freedom ring from the heightening Alleghenies of Pennsylvania!   21

Let freedom ring from the snowcapped Rockies of Colorado!   22

Let freedom ring from the curvaceous peaks of California!   23

But not only that; let freedom ring from Stone Mountain of Georgia!　24
Let freedom ring from Lookout Mountain of Tennessee!　25

Let freedom ring from every hill and molehill of Mississippi. From every mountainside, let freedom ring.　26

When we let freedom ring, when we let it ring from every village and every hamlet, from every state and every city, we will be able to speed up that day when all of God's children, black men and white men, Jews and Gentiles, Protestants and Catholics, will be able to join hands and sing in the words of the old Negro spiritual, "Free at last; free at last! thank God almighty, we are free at last!"　27

1,800 words

Vocabulary

Paragraph	5. invigorating	17. nullification
1. momentous	7. devotees	18. exalted
2. manacles	8. redemptive	21. prodigious
3. inalienable	16. interposition	

YOU FORCE KIDS TO REBEL
STEVEN KELMAN

On both high-school and college campuses, the official statements about almost any subject are so widely distrusted nowadays that citing them is the best way to have yourself marked as a dupe or a simpleton. Adults might understand how serious this problem is if they listen to the words of the songs of somebody like Bob Dylan. His most popular songs are talking about skepticism, about what's really going on in the world as compared to what we're being taught is going on in the world. When we take a look for ourselves, the facts we see are so different from what we've been taught that we have no choice but to turn into rebels or at least skeptics.   1

Kids grow up "tryin'a be so good"—in the words of one Dylan song. When we fall from this "good" innocence it's like going through an earthquake; the ground under you just isn't solid anymore. And it's a quick jump from saying to yourself, "What they taught me is a lie," to saying, "So they must be liars." The feeling is that the adult Establishment is phony or self-interested, composed of people you can't trust.   2

Most parents don't want to accept this explanation. It's said that we're know-it-alls, though we're really know-nothings, and it's said that an affluent society produces spoiled brats who have no sense of values and no appreciation of all the things being done for them.   3

There are a number of facts that show this isn't true. For instance, philosophy courses in almost every college are in unprecedented demand (as I just discovered when I unsuccessfully tried to get into one with a "limited" enrollment of 325). At Harvard, where I am now, the Phillips Brooks House, which does all sorts of social service and community-assistance projects, is the largest organization on campus.   4

Perhaps the most popular theory for the kids' rebellion is that the "conflict of generations" is inevitable, and that we will "outgrow it." However, even if some sort of reaction of young people against their parents is inevitable, the revolt is now taking a particular form—skepticism. It took the same form, by the way, in 19th-century Russia. When youths get skeptical, I submit, it does not indicate that anything is wrong with youth, but rather that something is wrong with adults.   5

And that "something" is the way you usually look at and react to what's going on in the world. "Hypocrisy" is a big word with us, and it's a mortal sin in our moral code, dooming the sinner to our version of hell— permanent eclipse of any moral influence he might have on us.   6

If kids were taught that the world is flat, any reasonably sane person would expect us to revolt against those responsible for teaching that particular "fact." So what else but skepticism and revolt should anybody expect from us when we are being taught a view of the world which is little more sophisticated than the flat-earth theory? 7

It all starts in first grade. There we are treated to a candy-cane world where all the children in the textbooks are white tots living in suburbia with a dog running around the lawn. When suburban kids find out about slums, they're apt to get skeptical. When slum kids are taught about a world that has nothing to do with the world in which they live, they have to do the same. A song which has been a hit among students—is a parody—perhaps unconscious—of those first-grade primers:

> Little boxes on the hillside.
> Little boxes made of ticky-tacky,
> Little boxes, little boxes, little boxes
> All the same.
> There's a green one, and a pink one,
> And a blue one, and a yellow one,
> And they're all made out of ticky-tacky,
> And they all look just the same.[1]   8

Many of us come to realize just how unreal the classroom world is when our thoughts turn to boy-girl relationships. No teen-ager can escape knowing that love and sex are part of the real world. So how does society's agent, the school, present this part of reality? It ignores it. For instance, one biology teacher I heard about treated his students to the obscene spectacle of his own sniggering while he described sexual reproduction in algae. Health teachers reduce puberty to a section of an inane chart on "stages of human development." When we find out the facts and feel the emotions, how can anyone expect us not to be skeptical about an adult world which tries to act as if none of this existed? And the moral code that we have developed, "sex with love," seems to us to be more logical than anything you've put up. 9

The whole idea the school seems to try to get across is that if you don't teach it to us, it doesn't exist. This can sometimes go to extreme length. In junior high school we had a thing called a "Reading Record Card." This was supposed to be a list (and brief discussion) of all the books you had read each year. But "all the books" actually meant all the books that were in the school library. And when students protested against the refusal to allow listing of books like *1984* and *The Grapes of Wrath*, we were treated like people in China who try to whisper that Mao Tse-tung is not the only recognized writer in the world. And what are we taught about literature? We are often required to memorize such details as "What color was Ivanhoe's horse?" and "What hotel did Gatsby and the Buchanans meet in?" rather than talking about how a book means something in help-

---

[1] *Little Boxes*, words and music by Malvina Reynolds, used by permission of Schroeder Music Co., Berkeley, Calif. © 1962.

ing us to figure out ourselves or other people. So kids often give up the classics. One kid told me that he feared becoming a writer because of what high-school English teachers would do to his books. 10

And how about student government? I was active in it during high school, but the majority attitude of indifference was a pretty good instinctive reaction. In most schools the "governments" must restrict themselves to planning social extravaganzas. When they try to do something—as when ours voted to fast for a lunch in sympathy with the people of India—the administration vetoed our plans. You say that we should act responsibly, and when we try to, you act as if youthful hordes were trying to take over the school. Is the world like that? 11

It sometimes seems to us that myths are peddled to us about *everything* we are taught. For example, the quaint myth of the American family farm—enshrined in numerous references in our courses—obscures the reality of giant agricultural industries and underpaid migrant labor. The history of American cities as it is generally presented comes to a screeching halt at the turn of the century. American history textbooks I've seen are at least 30 years behind the latest historical investigations. Thus one widely used junior-high history text states that the sole purpose of American intervention in Latin America in the early part of the century was to "lend a helping hand" to the people by building roads, bridges, and hospitals. This is a little hard to believe. More than one kid I know has reacted by taking the position that our only motive in Latin America was financial greed. From my experience, American-history courses generally produce more anti-Americanism than understanding of history. 12

And what about the presentation of the one problem which concerns kids most of all—race? Well, one junior-high-school civics book devotes a total of four paragraphs to the history of the Negro in the United States. The last hundred years of Negro history are summed up like this:

> During the War Between the States, all Negro slaves were set free. Since then American Negroes have gone through a difficult period of adjustment to new ways of life. They have made remarkable progress in a short time.
>
> 13

Now, when we leave such textbooks and look at the world, it is entirely natural that we think someone has been trying to put something over on us. Our world includes Watts and also suburbia, grape pickers as well as family farms, Latin Americans whose memories of American troops often center on the two-bit dictators the troops installed rather than the roads they built. And why would you teach us unreality if you didn't accept it? 14

A sort of "textbook case" (if the pun is acceptable) of codified obscuritanism being peddled under the guise of education is the high-school courses designed to teach us about Communism. In the world presented in most "Communism" courses, "Democracy" and "Communism" fight each other out on a wooden stage. After going through one of these courses, it takes someone with a vivid imagination to realize that these things are ideas millions of people around the world are living and sometimes dying for. The "Comparison Charts" commonly used are of varying lengths (the one in J. Edgar Hoover's high-school guide, *A Study of Communism*, takes the prize, filling up eight pages of text). They are designed to contrast the beliefs of Communism vs. Freedom in such fields as government, economics, education, morality, etc. Considering the debates which have gone on about such fundamental questions, it should come as no shock that these "contrasts" can seem ludicrous. Take this example from Hoover's book:

> Communism: There is a total disregard for the inherent dignity of the individual.
> Freedom: There is a deep and abiding respect for the inherent dignity and worth of the individual. 15

Most students who are paying attention to this react by murmuring, "You must be putting me on," or a less polite variant. For we know that in this world nothing is so simple. And we only have to look at the pictures of the Alabama police dogs to know that things are not simple at all. So a lot of kids react by concluding that there's no difference between "Communism" and "Freedom" in this respect. And if we try to argue, we get Hoover thrown back at our face. 16

Almost every "Communism" course repeats an account of Marxism. When it centers on doctrines like "dialectical materialism," which even Communists have trouble understanding, the course usually turns into a farce. Afterward we often get the accompanying horror images. One widely used film states that the only three non-Communist countries in the West are Spain, Switzerland and America! In an attempt to get down to what is presumed to be our level, one text shows a cartoon of an Oriental-looking Lenin, left hand on a cannon, leading regimented lines of darkly colored robot people against others who, huddled in small groups around the base of the Statue of Liberty, are riding in a car, watching TV, debating, and mowing a lawn. Most of us think that such things insult our intelligence. 17

As we go through school, we are subjected to lots more of this evidence that the real world and the world being taught us aren't the same. Of course, some of us never rebel. They will form the shock troops of the older generation and in our vocabulary are "finks." Or, they will just "cop out" to boredom. 18

But for the others, an overdose of unreality, just like an overdose of anything else, can produce crazy results—even a sickness. Flirtations with things like LSD and "pot" are merely escaping reality, not trying to refuse to adapt to it. It is, for example, a tragedy that anti-Communism is becoming a dirty word on the American campus. It is also a tragedy that the political activism of a generation concerned with the world is in danger of being wasted in the pursuit of semi-anarchist dreams. And the refusal to believe anything people in authority say is only a reaction to the fact that last time we believed we were deceived.   19

What can be done to prevent this revolt against the future? Actually, what is really needed is a revamping of the way we are taught. One suggestion might be to drop our fetish with "objectivity" in subjects toward which we are not objective. Politics are not objective. Love is not objective. People are not objective. Instead of objectivity, the guiding word in our schools should be democracy—which is, as far as I can tell, the prevailing philosophy in our country. Democracy means trusting us to make up our minds. Using democracy in a course about Communism, for example, could mean matching a text that defends a free society with one defending Communism. To the nervous Nellies who recoil, I ask, "Don't you think that the case for Democracy is the better one?" Don't you realize that in the Vietnam war we are given absurd analogies to European history and opponents tend to view the Viet Cong as 20th-century versions of Robin Hood?   20

These are only random examples. The point is this: Adults often like to pretend the real world doesn't exist. Kids can't. We might want to escape from it, but we can't forget about it. And we know the difference between the world we're taught and the world we experience. And if we blame you for trying to put something over on us, it's only because we're taught what, alas, most Americans seem to think. If the school is trying to turn its back on reality, it only represents an America that's doing the same thing. And that's what really worries us.   21

2,000 words

Vocabulary

Paragraph	inane	15. codified
3. affluent	11. indifference	obscuritanism
4. unprecedented	instinctive	ludicrous
5. skepticism	vetoed	16. variant
8. parody	hordes	17. farce
9. sniggering	12. enshrined	19. flirtations
logical	14. unreality	20. objectivity

THE *SERENOS:* LINDA CUSAMANO
DON McNEILL

The girl burst into the storefront of the Visiting Mothers, like a guerrilla into a nursery. 1

"There's going to be some trouble in the park," she said. She paused to catch her breath. "The kids in the park are really up-tight." 2

Riots had almost become routine for Linda Cusamano. "We've got to get the *Serenos,*" she said. She went to the kitchen and began to rummage around for the white armbands which have become the symbol of armistice on the East Side. 3

Linda Cusamano returned to the room with an armful of sheets torn into strips. She passed them out, tied one on her right arm, and began to walk toward Tompkins Square Park. On the way, she paused to talk to kids standing in the doorways of the tenements, taking the temperature of the street. 4

A large crowd had gathered around the bandshell in the park. Enclosed by a sea of heads were several rows of benches filled with a rather elegant audience which had come that warm spring evening to enjoy a classical recital. On the edge of the crowd, the kids were restless. The Puerto Ricans are down on long hair, whether Haydn or hippie. 5

A tight pack of twelve kids had been roaming the park. Now they stood next to the crowd. Linda Cusamano went up to them, and they talked vigorously for a few minutes. They knew her. They had seen her every day on the street. 6

The kids split, to continue roaming through the mazes of Tompkins Square. "They're not telling me anything," she laughed. But every few minutes, like a cold-war diplomat, she would approach them again and they would talk some more. 7

She had passed out the armbands to a new corps of *Serenos.* All that went with the uniform was a name and instructions to link arms and surround any trouble. But, despite the rumors, when the recital ended at 11 p.m. the park seemed well below the riot threshold. 8

The steel mesh screen rattled down over the bandshell. The audience ambled to the west. The kids stampeded to the east. And Linda Cusamano returned to the Visiting Mothers storefront. 9

By two in the morning, 10th Street was quiet. Quiet enough so that Linda Cusamano could leave to go to WBAI for an all-night bail appeal. A kid from 10th Street was in jail, and she needed him. He had been at her side for a week, throughout all the turmoil in Tompkins Square, talking and getting people together and talking some more. A few days later he was busted by narcotics police. 10

The bail was raised, and by ten in the morning Linda Cusamano was in court, gloves in hand, to see him released. Now, while he is awaiting trial, he is working full-time for Visiting Mothers.

11

At noon, Linda Cusamano returned to the storefront. It was full of children now, left in the care of mothers on welfare while other mothers went to work or search for work.

12

She went to the back room, which is her home, to sleep.

13

Linda Cusamano is a teacher. She is teaching people how to survive in the city. She has little use for the Horatio Alger fantasies that so often inspire the professional social worker. Horatio Alger was a freak. The escapee is no help to the inmate. The success story is a television cliché to the kids on Avenue C, and high school equivalency tests are a drag. Bail when they're busted is something else.

14

She is working in the meantime, before the long-range goals of the vocational training-remedial education programs are realized. She is moved by the families that fall apart in the meantime, by the mothers who give up their babies for lack of immediate relief. With armbands and milk and a few friends from the street, Linda Cusamano is hacking at the here and now.

15

She knows what she's up against. She is pretty and twenty-two and has lived on the Lower East Side all her life. She hasn't been through it; she is still in it. She dropped out of Seward Park High School in the tenth grade, and has never been rehabilitated. She has trouble with progress reports, but she talks beautifully and eloquently. And some of the City's most powerful officials come by the storefront to listen, because Linda Cusamano knows the Lower East Side.

16

Visiting Mothers began as a salvage operation after an ambitious plan for a Lower East Side Day-Care Center was rejected by the Federal Welfare Administration a year ago. Linda envisioned a day-care center to relieve mothers of infant children so they could work, look for work, take advantage of opportunities offered by the poverty program, or simply shop for groceries. Without such crèche services, as are available throughout Europe for working mothers, many mothers face no alternative but to give up children to foster homes or go on welfare. The Welfare Administration praised her efforts, but declined the funds. A year ago, Linda joined with the Real Great Society, a self-help organization of former gang members financed by a grant from the Astor Foundation, and opened a storefront at 370 East 10th Street. But it was an uneasy alliance and on June 12 they parted ways. Now Linda is desperate for funds for the summer.

17

The day-care service is the nucleus of Visiting Mothers. At eight each weekday morning, the storefront opens to receive children of working mothers who pay $15.00 a week for the service. The children are cared for by mothers on welfare, who work full time for $30.00 a week. Now it's a hand-to-mouth operation. The working mothers bring milk and cookies, and lunch has lately been bologna sandwiches. A few weeks ago, Visiting Mothers ran out of milk. WBAI responded with an all-night "Milk-In" on the Bob Fass Show. "We had milk in every freezer on 10th Street," Linda recalled. 18

But the Visiting Mothers do more than day-care. When tension in the Puerto Rican community reached the riot level several weeks ago, Linda conceived the *Serenos*. While the Tactical Patrol Force was still in Tompkins Square Park, Linda was on the phone to City Hall pleading for a chance to test the idea. She worked through the night and through the next day, talking with city officials and, with her friend Carmen Mateos, talking with the kids in the street. The next night, hundreds of people in Tompkins Square Park wore the white armbands, ready to join together to stop any trouble, and the riot that seemed inevitable never materialized. 19

Linda spends a lot of time in the street. Like any kid on the Lower East Side, she knows her block and she's proud of it. And the kids on the block know her. With a lot of respect for native knowledge, she has bridged the communications barrier that plagues the social worker who commutes to the slums. "I've got a good thing going with these kids," she said. "They never call me cop. They'd like to, but I'm on the street all the time. They see me. The kids that were really involved that night have been coming around to the storefront and we sit and drink beer and play guitar. They are really into a beautiful music thing. 20

"The kids down here are very alert," she said. "And they're sharp and they're smart. Don't tell me about high school equivalency tests. The kids don't want to be tied down to training programs. They want to work with things that will immediately affect their lives." 21

Immediately. A girl comes to the storefront late in the evening. She is out of money and her baby sister needs milk. Linda goes to the kitchen and gives her a quart. Immediately. The park is tense and mothers tear sheets into armbands. Immediately. A kid from 10th Street is busted and Linda Cusamano is out raising bail. 22

"I want people to learn to live in the city," she said. "They've got to accept the fact that they're going to be here for a while and make it better." 23

Her vision is a series of block centers which would encompass day-care, a twenty-four-hour communications service, workshops, job listings, small apartment repairs, health services, musical instruction, a bail fund, the *Serenos*, and a diaper service. It's not as ponderous as it sounds. The musical instruction, Linda explained, could be on stoops and in laundromats, "just to teach them a little bit more than they know." 24

The idea of a bail fund is now being tested by the hippie community. Linda likes it. "We need a bail fund for every block," she said. "I don't care what the rap is. Everybody should be out on bail. They could parole kids to the block center, and demote some of this absurd ego thing that's going on. 25

"The hippies could teach the kids carpentry," she mused. "They're good at that. They could show them how to build aerial beds, and then there would be a lot more room. The tenants could work with the landlords to renovate the buildings. Can you imagine? Eventually landlords might be hiring crews of these kids.

26

"You teach the kids carpentry in the city, and the next year take them to the country to build domes."

27

Domes in the country are an important part of Linda's vision. She feels that relief in the country is essential to survival in the city. She is already looking for land out of the city where families could stay for two weeks this summer. Next summer she hopes to have kids from the East Side assembling low-cost geodesic domes, which they could sell in the winter when they return to the city.

28

"We'll call it Camp *Sereno*," she said.

29

Meanwhile, the rent is due on the storefront and the frozen milk is nearly finished. Her funds were cut off in mid-June and it is now too late to apply for summer grants. Without some relief, without food or rent or minimal salaries, Visiting Mothers may have to close.

30

"I'm lost," she said quietly. "I need somebody to hold the ladder. I need people to stand behind me while I'm in the street.

31

"What are we? We're women in the community who are doing more than isolating our miseries."

32

1,600 words

Vocabulary

Paragraph	17. envisioned
5. elegant	crèche
Haydn	24. ponderous
7. mazes	28. geodesic domes
14. cliché	

Bomb threats plagued the nation again last week, but very few bombs were going off. Nonetheless, the reverberations of recent blasts could still be heard. In Washington and in state capitals, officials were searching for new means to control dynamite and dynamiters. In Maryland, where two black militants died in bomb blasts, the trial of Rap Brown was moved once more to a new site as an indirect result of the explosions. In Manhattan, police picked carefully through the rubble of the West 11th Street house, where at least three people died. There, in the ruins, they found a severed finger, which enabled them to identify one of the victims as Diana Oughton, 28, a talented, idealistic girl whose turn to radicalism brought her in the end to a rebel bomb factory.

Most Americans find it difficult to grasp that some of the brightest and best-cared-for young are so enraged that they have opted for the nihilism of blowing up society. Diana Oughton's story provides some answers—and engenders some pessimism as well: 1

Diana was born on Jan. 26, 1942, and raised in Dwight (pop. 3,100), a town set in the prairie cornfields of northern Illinois. Her conservative, Episcopal family is one of the community's most prominent. Her paternal great-great-grandfather established the Keeley Institute for alcoholics. Her maternal great-grandfather, W. D. Boyce, founded the American Boy Scouts. James Oughton, 55, Diana's father, is a Dartmouth graduate and restaurateur. Diana and her three sisters were cherished and deeply loved. Said her father: "The social life in Dwight has never separated adults from children. Dinner was a family affair, and there was a pretty wide discussion all the way through." 2

Storybook Child

Time Correspondent Frank Merrick met in Dwight last week with Oughton and one of Diana's sisters, Carol, 26, who now lives in Washington. At first, Jim Oughton was remarkably composed for a father who had just learned that his eldest child had been blown apart. He told of her storybook childhood, of how she became a good horsewoman and swimmer, played a social game of tennis, studied piano and the flute. Her father remembers Diana as "independent in her thinking. She always had her own ideas, and they were sound ideas." About what? "A picture she liked, the best way to treat an animal, which was the finest season of the year—almost anything." 3

Aware of the limitations of Dwight, Oughton sent Diana off to Madeira School in Greenway, Va., and Bryn Mawr. She spent her junior year at the

University of Munich. It was at Bryn Mawr that Diana first showed an interest in social problems. Like many collegians, she was active in voter registration and tutored junior high school students. At night she would go by train to Philadelphia, where for two years she tutored two ghetto boys. Said Carol: "I remember how incredulous Diana was that a seventh- or eighth-grade child couldn't read, didn't even know the alphabet." A Princeton football player proposed marriage, but Diana said: "I don't want to get married now. There are too many things to do." 4

During her year in Germany, Diana made the turn away from affluence that so often marks the contemporary young. She preferred a *Pension* to a luxury hotel, a bicycle to a taxicab. On a trip with her father, she carried a Michelin guidebook because, he recalled, she "didn't want to go to any of those places, she wanted to go to places unknown." 5

After graduating, Diana signed on with the American Friends Service Committee, took a crash course in Spanish and was sent to Guatemala. Stationed in Chichicastenango, she taught Spanish to the local Indians, who were mostly limited to their native dialect. Her eyes widened at the vast poverty and the class hatred between the wealthy few and the impoverished many. She was particularly troubled that a regime she viewed as oppressive was so strongly supported by the U.S. But she was still willing to give the U.S. Establishment a chance. 6

Diana went on to the University of Michigan to earn a teaching certificate. This was the critical year of 1966, when U.S. students were being radicalized by the Viet Nam War. While at Ann Arbor, Diana joined the Children's Community School, an unstructured, permissive experiment in education for children from four to eight. There, she worked with Bill Ayers, son of the board chairman of Chicago's Commonwealth Edison Co., and with Eric Mann—who later became luminaries of the Students for a Democratic Society. The school, operating on Great Society money, folded in 1968, when its funds were cut off. 7

Stormy Days

"It was about this time," said Jim Oughton, "that there was less and less communication between Diana and any of us. She'd call and we'd call. She'd be home briefly from time to time." Diana joined S.D.S., and she was in Chicago for the stormy days and nights of the Democratic Convention. Sometimes she would stop in Dwight. She brought Bill Ayers and other radicals, and she would talk politics with her father, defending the revolutionary's approach to social ills. 8

"That was one of the tense things we did. I was so eager to find out the rationale of her thinking and activities that I probably pressed her harder than I should have. It was a complete stalemate, and she would just change the subject. I deeply loved Diana, and I certainly didn't want to break the communication for the future. I felt that sooner or later there'd be a maturity of thinking, a change of thinking." 9

Oughton, losing his composure at last, said: "This is as much as we know. Anything that happened with Diana in the last two years we don't have information on." He did become convinced that Diana was "completely carried away. It was almost an intellectual hysteria." The years unknown to her father were intensely political for Diana. When factionalism shattered S.D.S. in 1969, she and Bill Ayers joined the most radical, extreme, violence-prone faction, the Weathermen. She began to build an arrest record, once in Flint, Mich., for passing out pamphlets to high school students and again in Chicago in the Weathermen's "days of rage" forays against the police. Detroit police say that Diana was present at the small, secret conclave of Weathermen last December in Flint, at which a decision was reportedly made to begin a bombing wave. As one of the leading activists, gifted and smoldering Diana Oughton went on to her death in Manhattan.   10

To people in Dwight, what happened to Diana seems to be news from another planet. As one elder explained: "There is no radicalism in Dwight. It was a contact she made outside of this town, and thank God, she didn't bring it back." Diana's father is equally puzzled, but absolutely sure of one thing: "Even though there is a big difference of opinion as to whether she's right or wrong, I'm sure that in her own heart she conscientiously felt she was right. She wasn't doing this for any other gain than—well—you might say the good of the world."   11

1,200 words

Vocabulary

Paragraph	permissive
1. nihilism	luminaries
4. incredulous	9. stalemate
5. affluence	10. composure
Pension	conclave
7. unstructured	smoldering

DR. CALHOUN'S HORRIBLE MOUSERY
STEWART ALSOP

WASHINGTON—It was a lovely day—much too lovely to spend in an office. In fact, it seemed a perfect day to visit Dr. John Calhoun's mousery. 1

Dr. Calhoun is a distinguished ecologist, who works for the National Institute of Mental Health. His laboratory is located out beyond the suburbs, in rolling Maryland farmland. I had heard that Dr. Calhoun was conducting some fascinating experiments on the effects of overcrowding on mice. The experiments were fascinating, all right, but they spoiled that beautiful day for me. 2

Dr. Calhoun is a smallish, cheerful man with bright blue eyes, a goatee and mouse-colored hair that looks as though it had never been combed. His chief interest, he soon made clear, is not in mice but in men. 3

What was happening to the human race, he said, was really nothing new. "There have been ten doublings of the human population in the last 4 million years, and each doubling required half the time of the previous doubling." The trouble is that the doubling process is now down to about 40 years, and next time round it will be down to about twenty years. 4

Dr. Calhoun estimates that the world will be nudging the "upper threshold" of population, at the present rate, around the years 2008 to 2010. After that, population simply can't continue to go on growing as it has since the days when men lived in little hunter bands 40,000 years ago. Something will have to happen to stop the growth. 5

Familiar

All this was familiar, and because familiar, not really disturbing. But then Dr. Calhoun led me upstairs to his mousery, and gave me a horrible glimpse of what may be, after all, just around time's corner. 6

Dr. Calhoun's mousery consists of a series of big steel-sided boxes, equipped to provide their occupants with everything the most affluent mouse might want. There are comfortable nesting boxes, fine crawl spaces up the sides of the box, and unlimited food and water. There is only one thing wrong with this rodential paradise. There are too many mice in it. 7

With some 2,600 mice in a box 9 feet square, there are about sixteen times as many mice in the box as occur under the most ideal natural conditions. Peering down from the sides of the box at the squirming, flowing mass of tiny bodies, smelling the rank mouse smell, which is at first overpowering, I had a strong impulse to get out again, into the sunlight. But Dr. Calhoun started to explain his experiment and I stayed, fascinated and appalled. 8

The mice, as soon as they were put into the box, established their hierarchy, or pecking order, Dr. Calhoun explained. The top mice—the rodential bourgeoisie—established themselves with their consorts in the higher nesting boxes, nearest the food and water. Lower-grade mice found less desirable nesting sites. The lowest of all—the proles—were the mice who found no nesting sites at all. They swarmed over the bottom of the box—sad, scruffy little animals, mostly rejected males, a few viciously aggressive females. 9

Withdrawal

All the mice are afflicted in varying degrees with what Dr. Calhoun calls a "withdrawal syndrome." Only the proles on the open floor retain the capacity for "little bursts of violence," Dr. Calhoun said. "They chew on each other, and the ones being chewed on don't run away." He pointed out a couple of mice on the floor, and sure enough, one was gnawing on another's bottom, while the other sat passive. 10

The withdrawal syndrome of the mice bourgeoisie takes a different form. These mice become what Dr. Calhoun calls the "beautiful ones." Dr. Calhoun picked up two of the beautiful ones, and two of the proles, and held all four in one hand. The difference was obvious. The proles were scruffy and chewed up—one had lost half its tail—while the beautiful ones were sleek, unharmed and utterly passive. 11

Enzyme tests, Dr. Calhoun explained, have established that the beautiful ones are "completely unstressed." They simply eat, drink and sleep—and do nothing else. They build no nests, they never fight, they never forage, they rear no children, and they neither copulate nor conceive. They have ceased to be mice, in the same sense that a man who performs none of the functions of a man has ceased to be a man. 12

"We've had no live births for six months, and no conceptions for almost as long," said Dr. Calhoun. Perhaps as a result, many females take over a male role, becoming hunters and aggressors. Dr. Calhoun suspects there is an actual endocrine change. 13

"Aren't we maybe seeing the phenomenon of the beautiful ones, already, in the dropout, drug culture?" I asked. 14

Dr. Calhoun replied that he could give no scientifically provable reply to my question, but rather to my surprise, he did not think the question ridiculous. He led me on to a couple of uncrowded mouse boxes—the mice in these boxes were the carefully culled survivors of overcrowded mouse populations. Their fellows had found the release of death in the "carbobox," a mouse Auschwitz filled with carbon dioxide. 15

In one of the boxes, six survivors, terrified of the unaccustomed surrounding space, huddled together, clinging to each other desperately as though in a great cold. In another, a male mouse—the dye on his fur identified his sex—viciously attacked first one female, then another. In nature, Dr. Calhoun said, a male never attacked a female. 16

The experience of overcrowding, he explained, did something to the "programing" of the central nervous system of the surviving mice. It remained to be seen whether these survivors would reproduce. In three similar experiments with rats, there had been no reproduction at all.   17

Different

Thinking back on my afternoon at Dr. Calhoun's mousery, I recalled two remarks I had heard during a visit in May to Yale University. John Hersey, distinguished novelist and master of Pierson College, had said that there really did seem to be something different about this generation of the young. Perhaps one reason, he said, was "the sense of crowding—the feeling of too many elbows." William Kesen, a brilliant psychology professor, agreed, and added that today's young had "an odd sense of futurelessness —they never seem to want to talk about their own futures at all."   18

It is very farfetched, no doubt, to see any connection between these remarks and Dr. Calhoun's experiments. But the fact remains that this generation of the young, unlike their elders, will live to see Dr. Calhoun's "upper threshold" reached. Is it possible that when the threshold is reached, population growth will be ended, not by birth control or the bomb, but by the mysterious and terrible process that ended all reproduction in Dr. Calhoun's horrible mousery? Is it possible that the young have some sort of subconscious prescience of what lies in store?   19

1,200 words

Vocabulary

Paragraph	bourgeoisie	13. endocrine
8. appalled	10. syndrome	19. prescience
9. hierarchy	12. unstressed	

I THINK I MAY HAVE BEEN LISTENING
WILLIE MORRIS

What strikes me most in reading books like Alfred Kazin's haunting poetic reminiscences of boyhood in an immigrant Jewish neighborhood in the East, is the vast gulf which separates that kind of growing up and the childhood and adolescence of those of us who came out of the towns of the American South and Southwest a generation later. With the Eastern Jewish intellectuals who play such a substantial part in American cultural life, perhaps in the late 1960s a dominant part, the struggle as they grew up in the 1930s was for one set of ideas over others, for a fierce acceptance or rejection of one man's theories or another man's poetry—and with all this a driving determination to master the language which had not been their parents' and to find a place in a culture not quite theirs. For other Eastern intellectuals and writers whom I later was to know, going to the Ivy League schools involved, if not a finishing, then a deepening of perceptions, or of learning, or culture.

1

But for so many of us who converged on Austin, Texas, in the early 1950s, from places like Karnes City or Big Spring or Abileen or Rockdale or Yazoo City, the awakening we were to experience, or to have jolted into us, or to undergo by some more subtle chemistry, did not mean a mere finishing or deepening, and most emphatically did not imply the victory of one set of ideologies over another, one way of viewing literature or politics over another, but something more basic and simple. This was the acceptance of ideas themselves as something worth living by. It was a matter, at the age of eighteen or nineteen, not of discovering *certain* books, but the simple *presence* of books, not the nuances of idea and feeling, but idea and feeling on their own terms. It is this late coming to this kind of awareness that still gives the intellectuals from the small towns of our region a hungry, naïve quality, as opposed to the sharp-elbowed overintellectuality of some Easterners, as if those from down there who made it were lucky, or chosen, out of all the disastrous alternatives of their isolated lower- or middle-class upbringings, to enjoy and benefit from the fruits of simply being educated and liberal-minded.

2

What we brought to the University of Texas in the 1950s, to an enormous, only partially formed state university, was a great awe before the splendid quotations on its buildings and the walls of its libraries, along with an absolutely prodigious insensitivity as to what they implied beyond decoration. Minds awakened slowly, painfully, and with pretentious and damaging inner searches. Where an Alfred Kazin at the age of nineteen might become aroused in the subway by reading a review by John Chamberlain in the *New York Times* and rush to his office to complain, we at eighteen or nineteen were only barely beginning to learn that there were ideas, much less ideas to arouse one from one's self. If places like City College or Columbia galvanized the young New York intellectuals already drenched in literature and polemics, the University of Texas had, in its halting, unsure, and often frivolous way, to teach those of us with good minds and small-town high school diplomas that we were intelligent human beings, with minds and hearts of our own that we might learn to call our own, that there were some things, many things—ideas, values, choices of action—worth committing one's self to and fighting for, that a man in some instances might become morally committed to honoring every manifestation of individual conscience and courage. Yet the hardest task at the University of Texas, as many of us were to learn, was to separate all the extraneous and empty things that can drown a young person there, as all big universities can drown its young people, from the few simple things that are worth living a life by. Without wishing to sound histrionic, I believe I am thinking of something approaching the Western cultural tradition; yet if someone had suggested that to me that September night in 1952, as I stepped off the bus in Austin to be greeted by three fraternity men anxious to look me over, I would have thought him either a fool or a con man. 3

I emerged from that bus frightened and tired, after having come 500 miles non-stop over the red hills of Louisiana and the pine forests of East Texas. The three men who met me—appalled, I was told later, by my green trousers and the National Honor Society medal on my gold-plated watch chain—were the kind that I briefly liked and admired, for their facility at small talk, their clothes, their manner, but whom I soon grew to deplore and finally to be bored by. They were the kind who made fraternities tick, the favorites of the Dean of Men at the time, respectable B or C-plus students, tolerable athletes, good with the Thetas or the Pi Phis; but one would find later, lurking there inside of them despite—or maybe because of—their good fun and jollity, the ideals of the insurance salesman and an aggressive distrust of anything approaching thought. One of them later told me, with the seriousness of an early disciple, that my table manners had become a source of acute embarrassment to all of them. That night they drove me around the campus, and they were impressed that I knew from my map-reading where the University library was, for two of them were not sure. 4

. . .

Once I was invited to the apartment of a young graduate student and his wife. The walls of their apartment were lined with books, more books than I had ever seen before in a private dwelling—books everywhere and on everything. I was astonished; I tried to talk with those people, but I was unaccountably shy, and I kept looking at their books out of the corner of my eye, and wondering if I should say something about them, or ask perhaps if they were for sale or if they formed some kind of special exhibit. It is a rare experience for certain young people to see great quantities of books in a private habitat for the first time, and to hear ideas talked about seriously in the off hours. Good God, they were doing it for pleasure, or so it seemed. The wife, who was also a graduate student, asked me what I wanted to do with myself when I graduated from college. "I want to be a writer," I said, but not even thinking about it until the words were out; my reply surprised me most of all, but it was much more appropriate in those surroundings to have said that instead of "sports announcer," which probably constituted my first choice. "What do you want to write about?" she persisted. "Just . . . *things*," I said, turning red. That night, stirred by the conversation and by all the books I had seen, I went to the library, promising myself to read every important book that had ever been written. I was at a loss, because I did not have the faintest notion where to start. I picked out the most imposing volumes I could find—Lord Bryce on the American Commonwealth, which put me to sleep for ten nights in a row. But once this fire is lit, to consume and to know, it can burn on and on. I kept going back to the library, taking out tall stacks of books and reading them in a great undigested fury: Hemingway, Faulkner, Wolfe, Dreiser, anything in the American literature and American history shelves that looked promising. I started buying Modern Library books with the money I made writing for the newspaper, and I pledged to myself, as Marilyn Monroe had, that I would read them all, and in alphabetical order.   5

I believe now that the University of Texas was somehow beginning to give me an interest and a curiosity in something outside my own parochial ego. It was beginning to suggest the power not merely of language, but the whole unfamiliar world of experience and evocation which language served. That world was new, and the recognition of its existence was slow, uncertain, and immature. Books and literature, I was beginning to see, were not for getting a grade, not for the utilitarian purpose of being considered a nice and versatile boy, not just for casual pleasure, but subversive as Socrates and expressions of man's soul. It took me years to understand that words are often as important as experience, because words make experience last, but here, in the spring of my freshman year, there were men who were teaching me these things, perhaps with very little hope that anyone in their classrooms remotely cared, and I think perhaps I may have been listening. Freshman English was the first step; it was often the first and last time that many young people, headed in a state like Texas for insurance or business or the Junior League, might have had for a kind of small internal salvation.   6

1,500 words

Vocabulary

Paragraph

1. reminiscences
   perceptions
2. converged
   nuances
   alternatives
3. pretentious
   prodigious
   polemics

extraneous
histrionic
4. facility
6. parochial
   evocation
   utilitarian
   versatile
   subversive

When I was a little girl, we lived in a shabby neighborhood in Detroit that tried to pass itself off as middle class. It wasn't downright poor, it didn't even have that kind of dramatic look to it; it was just cheap-looking, old-fashioned frame houses, choked up close to each other—the kind of neighborhood a child is so embarrassed about that as I grew older and began high school, I had to pass up rides home (even when it snowed) with good looking American boys who thought my dark looks were exotic if irregular.   1

We had a neighborhood *show*, a huge brick building that took up a whole lot at the end of our block. It had a long, dark alley that crept along its side, not exactly filled with garbage, but sort of haunted with old tin cans, rusty nails and occasional tarnished pennies in the dust that you didn't even bother to pick up because you had a little dignity. How many times I walked that alley that led to the theater; to have approached the show from its glossy front would have been just another lie about where I came from.   2

Empty Promises

With 12 cents, I could see two full-length features, and every Saturday I did, sitting a phenomenal five hours—catching the beginnings of films I had just seen so as to prolong my return home. I remember the theater lobby. It had a shabbiness that was perked up a little by the huge glossy film posters that promised a lot next Saturday, and the films, too, were filled with empty promises.   3

I remember those movies with Ann Blyth, June Haver, Debbie Reynolds, Jeanne Crain, Diana Lynn, June Allyson, Piper Laurie and name-less bland starlets, the rage of America's virgin cult.   4

Because of my dark looks, my feelings of ethnic inferiority, I was fascinated by the fair, regular, perfect-looking Americans who lived such orderly lives. I say it was a fascination, but it left in me a longing which made my return home tough to face.   5

Having strung out a box of popcorn from noon till 5, I would leave the theater sick to my stomach, passing the faded carpets of the lobby. The wholesome family scenes drawn in the clean, crisp lines of Hollywood Technicolor gave way to seedy Finkell Ave. littered with garbage along its edges. 6

These films were designed as escapist dreams for the deprived masses, but they hurt and pained me because their graceful settings and their characters who never gave way to passion, who spoke quietly without yelling, tantalized me with an American ideal I couldn't hope to emulate. But it was a long time before I realized how much energy I wasted in pursuing dreams not worth emulating.   7

(Years later, when I was teaching literature to black students from the ghetto, I tried to push them into reading stories about their own culture and heroes. But they were stubbornly mad for "Mama's Bank Account." At first stupefied, I realized it was just the slow, mundane pace of American family life, the orderly routine of the average sanitary household that seemed Paradise to them, as it once had seemed to me. The spell of Americana still worked its crude power.)   8

Seeing "Love Story" (Village Westwood) pulled me back to those Saturday matinees. Its American wholesomeness was so reminiscent of the films that fired my adolescent fantasies and set me to longing: "A Date With Judy," "Our Very Own," "Mother Is a Freshman," "Father of the Bride," "By the Light of the Silvery Moon," "Cheaper by the Dozen," "Father's Little Dividend." "Love Story" takes place in the East, America's most prestigious romance-land, and is filled with New England purity— snow scenes, hockey games, red brick houses and sturdy apple-cheeked people. Everything is clean, orderly crisp, white antiseptic. But "Love Story" is more treacherous than the films that made me envious in my youth because it coats its sentimentality for the ordinary life with a contemporary gloss that seduces the audience into believing it is a modern story about young people today. The settings are all authentic. The dialog, cheap imitation Salinger, has a spare, cool, terse, sarcastic glibness that people mistake for honesty:

What about my scholarship? What about Paris, which I've never seen in my whole goddamn life?
What about our marriage?
What about my marriage?
Me. I'm saying it now.
You want to marry me?
Yes.
Why?
Because.
Oh. That's a very good reason.   9

Audiences have no trouble mocking more extravagant romantic films. But when the same soap opera romance it concealed under cynical wisecracks, they swallow the pap as if it were a profound revelation. This contemporary understatement plus its hard sell on old-fashioned American values will undoubtedly win "Love Story" a wide audience.   10

But the reasons for its strong appeal go deeper, I think. "Love Story" is a novel and a film of our times, an affirmation of the values of the Nixon era, a celebration of apathy. Americans, we hear, are tired of bitter things; they want honest, simple love stories. And here is a modern couple young people *can* emulate. These kids have all the respectable goals; they aren't against America. In fact, they never allow a single important social issue to pierce their stolid domesticity or detract them from total absorption in themselves and their limited life.   11

Their world is as wide as the hockey field and the squash courts. They're aggressive, competitive, acquisitive—their conversation centers on hockey scores, grades, class rank, dean's list, scholarships—like the go-getters who ran for school office in my high school during the 50s.   12

(While we grow more alarmed at the proliferation of hippie communes and the isolation of our young people, the life-style of this couple—as thoroughly impervious to the urgent problems of our society as their downbeat contemporaries—is reassuring: they are perpetuating our urban, materialistic technocracy.)   13

The short-lived heroine of "Love Story" is a second-generation Italian girl (about as foreign-looking as Deanna Durbin) who comes from a crowded, frame-house neighborhood very much like mine, but seen with a romantic eye—everything is alive with bustling people, and colorful in its humble way. Besides being poor, Jenny is beautiful, talented, confident, witty and gay, but this doesn't deter her one bit from pursuing the same goals that inspired June Allyson, Ann Blyth or Virginia Mayo. Her aggressive snottiness and air of superiority—which, we are led to believe, are natural by-products of her humble, impoverished, blue-collar background—dazzle the handsome Harvard Magna and WASP princeling, millionaire, who proposes. 14

Jenny gratefully settles down to a cocoon-like existence with Oliver Barrett IV, trading a scholarship to Paris and graduate school for a Camp Tuckahoe T-shirt. It must satisfy the audience that someone so extraordinary can embrace the most ordinary dreams of suburban domesticity; this girl knows her place. She is headed for the same anonymity as you and me. 15

Life drones on. The heroine is mercifully saved from this Nixonian nightmare and the dull drift into middle age when she suddenly is struck down by an incurable disease. At least things do pick up when Jenny begins to expire. America's sexless, passionless, ideal young lovers find their supreme moment on Jenny's deathbed, when they come together for what is only the second explicit love scene in the entire film.   16

Wired and taped and looking pale and ghastly, Jenny asks Oliver to take her in his arms. He creeps in, careful not to knock the tubes that have her hooked up to bottles and machines. As Oliver embraces the corpse, the all-American girl who croaks with a wisecrack on her lips, the sobbing in the audience reaches its peak. Death in this morbid little tearjerker seems so natural to the lovers' lives, so easily assimilated and so passively accepted that it makes me shudder.   17

Congratulates Film

Charles Champlin, writing in the *Times*, congratulates the film for its power to make us feel "good rather than depressed." Does he mean that the film makes death appetizing? Instead of raging against death, our vital young lovers embrace it stoically, and the film encourages us to wallow in the pathetic spectacle of a girl punished for being simply too good, too beautiful.

18

Death in "Love Story," as in the most popular of Victorian salon literature, has no connection whatsoever to the characters and their actions. It is a dramatic convenience.

19

Jenny's death isn't tragic; it is simple catastrophe, a creaky *deus ex machina* that gets author Erich Segal off the hook and is, at the same time, a weirdly appropriate conclusion to this complacent and passive vision of American life. What more could these lovers do but die?

20

"Love Story" is the 50s, sorority and fraternity row, a corpse from the Eisenhower years that the Nixon era somehow managed to resuscitate. I thought we had put all that behind us!

21

1,750 words

Vocabulary

Paragraph
1. shabby
   exotic
4. bland
7. emulate
8. mundane
9. prestigious

authentic
glibness
10. pap
   understatement
11. apathy
12. acquisitive

14. deter
15. anonymity
16. drones
17. assimilated
20. *deus ex machina*
21. resuscitate

CESAR CHAVEZ
STUDS TERKEL

(Editor's note: What follows is the transcription of an interview with Cesar Chavez. It appears in *Hard Times: An Oral History of the Great Depression* by Studs Terkel who poses the questions to which Chavez responds.)

Like so many who have worked from early childhood, particularly in the open country, he appears older than his forty-one years. His manner is diffident, his voice soft. 1

He is president of the United Farm Workers of America (UFWA). It is, unlike craft and industrial unions, a quite new labor fraternity. In contrast to these others, agricultural workers—those who "follow the crops"—had been excluded from many of the benefits that came along with the New Deal. 2

Oh, I remember having to move out of our house. My father had brought in a team of horses and wagon. We had always lived in that house, and we couldn't understand why we were moving out. When we got to the other house, it was a worse house, a poor house. That must have been around 1934. I was about six years old. 3

It's known as the North Gila Valley, about fifty miles north of Yuma. My dad was being turned out of his small plot of land. He had inherited this from his father, who had homesteaded it. I saw my two, three other uncles also moving out. And for the same reason. The bank had foreclosed on the loan. 4

If the local bank approved, the Government would guarantee the loan and small farmers like my father would continue in business. It so happened the president of the bank was the guy who most wanted our land. We were surrounded by him: he owned all the land around us. Of course, he wouldn't pass the loan. 5

One morning a giant tractor came in, like we had never seen before. My daddy used to do all his work with horses. So this huge tractor came in and began to knock down this corral, this small corral where my father kept his horses. We didn't understand why. In the matter of a week, the whole face of the land was changed. Ditches were dug, and it was different. I didn't like it as much. 6

We all of us climbed into an old Chevy that my dad had. And then we were in California, and migratory workers. There were five kids—a small family by those standards. It must have been around '36. I was about eight. Well, it was a strange life. We had been poor, but we knew every night there was a bed *there,* and that *this* was our room. There was a kitchen. It was sort of a settled life, and we had chickens and hogs, eggs and all those things. But that all of a sudden changed. When you're small, you can't figure these things out. You know something's not right and you don't like it, but you don't question it and you don't let that get you down. You sort of just continue to move. 7

But this had quite an impact on my father. He had been used to owning the land and all of a sudden there was no more land. What I heard . . . what I made out of conversations between my mother and my father—things like, we'll work this season and then we'll get enough money and we'll go and buy a piece of land in Arizona. Things like that. Became like a habit. He never gave up hope that some day he would come back and get a little piece of land. 8

I can understand very, very well this feeling. These conversations were sort of melancholy. I guess my brothers and my sisters could also see this very sad look on my father's face. 9

That piece of land he wanted . . . ?

No, never. It never happened. He stopped talking about that some years ago. The drive for land, it's a very powerful drive. 10

When we moved to California, we would work after school. Sometimes we wouldn't go. "Following the crops," we missed much school. Trying to get enough money to stay alive the following winter, the whole family picking apricots, walnuts, prunes. We were pretty new, we had never been migratory workers. We were taken advantage of quite a bit by the labor contractor and the crew pusher.* In some pretty silly ways. (Laughs.) 11

Sometimes we can't help but laugh about it. We trusted everybody that came around. You're traveling in California with all your belongings in your car: it's obvious. Those days we didn't have a trailer. This is bait for the labor contractor. Anywhere we stopped, there was a labor contractor offering all kinds of jobs and good wages, and we were always deceived by them and we always went. Trust them. 12

Coming into San Jose, not finding—being lied to, that there was work. We had no money at all, and had to live on the outskirts of town under a bridge and dry creek. That wasn't really unbearable. What was unbearable was so many families living just a quarter of a mile. And you know how kids are. They'd bring in those things that really hurt us quite a bit. Most of those kids were middle-class families. 13

We got hooked on a real scheme once. We were going by Fresno on our way to Delano. We stopped at some service station and this labor contractor saw the car. He offered a lot of money. We went. We worked the first week: the grapes were pretty bad and we couldn't make much. We all stayed off from school in order to make some money. Saturday we were to be paid and we didn't get paid. He came and said the winery hadn't paid

---

* "That's a man who specializes in contracting human beings to do cheap labor."

him. We'd have money next week. He gave us $10. My dad took the $10 and went to the store and bought $10 worth of groceries. So we worked another week and in the middle of the second week, my father was asking him for his last week's pay, and he had the same excuse. This went on and we'd get $5 or $10 or $7 a week for about four weeks. For the whole family. 14

So one morning my father made the resolution no more work. If he doesn't pay us, we won't work. We got in a car and went over to see him. The house was empty. He had left. The winery said they had paid him and they showed us where they had paid him. This man had taken it. 15

Labor strikes were everywhere. We were one of the strikingest families, I guess. My dad didn't like the conditions, and he began to agitate. Some families would follow, and we'd go elsewhere. Sometimes we'd come back. We couldn't find a job elsewhere, so we'd come back. Sort of beg for a job. Employers would know and they would make it very humiliating 16

Did these strikes ever win? 17

Never. 18
We were among these families who always honored somebody else's grievance. Somebody would have a personal grievance with the employer. He'd say I'm not gonna work for this man. Even though we were working, we'd honor it. We felt we had to. So we'd walk out, too. Because we were prepared to honor those things, we caused many of the things ourselves. If we were picking at a piece rate and we knew they were cheating on the weight, we wouldn't stand for it. So we'd lose the job, and we'd go elsewhere. There were other families like that. 19

Sometimes when you had to come back, the contractor knew this . . . ? 20

They knew it, and they rubbed it in quite well. Sort of shameful to come back. We were trapped. We'd have to do it for a few days to get enough money to get enough gas. 21

One of the experiences I had. We went through Indio, California. Along the highway there were signs in most of the small restaurants that said "White Trade Only." My dad read English, but he didn't really know the meaning. He went in to get some coffee—a pot that he had, to get some coffee for my mother. He asked us not to come in, but we followed him anyway. And this young waitress said, "We don't serve Mexicans here. Get out of here." I was there, and I saw it and heard it. She paid no more attention. I'm sure for the rest of her life she never thought of it again. But every time we thought of it, it hurt us. So we got back in the car and we had a difficult time trying—in fact, we never got the coffee. These are sort of unimportant, but they're . . . you remember 'em very well. 22

One time there was a little diner across the tracks in Brawley. We used to shine shoes after school. Saturday was a good day. We used to shine shoes for three cents, two cents. Hamburgers were then, as I remember, seven cents. There was this little diner all the way across town. The moment we stepped across the tracks, the police stopped us. They would let us go there, to what we called "the American town," the Anglo town, with a shoe shine box. We went to this little place and we walked in. 23

There was this young waitress again. With either her boyfriend or someone close, because they were involved in conversation. And there was this familiar sign again, but we paid no attention to it. She looked up at us and she sort of—it wasn't what she said, it was just a gesture. A sort of gesture of total rejection. Her hand, you know, and the way she turned her face away from us. She said: "Wattaya want?" So we told her we'd like to buy two hamburgers. She sort of laughed, a sarcastic sort of laugh. And she said, "Oh, we don't sell to Mexicans. Why don't you go across to Mexican town, you can buy 'em over there." And then she turned around and continued her conversation. 24

She never knew how much she was hurting us. But it stayed with us.

We'd go to school two days sometimes, a week, two weeks, three weeks at most. This is when we were migrating. We'd come back to our winter base, and if we were lucky, we'd get in a good solid all of January, February, March, April, May. So we had five months out of a possible nine months. We started counting how many schools we'd been to and we counted thirty-seven. Elementary schools. From first to eighth grade. Thirty-seven. We never got a transfer. Friday we didn't tell the teacher or anything. We'd just go home. And they accepted this. 25

I remember one teacher—I wondered why she was asking so many questions. (In those days anybody asked questions, you became suspicious. Either a cop or a social worker.) She was a young teacher, and she just wanted to know why we were behind. One day she drove into the camp. That was quite an event, because we never had a teacher come over. Never. So it was, you know, a very meaningful day for us. 26

This I remember. Some people put this out of their minds and forget it. I don't. I don't want to forget it. I don't want it to take the best of me, but I want to be there because this is what happened. This is the truth, you know. History. 27

2,200 words

Vocabulary

Paragraph
4. homesteaded
8. impact

9. melancholy
15. resolution
19. grievance

FINALLY FREE
FRANK CONROY

Now the road began to curve and houses appeared on either side—houses with lawns, driveways, and hedges. Sprinklers turned, throwing spray into the air and dark half-moons on the sidewalk. In the quiet and coolness pedaling seemed easier. Sitting straight I followed the smooth curves effort-lessly, my arms hanging at my sides. A group of kids playing on the side-walk stopped to watch me go by, automatically falling silent until I was past. They took me for a redneck. I heard their voices starting up behind me once I was out of sight.   1

Mile after mile of well-kept houses slipped by. At the first gas station I stopped for a Coke and checked the tire pressure. I liked gas stations. You could hang around as long as you wanted and no one took any notice. Sitting on the ground in a shady corner with my back against the wall, I took small sips at the Coke and made it last.   2

Is it the mindlessness of childhood that opens up the world? Today nothing happens in a gas station. I'm eager to leave, to get where I'm going, and the station, like some huge paper cutout, or a Hollywood set, is simply a facade. But at thirteen, sitting with my back against the wall, it was a marvelous place to be. The delicious smell of gasoline, the cars com-ing and going, the free air hose, the half-heard voices buzzing in the back-ground—these things hung musically in the air, filling me with a sense of well-being. In ten minutes my psyche would be topped up like the tanks of the automobiles.   3

Downtown the streets were crowded with shoppers. I cut in and out between the slow-moving cars, enjoying my superior mobility. At a red light I took hold of the tailgate of a chicken truck and let it pull me a couple of blocks. Peeling off at the foot of Los Olas Boulevard, I coasted up to the bike rack in front of the Sunset Theater.   4

It cost nine cents to get in. I bought my ticket, paused in the lobby to select a Powerhouse candy bar, and climbed to the balcony. The theater was almost empty and no one objected when I draped my legs over the seat in front. On the screen was a western, with Randolph Scott as the sheriff. I recognized a cheap process called Trucolor and hissed spontaneously, smiling foolishly at the empty darkness around me afterwards. Except for the gunfights the film was dull and I amused myself finding anachronisms. 5

The feature was better, an English movie with Ann Todd as a neurotic pianist and James Mason as her teacher. I was sorry when the house lights came on.   6

Outside, blinking against the sun, I left my bike in the rack and wan-dered down the street. Something was happening in front of the dime store.

I could see a crowd of kids gathered at the doors and a policeman attempting to keep order. I slipped inside behind his back. The place was a madhouse, jammed with hundreds of shrieking children, all pressing toward one of the aisles where some kind of demonstration was going on.   7

"What's happening?" I asked a kid as I elbowed past.   8

"It's Ramos and Ricardo," he shouted. "The twins from California."   9

I pushed my way to the front rank and looked up at the raised platform.   10

There, under a spotlight, two Oriental gentlemen in natty blue suits were doing some amazing things with yo-yos. Tiny, neat men, no bigger than children, they stared abstractedly off into space while yo-yos flew from their hands, zooming in every direction as if under their own power, leaping out from small fists in arcs, circles, and straight lines. I stared openmouthed as a yo-yo was thrown down and *stayed down,* spinning at the end of its string a fraction of an inch above the floor.   11

"Walking the Dog," said the twin, and lowered his yo-yo to the floor. It skipped along beside him for a yard or so and mysteriously returned to his palm.   12

"The Pendulum," said the other twin, and threw down a yo-yo. "Sleeping," he said, pointing to the toy as it spun at the end of its string. He gathered the line like so much loose spaghetti, making a kind of cat's cradle with his fingers, and gently rocked the spinning yo-yo back and forth through the center. "Watch end of trick closely," he said smiling, and suddenly dropped everything. Instead of the tangled mess we'd all expected the yo-yo wound up safely in his palm.   13

"Loop-the-Loop." He threw a yo-yo straight ahead. When it returned he didn't catch it, but executed a subtle flick of his wrist and sent it back out again. Five, ten, twenty times. "Two Hands Loop-the-Loop," he said, adding another, alternating so that as one flew away from his right hand the other flew in toward his left.   14

"Pickpocket," said the other twin, raising the flap of his jacket. He threw the yo-yo between his legs, wrapping the string around his thigh. As he looked out over the crowd the yo-yo dropped, perfectly placed, into his trouser pocket. Laughing, the kids applauded.   15

I spent the whole afternoon in one spot, watching them, not even moving when they took breaks for fear I'd lose my place. When it was over I spent my last money on a yo-yo, a set of extra strings, and a pamphlet explaining all the tricks, starting from the easiest and working up to the hardest.   16

Walking back to the bike I was so absorbed a mail truck almost ran me down. I did my first successful trick standing by the rack, a simple but rather spectacular exercise called Around the World. Smiling, I put the yo-yo in my pocket and pulled out the bike. I knew I was going to be good at it.   17

The common yo-yo is crudely made, with a thick shank between two widely spaced wooden disks. The string is knotted or stapled to the shank. With such an instrument nothing can be done except the simple up-down movement. My yo-yo, on the other hand, was a perfectly balanced construction of hard wood, slightly weighted, flat, with only a sixteenth of an inch between the halves. The string was not attached to the shank, but looped over it in such a way as to allow the wooden part to spin freely on its own axis. The gyroscopic effect thus created kept the yo-yo stable in all attitudes. 18

I started at the beginning of the book and quickly mastered the novice, intermediate, and advanced stages, practicing all day every day in the woods across the street from my house. Hour after hour of practice, never moving to the next trick until the one at hand was mastered. 19

The string was tied to my middle finger, just behind the nail. As I threw—with your palm up, make a fist; throw down your hand, fingers unfolding, as if you were casting grain—a short bit of string would tighten across the sensitive pad of flesh at the tip of my finger. That was the critical area. After a number of weeks I could interpret the condition of the string, the presence of any imperfections on the shank, but most importantly the exact amount of spin or inertial energy left in the yo-yo at any given moment—all from that bit of string on my fingertip. As the throwing motion became more and more natural I found I could make the yo-yo "sleep" for an astonishing length of time—fourteen or fifteen seconds— and still have enough spin left to bring it back to my hand. Gradually the basic moves became reflexes. Sleeping, twirling, swinging, and precise aim. Without thinking, without even looking, I could run through trick after trick involving various combinations of the elemental skills, switching from one to the other in a smooth continuous flow. On particularly good days I would hum a tune under my breath and do it all in time to the music. 20

Flicking the yo-yo expressed something. The sudden, potentially comic extension of one's arm to twice its length. The precise neatness of it, intrinsically soothing, as if relieving an inner tension too slight to be noticeable, the way a man might hitch up his pants simply to enact a reassuring gesture. It felt good. The comfortable weight in one's hand, the smooth, rapid descent down the string, ending with a barely audible snap as the yo-yo hung balanced, spinning, pregnant with force and the slave of one's fingertip. That it was vaguely masturbatory seems inescapable. I doubt that half the pubescent boys in America could have been captured by any other means, as, in the heat of the fad, half of them were. A single Loop-the-Loop might represent, in some mysterious way, the act of masturbation, but to break down the entire repertoire into the three stages of throw, trick, and return representing erection, climax, and detumescence seems immoderate. 21

The greatest pleasure in yo-yoing was an abstract pleasure—watching the dramatization of simple physical laws, and realizing they would never fail if a trick was done correctly. The geometric purity of it! The string wasn't just a string, it was a tool in the enactment of theorems. It was a line, an idea. And the top was an entirely different sort of idea, a gyroscope, capable of storing energy and of interacting with the line. I remember the first time I did a particularly lovely trick, one in which the sleeping yo-yo is swung from right to left while the string is interrupted by an extended index finger. Momentum carries the yo-yo in a circular path around the finger, but instead of completing the arc the yo-yo falls on the taut string between the performer's hands, where it continues to spin in an upright position. My pleasure at that moment was as much from the beauty of the experiment as from pride. Snapping apart my hands I sent the yo-yo into the air above my head, bouncing if off nothing, back into my palm.   22

I practiced the yo-yo because it pleased me to do so, without the slightest application of will power. It wasn't ambition that drove me but the nature of yo-yoing. The yo-yo represented my first organized attempt to control the outside world. It fascinated me because I could see my progress in clearly defined stages, and because the intimacy of it, the almost spooky closeness I began to feel with the instrument in my hand, seemed to ensure that nothing irrelevant would interfere. I was, in the language of jazz, "up tight" with my yo-yo, and finally free, in one small area at least, of the paralyzing sloppiness of life in general.   23

1,800 words

Vocabulary

Paragraph	20. inertial	gesture
3. facade	reflexes	22. enactment
psyche	21. intrinsically	gyroscope
5. anachronisms		

TITANIC THOMPSON
JOHN LARDNER

One day not long ago, a St. Louis hotel detective tipped off a cop friend of his that there was a fellow in a room on the eighth floor who packed a gun. They decided to do a little further research. They went into the room without knocking, and it didn't take long to find the gun. It was pointing at them. The man who held it was tall, dark, thin, well dressed and fiftyish.   1

"Take it easy," he said. Then, observing the cop's uniform, he set down the gun, a small Army model, on a table, and smiled pleasantly. "I thought it might be a stick-up," he said. "I have to be careful."   2

Down at the station house, where the man was taken to explain why he was armed and why he drew his hardware so quickly, they got a polite and possibly a truthful answer. He happened to have $3,930 on him. He was expecting to claim a race horse with it. When he carried cash, he liked to feel protected. He had a license for the gun. His name was Alvin C. Thomas. At this point, the police lost interest in the details of the story and merely sat looking at the speaker with the frank curiosity of zoo-goers looking at a duck-billed platypus—for Alvin C. Thomas, as they knew and as he readily confirmed, is also Titanic Thompson. All the cops in the house took a good, long stare. Then they released him, and he went on his way.   3

On a small scale, Titanic Thompson is an American legend. I say a small scale, because an overpowering majority of the public has never heard of him. That is the way Titanic likes it. He is a professional gambler. He has sometimes been called the gamblers' gambler. He does not resent his fame among fellow hustlers as a "man with a million propositions," as a master of percentage, but he likes to have it kept within the lodge. In the years of his early manhood, no one knew of him except gamblers, a few rich suckers, a few golf pros, and, by rumor, the police of New York City, the Middle West, and California, his favorite bases of operation. The cops had heard that he clipped people at everything, from golf to throwing quarters at a crack in the floor. But the people he clipped were mostly members of his own profession. Those outside it, honest suckers, did not complain. Suckers seldom do. Besides, they believed—and often they were right—that they had been beaten by pure skill.   4

One night in 1928, the most celebrated card game in American criminal history took place. As a result of it, Arnold Rothstein, a so-called underworld king, was murdered. And then it turned out that someone named Titanic Thompson had sat in on the game, and might know something about the killing.   5

That was the end, for a while, of Titanic's obscurity. Members of the

Grassy Sprain Country Club, near New York City, blurted out a story that had been on their minds for a month. One day, some time between the Rothstein killing and Titanic's arrest as a material witness, Leo P. Flynn, a big-time fight manager and matchmaker who once handled Jack Dempsey, had brought a stranger out to the club. Leo was known there as a sport and a pretty fair golfer. This time though, he didn't want to play golf himself. He wanted to match the stranger, whom he called Titanic, against the club professional, George McLean.   6

A side bet of $2,500 was arranged, with Flynn backing Thompson and several members pooling their funds in support of the local pride. That day, McLean won. He won with ease—the stranger, though he hit some good shots, did not seem to be in George's class. Besides, he was left-handed, and top-notch left-handed golfers are almost as rare as left-handed catchers. The McLean faction listened to Flynn's talk of a return match. McLean listened to the stranger's mild appeal for a ten-stroke handicap.   7

"I'm not in your league," said the unknown, running his hand through his floppy dark hair, "but I think I can do better than I did today. Give me a real edge in strokes, and we'll bet real dough."   8

The handicap, after some needling back and forth, was fixed at eight strokes. The real dough, supplied mostly by Mr. Flynn and another golfing sport, a Mr. Duffy, was $13,000, and the members covered every dime of it in behalf of their pro. Mr. Duffy, it happened, was Big Bill Duffy, a jolly henchman of Owney Madden, the racketeer. The members did not know this, but it would probably have made no difference if they had. They did not see how you could fix a golf match, and they did not see how an amateur could beat a good pro. It may not have occurred to them that for $13,000 Titanic was not, strictly speaking, an amateur.   9

The stranger shot much better, or luckier, golf this time than he had in the first match, but at the end of sixteen holes he had used up his eight-stroke advantage. The match was dead even, and McLean prepared to close in. On the short seventeenth, his tee shot stopped six feet from the pin. Titanic studied the distance and dropped one four feet closer. Perhaps that shot unnerved McLean. At any rate, he missed his putt. The stranger sank his. Titanic stood one up. He halved the last hole in par, and Mr. Flynn and Mr. Duffy picked up the $13,000—of which they gaily gave Mr. Thompson his share—and called for drinks for the house. The members went home to brood on the fact that a golf match can indeed be fixed— "fixed upward," as gamblers say—if the fixer is a talented athlete who knows how to hide the symptoms until the price is right.   10

On the day the news broke of Titanic's arrest in the Rothstein case, Grassy Sprain started the legend rolling. It has been gathering strength ever since. Generally speaking, New York newspaper readers forgot Thompson soon after the trial of George A. McManus for Rothstein's murder (Titanic was a state witness who gave the state no help at all). To most of the rest of the world, he was then, and still is, unknown. But in the small circle in which his name is famous Titanic Thompson stories have been collected, pooled, and warmed over slow fires for nearly a quarter of a century, till now they amount to a kind of saga—the sharpshooter's Adventures of Robin Hood.   11

Rothstein's death reminded Broadway story-swappers of what might on other levels be called the Adventure of the White Horses. The horse-playing set to which Titanic and Rothstein belonged had formed the habit of spotting white horses from the train that took them to the Belmont or Jamaica track. One morning, some twenty of these smoking-car handicap-pers made up a pool, of $50 each, on the number of white horses that would be counted on the trip that day. Rothstein's estimate was surprisingly high; Titanic studied the tycoon thoughtfully before he made his own guess, just one horse above Rothstein's. There was an outburst of white horsemeat along the Long Island Rail Road tracks that day—a batch of fifteen animals at one crossing, a batch of twelve at another. The first batch had been planted by Titanic, the second by Rothstein.   12

"That will teach you not to be close with your money," said Titanic to Rothstein, as he pocketed the pool. "For thirty bucks, you could have had a whole livery stable."   13

Bear in mind that if Titanic had taken from the rich to give to the poor, as Robin Hood and Jesse James are said to have done, the legend-makers of the gambling world would want no part of him. He would be the wrong kind of hero. But Mr. Thompson has always taken very frankly to give to himself, or to split with the people who stake him. He has seldom made a bet he wasn't sure of winning. He always carries a gimmick—some-times his hidden athletic skill, sometimes his trained knowledge of percent-age, and occasionally a little something extra.   14

Here are some of the tales they tell:

1. Titanic once bet a peanut vendor $10 he could throw a peanut across Times Square in New York. He took a peanut from the vendor's stack, palmed a loaded one in its place, and pitched the phony goober up against the marquee of the Hotel Astor, across the street.   15

2. Billy Duffy once backed Titanic in a bet against a powerful amateur golfer, noted for his long drives. Titanic offered to let his opponent make three drives on each hole and play the best drive of the three. It sounded like a big margin to spot a strong hitter, and the party of the second part snapped the bet up. Playing his best drive, he piled up a big lead on the first nine holes. By that time, his arms were so tired from three full swings a hole that he could hardly knock the ball off the tee. Titanic breezed home in the last nine.   16

3. Titanic once bet $10,000 that Nick (the Greek) Dandolos, another high operator, would not sink a 25-foot putt. Kissed by the goddess Athena, the Greek holed the ball. Thompson, however, was not one to let $10,000 of his money rest long in someone else's jeans. He bet Nick double or

nothing that he could hit a silver dollar with a gun eight times out of eight, from ten feet away. After the ceremony, the Greek gave back the ten grand and kept what was left of the dollar for a souvenir. 17

4. Titanic's mathematics were as sound as Pascal's. In fact, they were based on the reasoning of the great seventeenth-century Frenchman. He once bet a fellow gambler that two of the first thirty persons they met and spoke to would prove to have the same birthday. Strong in the thought that he had 365 days running for him, the second hustler was pleased to accept. Suspecting, not unnaturally, a frame-up, he was careful to approach total strangers and chance passers-by, who could not be known to Titanic. He lost the bet on the twenty-eighth question, when a duplicate birthday turned up. 18

"To tell you the truth," said Titanic afterward, "on each of the last five guys we spoke to, the odds were better than even money in my favor. I'll explain the mathematics to you some time."

Your correspondent will also be glad to explain the mathematics some time, to any reader. He does not quite understand them, but he knows what they are. Titanic's reasoning on the birthday proposition was founded on the fact that the chance against him at first was 364/365th, which, when multiplied by the succeeding chances—363/365th, 362/365th, and so forth—came fairly soon to represent 1/2, or one chance in two, or even money. 19

5. Tony Penna, the golf professional, tells of a bet by Titanic that he could throw a pumpkin over a three-story house. The pumpkin, when he produced it, was the size of an orange—but still a pumpkin. Going perhaps into the realm of pure myth, Penna adds that Titanic once bet he could throw a baseball over the Empire State Building. He won it (says Penna) by taking an elevator to the top platform and throwing from there. 20

6. Titanic once bet a dice impresario named Nutts Nitti that he could find a hairpin in each block of a stretch of twenty consecutive New York City blocks. He won. The hairpins had been planted in advance. 21

7. Titanic once bet he could throw a quarter at a potato, from fifteen feet away, and make it stick in the potato at least once in ten tries. Encountering resistance from his opponent, he agreed to settle for seven tries, and scored on the fourth one. 22

8. Titanic was motoring into Omaha, his temporary base, with a friend one day. As they passed a signpost on the road, Titanic, without looking at it, offered to bet that they would reach the city limits within ten minutes. The signpost made it ten miles to town. The friend, a noticing sort of man, took the bet. He lost. Titanic had moved the signpost five miles closer that morning. 23

9. There is a standard prop in Titanic's repertory—a two-headed quarter, which he uses with more than standard speed, skill, and acting talent. His opening line, after dinner, is "Let's toss for the check." His next line, while the coin is in the air, is "You cry." If his opponent cries tails, Titanic lets the quarter fall—heads. If the other fellow cries heads, Titanic swings

his hand nonchalantly, catches the coin, puts it back in his pocket, and speaks to this effect: "Oh, to hell with gambling for ham and eggs. Let's go Dutch." 24

10. Titanic is credited with being the man who introduced Rothstein to the art of betting on automobile license plates, at Rothstein's expense. He bet Rothstein, as they stood on a Broadway corner, that the first New Jersey plate to come along would make a better poker hand than the first New York plate. Thirty seconds later, from his parking spot around the corner (there were parking spots in those days), a colleague of Titanic's drove into view in a New Jersey car. His plate number carried three threes. 25

11. In a Hot Springs, Arkansas, stud-poker game, a player named Burke became justly incensed one evening because he could not win. 26

"That deck is ice cold, and so is the other one," he bawled. "I ain't had a pair in an hour." 27

"You ought to know," said Titanic soothingly, "that the odds are against getting a pair in any five-card hand. Now, if you dealt yourself six cards—" 28

"With these cards," yelled Burke, "I couldn't pair myself if I dealt all night!"—and the way was paved for a Thompson proposition. Titanic offered to let Burke deal himself ten cold hands of six cards each. Before each hand, he offered to bet that there would be a pair in it. They say that the agony of Burke, as he paired himself in eight of the ten hands and thus lost $300 by the sweat of his own fingers, was something to see. Titanic had known that the addition of a sixth card changes the odds on catching a pair from 13 to 10 against to nearly 2 to 1 in favor. And to bet even money on a 2-to-1 favorite, he would walk quite a distance and stay quite a while. 29

12. In his early days, Titanic, going through a storeroom in the basement of a sporting club in Ohio on his way to the men's room, spotted a rat and nimbly tipped a barrel over the animal. Later, in the course of the dice game upstairs, he raised the subject of the prevalence of rats in Ohio sporting clubs and made a bet that he could find and shoot one any time. The bet was taken. Titanic returned to the cellar, shot the dead rat, and brought it back to the table with him. 30

13. Titanic, shooting right-handed, lost a close golf match to an amateur who played in the 90s. Next day, he bet the winner double their first bet that he could beat him playing left-handed. Left-handed, his natural style, Titanic shot an 80. The victim continued to shoot in the 90s. 31

14. Titanic once bet he could drive a golf ball 500 yards. The bet was popular on all sides, and the interested parties followed Titanic out to the golf course of his choice, on Long Island. He picked a tee on a hill overlooking a lake. It was wintertime. His drive hit the ice and, it seemed to his opponents, never did stop rolling. It went half a mile, if it went a yard. 32

Titanic, as the district attorney found out in the Rothstein case, does not talk much. All that anyone knows about his origins and early life comes from stray remarks, spaced far apart, that he has let fall to other gamblers on the golf course or at the card table. This writer has seen him only once. It was in the "private" or "upstairs" crap game at the old Chicago Club in Saratoga. Joe Madden, the literary barkeep, pointed him out to me from the sidelines. I saw a slender fellow about six feet tall, his dark hair cut long, wearing a neat gabardine suit and two fair-sized diamond rings. When Titanic left the game a little later, Madden said, "He's going down to the drugstore to get a load of ice cream. That's his dish." 33

"That's his dish for breakfast," corrected one of the gamblers at the table. "But he don't eat breakfast till he gets up for the races, maybe two o'clock in the afternoon." 34

A discussion of Titanic's habits ensued. It reminded me of a session of fight men on Jacobs Beach or in the press room at the Garden, discussing some figure of legend like Stanley Ketchel. I asked where the name Titanic had come from. The answer was one I'd heard before, the only one I've ever heard. It may or may not be true. 35

In a poker game in New York on Thompson's first tour of the East, one player said to another, "What's that guy's name?" 36

"It ought to be Titanic," said the second player. "He sinks everybody." 37

The logic here was a little unsound—if I remember the S.S. *Titanic* story, "Iceberg" would have been the right name. But gamblers are seldom good on names. Thompson, for instance, is an easy garbling of Titanic's real name, Thomas. There seems to be no doubt, judging by police files, that he was born Alvin Clarence Thomas, in the state of Arkansas, about 1893. He still talks with a slight Southwestern accent. As a boy, he once said, he acquired the throwing skill that served him handsomely later by killing quail with rocks. He was a good horseshoe pitcher and an expert shot. 38

Athletic talent is a rare thing in a professional gambler, but what surprised the golf pros of the Pacific Coast and the Southwest, who knew him in his early days and accepted him as an athlete to begin with, was his lightning speed of mind at gambling. He would make twelve to fifteen bets on a single hole, keeping track of them in his head while others took time to make notes. He would lose one bet and make another on the next shot that would bring his stake back doubled. Penna and others noticed that his bets during the match often were bigger than his bet on the match as a whole. 39

"Yeah, that's right," said Titanic, when someone spoke of this. "I like to bet 'em when they're out there on the course with me. Especially on the greens. Why? Figure it out for yourself." 40

It was not hard to figure, When a golfer is out there on the course, any new bet he makes is probably made with his own money, without the help of a backer. When he bets with his own money, he gets nervous. Especially on the greens. 41

In Titanic's youth, they say, he was impatient with mental slowness of any kind, but it could not have been long before he came to recognize that quality, in the people around him, as so much bread and jam for him. Among the money golfers who knew him at one time and another were Penna, Dick Metz, Len Dodson and Ben Hogan. He always told them, as he often told the cops when they picked him up on the curious charge of shooting golf too well, that he was "a former pro." It may have been so, but the chances are that he was a former caddy who, on discovering his own skill at the game, almost immediately became a professional gambler rather than a professional golfer. It was a nice economic choice. The best professional golfers in the country, even in these days of rich prizes, do well to earn $30,000 in a year from tournaments. Titanic has sometimes made $50,000 in a few weeks of well-timed chipping and putting at golf resorts.   42

"I've been broke," he told a Coast newspaperman once, "but never for more than six hours at a time. When I tap out, somebody I once helped loans me a stake, and I'm back in action again."   43

Titanic Thompson broke into the Rothstein game, as a young man, because he was good company and a good player—though the state of New York tried to prove, a little later, that trained fingers had something to do with it. The fateful game that led to Rothstein's death and to Titanic's first appearance in print took place on the night of September 7–8, 1928. It was held at the apartment of Jimmy Meehan, a regular member of the circle, on the West Side of New York. Rothstein, because he was rumored to have a finger in every branch of organized crime in the city, was the best-known player in the game, but all the others were noted figures in the gambling, bookmaking, and horseplaying worlds. They included Martin "Red" Bowe, Nigger Nate Raymond, Sam and Meyer Boston, Abe Silverman, George A. McManus, and Titanic Thompson. The game was stud poker, but as it went along it took on a pattern familiar in that group—it became a "high-card" game, with the biggest money being bet on the size of the first-up card in the stud hand.   44

There were rumors along Broadway in the following week that Rothstein had lost a packet. There were also rumors that the winners had not been paid in full. It took a gunshot, however, to make the story public property. On November 4, 1928, someone put a revolver slug into Rothstein's body in Room 349 of the Park Central Hotel. Rothstein staggered from the room and died just outside it. The killer pushed aside a screen and threw the gun into the street below. The New York newspapers went to town. It became the biggest crime story since the murder of Herman Rosenthal by Whitey Lewis, Dago Frank, Lefty Louie, and Gyp the Blood.   45

The overcoat of George McManus, a smiling gambler, brother of a police lieutenant, had been found in Room 349. Soon afterward McManus was indicted for murder, along with three gunmen who never did show up for the trial. On November 26, the D.A., Joab H. Banton, arrested Jimmy

Meehan, Red Bowe, Sidney Stajer (Rothstein's secretary), Nigger Nate Raymond, and Titanic as material witnesses. All of them but Bowe were held in $100,000 bail. For some reason it was Titanic, then and later, who caught the public's fancy—maybe because he was to be a Westerner, a lone wolf, a romantic and single-duke gambler of the old school.   46

It turned out that Titanic had a wife, Mrs. Alice Thomas, who had been living with him at the Mayflower Hotel. A few days after his arrest, she paid him a tearful visit at the West Side prison on Fifty-fourth Street. Titanic then sent for the D.A.'s men, made "important disclosures" (the papers said), and was released in $10,000 bail. What kind of minstrel show he gave to win his freedom is not known. Unofficially it was reported that he had admitted to being in Room 349 just before the murder, leaving when he saw that there might be trouble. Whatever he said, it was plain that the D.A. thought he had laid hold of a fine, friendly witness. The D.A. was very wrong.   47

When the McManus murder case came to trial, in November 1929, Titanic was running a night club and gambling spot in Milwaukee. He was also running a fever in a Milwaukee hospital. So important was his evidence considered by the prosecution that the trial was delayed for a week. Titanic, in Milwaukee, showed for the first time that he was in no mood to blow whistles.   48

"I don't know what they want me as a witness for," he told reporters, whom he received in scarlet pajamas in the hospital. "I wasn't with Rothstein on the night of the murder and hadn't seen him or McManus for two months previously. We played cards at that time, and McManus lost a lot of money. That's all I know about the case."   49

When he did get to New York to testify, the courtroom was packed. Titanic sat in the rear of the room, twisting his fingers nervously, till he was called. The crowd buzzed as he took the stand. McManus, in the dock, sat up and smiled at Titanic. Titanic nodded to McManus. Ferdinand Pecora, later a famous judge, then an assistant D.A. and a strong trial lawyer, moved in on Titanic confidently. It has been established that McManus had lost $51,000 to Rothstein in the celebrated high-card game while Rothstein was losing about $219,000 to some of the others. Pecora's pitch was obvious. He implied that Rothstein, possibly with Titanic's help, had fleeced McManus of the fifty-one grand. Titanic would have no part of this hypothesis. After identifying himself by saying that he gambled on everything from golf to horse races, and referring to McManus as "a square and honest guy," he began to spar Pecora to a standstill.   50

"Was the game on the level?" asked the prosecutor.   51

"It couldn't be any other way on high cards," said Titanic with a deeply scornful gesture. "A man who never dealt in his life was peddling the papers. We had to show him how to shuffle."   52

To "peddle the papers" is to deal. The crowd was delighted with this local color.   53

"Now, think," said Pecora angrily, after a while. "Wasn't this game crooked?"   54

"Anyone ought to know," said Titanic, still scornful, "that that's impossible."   55

"Couldn't a clever dealer give the high card to any man he chose?"   56

"Certainly not," said Titanic. "It ain't being done."   57

On other questions, his memory failed.   58

"You see," he told Pecora patiently, "I just don't remember things. If I bet on a horse today and won ten grand, I probably would not be able to recall the horse's name tomorrow."   59

While the public gasped at this specious statement, the defense took over for cross-examination. At once, Titanic's memory improved, and his attitude got friendlier. He said that McManus had shown no ill will after the game.   60

"He's a swell loser," said Titanic tenderly. "Win or lose, he always smiles."   61

In short, he probably gave the state less change for its money than any state's witness in recent memory. And it's a matter of record that George A. McManus was acquitted of the murder of Arnold Rothstein.   62

It's a matter of record, too, that Titanic was annoyed by his notoriety during the trial. For several months afterward, he complained that he could no longer get a "good" game of golf, by which he meant a game with gravy on the side. He may have misstated the case a little. Recently I asked Oswald Jacoby, the card wizard, about a story in the newspapers that said that John R. Crawford, an ex-G.I. and a spectacular newcomer to card-playing circles, resented the publicity he got in a big Canasta game for charity because no one wanted to play cards with him any more.   63

"Don't you believe it," said Mr. Jacoby. "People always want to play with a man with a big reputation. The more money they have, the more they like it."   64

Be that as it may, Titanic, in Tulsa soon after the trial, was bothered by the galleries that followed him—but he did find one man who wanted to play golf with him just to be able to say he'd done it. Titanic fixed up "a little proposition" for him and won $2,000. There must have been other men with the same ambition, or else Ti's celebrity began to fade, for we cross his trail again in Little Rock, Arkansas, soon afterward, playing golf for $2,000 and $3,000 a round.   65

True, even a roving gambler likes to stop and run a "store" now and then, but since the time of his first fame, Titanic has found it more comfortable to keep on the move. He and a large restaurant operator and racketeer, whom we will call Tony Rizzo, were moving by train not long ago from California to Tony's base at Hot Springs.   66

"Tony," said Titanic, "do you ever regret being illiterate?"   67

"Whaddya mean?" said Tony, hurt. "I ain't so dumb."   68

"I'm going to teach you to spell two ten-letter words," said Titanic.

"The words are 'rhinoceros' and 'anthropoid.' If you can still spell them when we get off the train, I'll pick up the checks for this trip. But take a tip from me—keep spelling them or you'll forget them." 69

For the rest of the trip, Rizzo kept spelling out, in order, the letters r-h-i-n-o-c-e-r-o-s and a-n-t-h-r-o-p-o-i-d. He still knew them at the Hot Springs station. Titanic paid off. 70

The gambler set the second stage of the proposition for Tony's restaurant. He first brought an unknown partner, a respectable-looking fellow as shills go, into the act. He rehearsed the shill in the spelling of ten ten-letter words, including "rhinoceros" and "anthropoid." The next night he sat down in Rizzo's restaurant, as usual, with Owney Madden and other lovable tourists. Rizzo himself, as usual, was sitting at a table by himself, wolfing his pizza in solitary grandeur. 71

"Do you know," said Titanic confidentially, "that that Rizzo just pretends to be ignorant? He puts on a dumb front for business. The guy has got diplomas from two colleges." 72

This speech aroused great skepticism at Titanic's table, which in turn aroused bets. Titanic covered a thousand dollars' worth, his argument being that Tony could spell any ten-letter word, any one at all, that Mr. Madden and the boys chose to mention. As Titanic expected, a pause followed, while the boys tried to think of a ten-letter word to give Tony. They were somewhat embarrassed. At this point, Titanic's partner hove into view, and Titanic hailed him. 73

"Excuse me, sir," he said, "but you look as though you might be able to help us. May I ask your business? A lawyer? Fine. Would you mind writing down ten ten-letter words on a piece of paper here, for these gentlemen to choose from?" 74

The stranger obliged. Looking around, he wrote down the word "restaurant," which appeared on Tony's window. He wrote down several others he found on the bill of fare, such as "cacciatore." In and among the rest he inserted the words "rhinoceros" and "anthropoid." He turned the paper over to the boys, who immediately set to work making scratches in the morning line, to protect their bets. They scratched "restaurant"— Tony saw it on the window all day, he might know it. They scratched "cacciatore." "He's Eyetalian," said Mr. Madden, "and he might know all that kind of stuff." This left them, in the end, with "rhinoceros" and "anthropoid." At random, they scratched "rhinoceros." They summoned Mr. Rizzo and desired him to spell the word "anthropoid." 75

"Sure," said Tony, taking a deep breath. "R-h-i-n-o-c-e-r-o-s." 76

Titanic paid off the $1,000. The bet belongs to his legend partly because he lost it and partly because he won the money back, with galloping dominoes, the same night. As I said before, he is prosperous just now. A fellow gambler who ran across him in Evansville, Indiana—you are apt to find him anywhere—says that Titanic's pajamas and dressing gowns, always brilliant, are more brilliant than ever. His supply of jewels, rings, and stickpins is at high tide. A man like Ti, my informant explains, buys jewels whenever he is in the money, to sell or hock when times are hard. 77

The Titanic legend would not be so solidly honored in the gambling world, it would not be complete, if the quiet Mr. Thompson had never used the gun he always carries, in defense of the money he takes from the rich to give to himself. The police of Little Rock, years ago, found a letter in Titanic's room which demanded "2 thousand cash or you will be sorry." The police of St. Louis, more recently, found him ready to draw at the sound of a door being opened. 78

And in Tyler, Texas, a few years back, it was proved clearly that in matters involving Titanic Thompson and his money there is very little kidding. Titanic had had a good day on the golf course. His caddy noticed it. The caddy was sixteen years old, but he had grown-up ideas. At a late hour the same evening, a shot was fired in Tyler, and the police arrived to find the caddy with a bullet in him, while Titanic stood in attendance. 79

"I shot him," said the gambler. "It was self-defense. He tried to stick me up for my roll." 80

The young man died next day. A mask and an unfired gun were found on his person, and the plea of self-defense was allowed. Titanic moved along, with a stronger toehold on history than ever. 81

5,600 words

Vocabulary

Paragraph	amateur	24. colleague
4. legend	10. gaily	29. prevalence
overpowering	14. gimmick	37. garbling
6. obscurity	percentage	45. indicted
blurted	16. margin	62. notoriety
7. handicap	21. impresario	76. galloping dominoes
9. needling	resistance	

Speculations and Rumors

Myths have traditionally surrounded the dramatic assassinations of history. The rumors and theories about the assassination of Abraham Lincoln that are still being publicized were for the most part first bruited within months of his death. Whenever there is any element of mystery in such dramatic events misconceptions often result from sensational speculations.   1

Lacking the testimony of Lee Harvey Oswald, it has been necessary to reconstruct painstakingly all of the facts that led the Commission to the conclusion that Oswald assassinated President Kennedy, acting alone and without advice or assistance. The Commission has found no credible evidence that he was a member of a foreign or domestic conspiracy of any kind. Nor was there any evidence that he was involved with any criminal or underworld elements or that he had any association with his slayer, Jack Ruby, except as his victim. The evidence on these issues has been set forth in great detail in this report.   2

In addition the Commission has inquired into the various hypotheses, rumors, and speculations that have arisen from the tragic developments of November 22–24, 1963. It is recognized that the public judgment of these events has been influenced, at least to some extent, by these conjectures. 3

Many questions have been raised about the facts out of genuine puzzlement or because of misinformation which attended some of the early reporting of the fast-crowding events of these 3 days. Most of the speculation and attempted reconstruction of these events by the public centered on these basic questions: Was Lee Harvey Oswald really the assassin of the President; why did he do it; did he have any accomplices; and why did Ruby shoot Oswald? Many of the theories and hypotheses advanced have rested on premises which the Commission feels deserve critical examination.   4

Many people who witnessed the assassination and the killing of Oswald or were present in the area were a major source of diverse and often contradictory information. As is easily understood under such circumstances, all of the witnesses did not see and hear the same thing or interpret what they saw and heard the same way and many changed their stories as they repeated them. Moreover, they were interviewed at different times after the event by different people and often under circumstances which made accurate reporting extremely difficult.   5

Even the occupants of the cars in the Presidential motorcade were not entirely in agreement in their accounts because they, too, saw and heard what happened from different positions. Moreover, those closest to the assassination were subjected to a physical and emotional strain that tended to affect their recollections of what they thought they saw or heard. Consequently, the presentation of the news from Dallas included much misinformation. This, to some extent, was unavoidable, but the widespread and repetitive dissemination of every scrap of information about the President's assassination and its aftermath has helped to build up a large number of erroneous conclusions. The manner in which local authorities released information about the investigation, sometimes before it could be verified in all detail, has further contributed to the fund of ill-founded theories. Typographical mistakes in the press and failure to transcribe sound accurately from tapes resulted in errors, some of which have remained uncorrected in print at the time of the publication of this report.   6

Much of the speculation that has persisted in one form or another since November 22–24 came from people who usually spoke in good faith. Some of the errors have resulted simply from a lack of complete knowledge at the time of the event. In this category are the statements attributed to doctors at Parkland Memorial Hospital who attended the dying President and described his wounds to the press afterward. It remained for the autopsy in Washington, completed early the next morning, to ascertain the full facts concerning the wounds. The correction of earlier assertions of fact on the basis of later and fuller analysis or investigation is a normal part of the process of accumulation of evidence. But it is not often that the process is conducted in such an intense glare of worldwide publicity, and later corrections have difficulty overtaking the original sensational reports. . . .   7

This appendix is intended to clarify the most widespread factual misunderstandings. False or inaccurate speculations concerning the assassination and related events are set forth below together with brief summary statements of what the Commission has found to be the true facts. The citation following each Commission finding is either to that portion of the report in which the subject is discussed more fully, to the evidence in the record supporting the finding, or to both. For complete answers to these speculations, the sources cited in the footnotes should be consulted.*   8

The Source of the Shots

There have been speculations that some or all of the shots aimed at President Kennedy and Governor Connally came from the railroad overpass as the Presidential automobile approached it, or from somewhere other than the Texas School Book Depository Building. Related speculations maintain that the shots came from both the railroad overpass and the Texas School

---

* Editor's note: The footnotes, which appear at the end of the *Report*, will not be reproduced here. The numbers will, however, be included for anyone who wishes to further consult the original.

Book Depository Building. These are supported by a number of assertions that have been carefully examined by the Commission in the course of its investigation and rejected as being without foundation. They are set forth below, together with the results of the Commission's investigation.

Speculation.—The shots that killed the President came from the railroad overpass above the triple underpass.

Commission finding.—The shots that entered the neck and head of the President and wounded Governor Connally came from behind and above. There is no evidence that any shots were fired at the President from anywhere other than the Texas School Book Depository Building.[1]

Speculation.—The railroad overpass was left unguarded on November 22.

Commission finding.—On November 22 the railroad overpass was guarded by two Dallas policemen, Patrolmen J. W. Foster and J. C. White, who have testified that they permitted only railroad personnel on the overpass.[2]

Speculation.—There are witnesses who alleged that the shots came from the overpass.

Commission finding.—The Commission does not have knowledge of any witnesses who saw shots fired from the overpass. Statements or depositions from the 2 policemen and 13 railroad employees who were on the overpass all affirm that no shots were fired from the overpass. Most of these witnesses who discussed the source of the shots stated that they came from the direction of Elm and Houston Streets.[3]

Speculation.—A rifle cartridge was recovered on the overpass.

Commission finding.—No cartridge of any kind was found on the overpass nor has any witness come forward to claim having found one.[4]

Speculation.—A witness to the assassination said that she saw a man run behind the concrete wall of the overpass and disappear.

Commission finding.—Mrs. Jean L. Hill stated that after the firing stopped she saw a white man wearing a brown overcoat and a hat running west away from the Depository Building in the direction of the railroad tracks. There are no other witnesses who claim to have seen a man running toward the railroad tracks. Examination of all available films of the area following the shooting, reexamination of interviews with individuals in the vicinity of the shooting, and interviews with members of the Dallas Police Department and the Dallas County sheriff's office failed to corroborate Mrs. Hill's recollection or to reveal the identity of the man described by Mrs. Hill.[5]

Speculation.—Immediately after the shooting a motorcycle policeman was seen racing up the grassy embankment to the right of the shooting scene pursuing a couple seeking to flee from the overpass.

Commission finding.—There are no witnesses who have ever stated this and there is no evidence to support the claim. A motorcycle policeman, Clyde A. Haygood, dismounted in the street and ran up the incline. He stated that he saw no one running from the railroad yards adjacent to the overpass. Subsequently, at 12:37 p.m., Haygood reported that the shots had come from the Texas School Book Depository Building.[6] 13

Speculation.—More than three shots, perhaps as many as five or six, were fired at the President and Governor Connally. 14

Commission finding.—The weight of the evidence indicates that three shots were fired, of which two struck President Kennedy. There is persuasive evidence from the experts that one of these two bullets also struck Governor Connally. Some witnesses claimed that they heard more than three shots but, as fully described in Chapter III, the great majority heard only three shots.[7] 15

Speculation.—At least four or five bullets have been found. 16

Commission finding.—After the assassination, metal remains of bullets were recovered. These included an almost whole bullet of 158.6 grains, fragments weighing 44.6 grains and 21.0 grains, and other fragments too small be to identified. These metal remains indicate that at least two shots were fired. The Commission believes that three shots were fired.[8] 17

Speculation.—A bullet was found on the stretcher used for President Kennedy at Parkland Hospital. 18

Commission finding.—No bullet was found on the stretcher used by President Kennedy. An almost whole bullet was found when it rolled off the stretcher used by Governor Connally.[9] 19

Speculation.—A bullet was found in the grass near the scene of the assassination shortly afterward by a deputy sheriff of Dallas County, E. R. Walthers. 20

Commission finding.—Walthers has denied that he found a bullet at any time or that he told anyone that he had found one. With another deputy sheriff he made a diligent search for such a bullet 2 or 3 days after the assassination.[10] 21

Speculation.—The Presidential car stopped momentarily or almost came to a complete halt after the first shot. This is evidence that the driver had the impression that the first shot came from the front and therefore hesitated to drive closer to the overpass. 22

Commission finding.—The Presidential car did not stop or almost come to a complete halt after the firing of the first shot or any other shots. The driver, Special Agent William R. Greer, has testified that he accelerated the car after what was probably the second shot. Motion pictures of the scene show that the car slowed down momentarily after the shot that struck the President in the head and then speeded up rapidly.[11] 23

Speculation.—The Presidential car had a small round bullet hole in the front windshield. This is evidence that a shot or shots were fired at the President from the front of the car. 24

Commission finding.—The windshield was not penetrated by any bullet. A small residue of lead was found on the inside surface of the windshield; on the outside of the windshield was a very small pattern of cracks immediately in front of the lead residue on the inside. The bullet from which this lead residue came was probably one of those that struck the President and therefore came from overhead and to the rear. Experts established that the abrasion in the windshield came from impact on the inside of the glass.[12]

25

Speculation.—The throat wound sustained by the President was the result of a shot fired from the front according to doctors at Parkland Hospital.

26

Commission finding.—Doctors at Parkland Hospital originally believed that the throat wound could have been either an entry or exit wound, but they made no examination to determine entry and exit wounds. Subsequently, when the evidence of the autopsy became available, the doctors at Parkland agreed that it was an exit wound.[13]

27

Speculation.—It is inconceivable that the doctors at Parkland Hospital did not turn the President over on his face and notice the bullet hole in the back of his neck.

28

Commisson finding.—Doctors at Parkland Hospital have testified that the President remained on his back while he was at Parkland Hospital for treatment and that they did not turn him over at any time; they were busy trying to save his life. Consequently, they were never aware of the hole in the back of his neck until they were notified of it later.[14]

29

Speculation.—The first shot struck the President in the throat as the car was proceeding along Houston Street toward the Texas School Book Depository. The car then made a left turn on to Elm Street and proceeded for some distance before additional shots were fired at the President.

30

Commission finding.—Before the autopsy findings made it clear that the shots were fired from the rear, there was speculation that the first shot may have been fired before the Presidential car turned on to Elm Street. As this report demonstrates, all of the shots that struck the President were fired from the rear and in a time period inconsistent with the theory that the first shot struck him while his car was coming down Houston Street. Motion pictures taken at the time show that the first shot struck the President after the car had turned onto Elm Street and was proceeding away from the Depository.[15]

31

The Assassin

Speculations tending to support the theory that Oswald could not have assassinated President Kennedy are based on a wide variety of assertions. Among these are statements that Oswald could not have been acquainted with the motorcade route before he came to work on November 22, that he may well have carried curtain rods rather than a rifle in a brown paper package he brought with him, that there may have been other people in the building who could have fired the rifle, that Oswald could not have fired the shots in the time available to him, that he was not a good enough marksman to have scored the hits with the rifle, that there were other people in the lunchroom of the Depository Building when he was confronted by Patrol-man M. L. Baker, and that there are no eyewitnesses who could identify Oswald as having been in the window. Each of these speculations is dealt with below in the light of the testimony and evidence considered by the Commission.

Speculation.—Oswald could not have known the motorcade route before he arrived at work on November 22.

Commission finding.—The motorcade route was published in both Dallas papers on November 19 and was therefore available at least 72 hours before Oswald reported for work on November 22.[16]

Speculation.—The route as shown in the newspaper took the motorcade through the Triple Underpass via Main Street, a block away from the Depository. Therefore, Oswald could not have known that the motorcade would pass directly by the Texas School Book Depository Building.

Commission finding.—The motorcade route as published showed the motorcade turning right off Main Street onto Houston for one block and then left on Elm to the access road to the Stemmons Freeway. This route was clearly indicated in published descriptions and maps of the motorcade route. There was no mention of continuing on Main Street through the Triple Underpass.[17]

Speculation.—The motorcade route was changed on November 22 after the map had been printed. The motorcade was shifted from Main Street over to Elm Street to bring it by the Texas School Book Depository Building.

Commission finding.—The motorcade route was decided upon on November 18 and published in the Dallas newspapers on November 19. It was not changed in any way thereafter. The route called for the motorcade to turn off Main Street at Houston, go up to Elm, and then turn left on Elm Street.[18]

Speculation.—The normal and logical route would have been straight down Main Street through the Triple Underpass to the Stemmons Freeway. It is possible to drive from Main onto the access road to the Stemmons Freeway from a point beyond the underpass.

Commission finding.—The normal, direct, and only permissible route to the Stemmons Freeway from Main Street is via Houston and Elm Streets. Any attempt to turn onto the access road to the Stemmons Freeway from Main Street beyond the Triple Underpass would have been extremely diffi-cult because of a concrete strip dividing Elm and Main Streets. Such an attempt would have required making an S-turn beyond the strip at a very tight angle, thereby slowing the Presidential car almost to a stop.[19]

Speculation.—Oswald may well have carried curtain rods to work on November 22 in the brown paper package he was observed to bring into the building because he lived in a room where he needed them.

Commission finding.—According to Oswald's landlady at 1026 North Beckley Avenue, Mrs. A. C. Johnson, the room had venetian blinds, curtain rods, and curtains while Oswald was living there. The curtain rods in the Paine garage that belonged to Mrs. Paine were still there after Oswald went to work on November 22. Mrs. Paine and Marina Oswald testified that Oswald had not spoken to them about curtain rods. After the assassination the empty package was found near the window from which the shots were fired, but no curtain rods were found.[20]

11

Speculation.—Oswald spent the morning of November 22 in the company of other workers in the building and remained with them until they went downstairs to watch the President go by, no later probably than 12:15.

12

Commission finding.—Oswald did not spend the morning in the company of other workers in the building, and before the assassination he was last seen in the building on the sixth floor at about 11:55 a.m. by Charles Givens, another employee.[21]

13

Speculation.—It is probable that the chicken lunch, remains of which were found on the sixth floor, was eaten by an accomplice of Oswald who had hidden on the sixth floor overnight.

14

Commission finding.—The chicken lunch had been eaten shortly after noon on November 22 by Bonnie Ray Williams, an employee of the Texas School Book Depository, who after eating his lunch went to the fifth floor where he was when the shots were fired. Oswald did not eat the chicken lunch, nor did he drink from the soft drink bottle found near the chicken lunch.[22]

15

Speculation.—Laboratory tests showed remains of the chicken lunch found on the sixth floor were 2 days old.

16

Commission finding.—The chicken lunch remains had been left there shortly after noon on November 22 by Bonnie Ray Williams.[23]

17

Speculation.—An amateur 8-millimeter photograph taken at 12:20 p.m., 10 minutes before the assassination of President Kennedy, showed two silhouettes at the sixth-floor window of the Depository.

18

Commission finding.—A film taken by an amateur photographer, Robert J. H. Hughes, just before the assassination, shows a shadow in the southeast corner window of the sixth floor. This has been determined after examination by the FBI and the U.S. Navy Photographic Interpretation Center to be the shadow from the cartons near the window.[24]

19

Speculation.—A picture published widely in newspapers and magazines after the assassination showed Lee Harvey Oswald standing on the front steps of the Texas School Book Depository Building shortly before the President's motorcade passed by.

20

Commission finding.—The man on the front steps of the building, **thought** or alleged by some to be Lee Harvey Oswald, is actually Billy Lovelady, an employee of the Texas School Book Depository, who somewhat resembles Oswald. Lovelady has identified himself in the picture, and other employees of the Depository standing with him, as shown in the picture, have verified that he was the man in the picture and that Oswald was not there.[25]

21

Speculation.—The post office box in Dallas to which Oswald had the rifle mailed was kept under both his name and that of A. Hidell. 22

Commisson finding.—It is not known whether Oswald's application listed the name A. Hidell as one entitled to receive mail at the box. In accordance with U.S. Post Office regulations, the portion of the application listing the names of persons other than the applicant entitled to receive mail was discarded after the box was closed on May 14, 1963. During the summer of 1963, Oswald rented a post office box in New Orleans, listing the name "Hidell" in addition to his own name and that of his wife. Hidell was a favorite alias used by Oswald on a number of occasions. Diligent search has failed to reveal any person in Dallas or New Orleans by that name. It was merely a creation for his own purposes.[26] 23

Speculation.—The President's car was going at a speed estimated at from 12 to 20 miles per hour, thus presenting a target comparable to the most difficult that a soldier would encounter under battlefield conditions. 24

Commission finding.—During the period between the time that the first and second shots struck the President, the Presidential car was traveling at an average speed of approximately 11.2 miles per hour. Expert witnesses testified that the target is regarded as a favorable one because the car was going away from the marksman in a straight line.[27] 25

Speculation.—Oswald could not have fired three shots from the Mannlicher-Carcano rifle in 5½ seconds. 26

Commission finding.—According to expert witnesses, exacting tests conducted for the Commission demonstrated that it was possible to fire three shots from the rifle within 5½ seconds. It should be noted that the first loaded shell was already in the chamber ready for firing; Oswald had only to pull the trigger to fire the first shot and to work the bolt twice in order to fire the second and third shots. They testified that if the second shot missed, Oswald had between 4.8 and 5.6 seconds to fire the three shots. If either the first or third shot missed, Oswald had in excess of 7 seconds to fire the three shots.[28] 27

Speculation.—Oswald did not have the marksmanship ability demonstrated by the rifleman who fired the shots. 28

Commission finding.—Oswald qualified as a sharpshooter and a marksman with the M-1 rifle in the Marine Corps. Marina Oswald testified that in New Orleans her husband practiced operating the bolt of the rifle. Moreover, experts stated that the scope was a substantial aid for rapid, accurate firing. The Commission concluded that Oswald had the capability with a rifle to commit assassination.[29] 29

Speculation.—The name of the rifle used in the assassination appeared on the rifle. Therefore, the searchers who found the rifle on the sixth floor of the Texas School Book Depository should have been able to identify it correctly by name. 30

Commission finding.—An examination of the rifle does not reveal any manufacturer's name. An inscription on the rifle shows that it was made in

Italy. The rifle was identified by Captain Fritz and Lieutenant Day, who were the first to actually handle it.[30]

31

Speculation.—The rifle found on the sixth floor of the Texas School Book Depository was identified as a 7.65 Mauser by the man who found it, Deputy Constable Seymour Weitzman.

32

Commission finding.—Weitzman, the original source of the speculation that the rifle was a Mauser, and Deputy Sheriff Eugene Boone found the weapon. Weitzman did not handle the rifle and did not examine it at close range. He had little more than a glimpse of it and thought it was a Mauser, a German bolt-type rifle similar in appearance to the Mannlicher-Carcano. Police laboratory technicians subsequently arrived and correctly identified the weapon as a 6.5 Italian rifle.[31]

33

Speculation.—There is evidence that a second rifle was discovered on the roof of the Texas School Book Depository or on the overpass.

34

Commission finding.—No second rifle was found in either of these places or in any other place. The shots that struck President Kennedy and Governor Connally came from the rifle found on the sixth floor of the Texas School Book Depository.[32]

35

Speculation.—It is possible that there was a second Mannlicher-Carcano rifle involved in the assassination. The Irving Sports Shop mounted a scope on a rifle 3 weeks before the assassination.

36

Commission finding.—Dial D. Ryder, an employee of the Irving Sports Shop, has stated that he found on his workbench on November 23 an undated work tag with the name "Oswald" on it, indicating that sometime during the first 2 weeks of November three holes had been bored in a rifle and a telescopic sight mounted on it and bore-sighted. However, Ryder and his employer, Charles W. Greener, had no recollection of Oswald, of his Mannlicher-Carcano rifle, of the transaction allegedly represented by the repair tag, or of any person for whom such a repair was supposedly made. The rifle found on the sixth floor of the Texas School Book Depository had two holes in it bored for the installation of a scope prior to shipment to Oswald in March 1963. The Commission concluded that it is doubtful whether the tag produced by Ryder was authentic. All of the evidence developed proves that Oswald owned only the one rifle—the Mannlicher-Carcano—and that he did not bring it or a second rifle to the Irving Sports Shop.[33]

37

Speculation.—Ammunition for the rifle found on the sixth floor of the Texas School Book Depository had not been manufactured since the end of World War II. The ammunition used by Oswald must, therefore, have been at least 20 years old, making it extremely unreliable.

38

Commission finding.—The ammunition used in the rifle was American ammunition recently made by the Western Cartridge Co., which manufactures such ammunition currently. In tests with the same kind of ammunition, experts fired Oswald's Mannlicher-Carcano rifle more than 100 times without any misfires.[34]

39

Speculation.—The assertion that Oswald's palmprint appeared on the rifle is false. The FBI told newsmen in an off-the-record briefing session that there was no palmprint on the rifle.   40

Commission finding.—The FBI confirmed that the palmprint lifted by the Dallas police from the rifle found on the sixth floor of the Texas School Book Depository Building was Oswald's palmprint. The FBI informed the Commission that no FBI agent made statements of any type to the press concerning the existence or nonexistence of this print.[35]   41

Speculation.—If Oswald had been gloveless, he would have left fingerprints on the rifle because he would not have had time to wipe the prints off the rifle after he had fired it.   42

Commission finding.—An FBI fingerprint expert testified that the poor quality of the metal and wooden parts would cause them to absorb moisture from the skin, thereby making a clear print unlikely. There is no evidence that Oswald wore gloves or that he wiped prints off the rifle. Latent fingerprints were found on the rifle but they were too incomplete to be identified.[36] 43

Speculation.—Gordon Shanklin, the special agent in charge of the Dallas office of the FBI, stated that the paraffin test of Oswald's face and hands was positive and proved that he had fired a rifle.   44

Commission finding.—The paraffin tests were conducted by members of the Dallas Police Department and the technical examinations by members of the Dallas City-County Criminal Investigation Laboratory. The FBI has notified the Commission that neither Shanklin nor any other representative of the FBI ever made such a statement. The Commission has found no evidence that Special Agent Shanklin ever made this statement publicly.[67]   45

Speculation.—Marina Oswald stated that she did not know that her husband owned a rifle nor did she know that he owned a pistol.   46

Commission finding.—There is no evidence that Marina Oswald ever told this to any authorities. On the afternoon of November 22, she told the police that her husband owned a rifle and that he kept it in the garage of the Paine house in Irving. Later, at Dallas police headquarters, she said that she could not identify as her husband's the rifle shown her by policemen. When Marina Oswald appeared before the Commission she was shown the Mannlicher-Carcano 6.5 rifle found on the sixth floor of the Depository and identified it as the "fateful rifle of Lee Oswald."[38]   47

Speculation.—The picture of Oswald taken by his wife in March or April 1963 and showing him with a rifle and a pistol was "doctored" when it appeared in magazines and newspapers in February 1964. The rifle held by Oswald in these pictures is not the same rifle that was found on the sixth floor of the Texas School Book Depository Building.   48

Commission finding.—Life magazine, Newsweek, and the New York Times notified the Commission that they had retouched this picture. In doing so, they inadvertently altered details of the configuration of the rifle. The original prints of this picture have been examined by the Commission and by photographic experts who have identified the rifle as a Mannlicher-

Carcano 6.5, the same kind as the one found on the sixth floor of the Texas School Book Depository. FBI experts testified that the picture was taken with Oswald's camera.[39]

49

Speculation.—The rifle picture of Oswald was a composite one with Oswald's face pasted on somebody else's body.

50

Commission finding.—Marina Oswald has testified that she took this picture with a camera owned by her husband and subsequently identified as Oswald's Imperial Reflex camera. She identified the man in the picture as her husband. Experts also state the picture was not a composite.[40]

51

Speculation.—After firing the shots, Oswald could not have disposed of the rifle and descended the stairs to the lunchroom in time to get a drink from a soft drink machine and be there when Patrolman Baker came in.

52

Commission finding.—A series of time tests made by investigators and by Roy S. Truly and Patrolman M. L. Baker at the request of the Commission, show that it was possible for Oswald to have placed the rifle behind a box and descended to the lunchroom on the second floor before Patrolman Baker and Truly got up there. Oswald did not have a soft drink bottle in his hand at the time he was confronted by Baker and he was not standing by the soft drink machine. He was just entering the lunchroom; Baker caught a glimpse of him through the glass panel in the door leading to the lunchroom vestibule.[41]

53

Speculation.—There were other people present in the lunchroom at the time that Baker and Truly saw Oswald there.

54

Commission finding.—Baker and Truly have both stated that there was no one in the lunchroom other than Oswald at the time that they entered. No other witness to this incident has been found.[42]

55

Speculation.—Police were sealing off all exits from the building by the time Oswald got to the second floor.

56

Commission finding.—Police may have begun to take up positions at the exits to the building as early as 12:33, but it is unlikely that they had blocked them off completely until 12:37 p.m. at the earliest. Oswald was seen in an office, walking toward an exit leading to the front stairway, at about 12:33 p.m. Oswald probably had at least 7 minutes in which to get out of the building without being stopped.[43]

57

5,200 words

Vocabulary: "Speculations and Rumors"

Paragraph		
1. assassination	credible	6. dissemination
bruited	conspiracy	verified
misconceptions	3. conjectures	typographical
speculations	4. genuine	transcribe
2. reconstruct	premises	7. assertions
painstakingly	5. contradictory	accumulation

"The Source of the Shots"

11. corroborate
13. adjacent

21. diligent
22. momentarily

27. subsequently
31. inconsistent

"The Assassin"

14. accomplice
23. alias

29. capability
49. inadvertently

51. composite

```
┌─────────────────────────────────────────────┐
│              CASUALTIES OF WAR                │
│                DANIEL LANG                    │
└─────────────────────────────────────────────┘
```

(Editor's note: This excerpt from the book of the same title summarizes the consequences of war and of one episode of the war in Vietnam. By definition, a casualty is a person captured, injured, missing, or killed in action against an enemy. Lang shows that the experience of war itself may become "the enemy" and generate casualties: Mao, whose misfortune it was to be the best-looking girl in her village the day a United States patrol passed through; the four men, having already perhaps become casualties, who raped, then murdered Mao; and Eriksson, the fifth member of the patrol, who felt impelled to report the atrocity—he too became a casualty: "He had yet to exonerate himself from the self-imposed charge of having failed to save Mao's life.")

Like their predecessors in all wars, American veterans of the Vietnamese campaign who are coming home to civilian life have their heads filled with memories that may last the rest of their days, for, no matter how far from the front a man may have spent his time as a soldier, he will remember it as a special time, when, fleetingly, his daily existence appeared to approach the heroic. Former Private First Class Sven Eriksson—as I shall call him, since to use his actual name might add to the danger he may be in—has also come back with his memories, but he has no idea what the future will do to them. Honorably discharged in April, 1968, this new war veteran, who is twenty-four and comes from a small farming community in northwestern Minnesota, isn't even sure that he would care to hold on to his recollections, if it were possible for him to control his memory. Naturally, Eriksson's experiences in Vietnam were varied, and many of them impressed themselves vividly on his mind. Just seeing an Asian country, for instance, was an adventure, Eriksson says, its landscape so different from the frozen plains of his corner of Minnesota; he had never before splashed through paddy fields, he told me, or stood blinking in the sudden sunlessness of lush, entangled jungle, or wandered uncertainly through imprisoning fields of towering elephant grass. An infantryman, Eriksson saw a fair amount of action, so, if he chose, he could reminisce about strong points he helped take and fire fights in which he was pinned down, and one ambush, in particular, in which half his unit was wounded. But, as Eriksson unhesitatingly acknowledges, the fact is that when he thinks of his tour of duty in Vietnam it is always a single image that comes to his mind. The image is that of a Vietnamese peasant girl, two or three years younger than he was, whom he met, so to speak, on November 18, 1966, in a remote hamlet in the Central Highlands, a few miles west of the South China Sea. Eriksson and four other enlisted men were then on a reconnaissance patrol in the vicinity of the girl's home. Eriksson considers himself hazy about the girl's looks. He does remember, though, that she had a prominent gold tooth, and that her eyes, which were dark brown, could be particularly expressive. He also remembers that she was wearing dusty earrings made of bluish glass; he noticed the trinkets because they gave off a dull glint one bright afternoon when he was assigned to stand guard over her. Like most rural women, she was dressed in loose-fitting black pajamas. They obscured her figure, Eriksson says, but he has the impression that she was slender and slight, and was perhaps five feet two or three inches tall. For as long as she lived, Eriksson did not know her name. He learned it, eventually, when the girl's sister identified her at court-martial proceedings—proceedings that Eriksson himself instigated and in which he served as the government's chief witness. The girl's name—her actual name—was Phan Thi Mao. Eriksson never exchanged a word with her; neither spoke the other's language. He knew Mao for slightly more than twenty-four hours. They were her last. The four soldiers with whom he was on patrol raped and killed her, abandoning her body in mountain brush. One of the soldiers stabbed her three times, and when defense counsel challenged Eriksson at the court-martial proceedings to describe the sound that the stabbings made, he testified, "Well, I've shot deer and I've gutted deer. It was just like when you stick a deer with a knife—sort of a thud—or something like this, sir."   1

At the very outset, Eriksson told me that the last thing he wished to do was discuss Mao's murder in any legalistic vein. It was certainly possible to do so, as I knew for myself from having read the court record of the trials he had brought about: seven bulky volumes in the offices of the Clerk of Courts, U.S. Army Judiciary, in Falls Church, Virginia, which included Eriksson's testimony against the members of the patrol; their convictions and appeals; interminable correspondence between judges and opposing counsel; and depositions concerning the character of individual defendants. Having appeared as a witness before four tribunals in Vietnam, Eriksson told me, he had had his fill of the judicial process—of the dogged grillings by lawyers and the repeated strictures of judges insisting on precise answers to questions that were often vague. As far as he was concerned, Eriksson said, it had all seemed a morass of cleverness, but then, he conceded, he may well have entered the military courtroom in the Central Highlands, where the four trials were held, with unwarranted expectations, for it had been his hope that the trials would help him unravel his reactions to Mao's fate. Unreasonably, he granted, he had come into court with the idea that he and the others on hand would wonder aloud, in a kind of corporate searching, how it was possible for the young girl to meet the end she did. He had imagined that he would be able to ask how it was that he alone of the patrol had come to act as he had. He had wanted to tell of the way the episode with Mao had affected him, and why it was that he had felt impelled to report the others—four young Americans like him, each dependent on the others for survival deep in enemy territory. He had wanted to unburden himself of his doubts about whether he had done all he might have done for Mao in her travail—doubts that gnaw at him to this day. With me, he said, he trusted he would be able to go into these matters freely, but he had early discovered that in a court of law they were of little interest. 2

Launching into his unlegalistic account, Eriksson told me that it seemed clear to him in retrospect that he should have been prepared for Mao's death. It had been preceded by any number of similar occurrences. In one form or another, he said, they took place almost daily, but he was slow, or reluctant, to perceive that they were as much a part of the war as shells and targets were. Eriksson now believes he should have foreseen that sooner or later one of these incidents was bound to strike him with special, climactic force. He had scarcely landed in Vietnam, in October, 1966, when he was made aware of these occurrences, each of them apparently impulsive and unrelated to military strategy. He told me that beatings were common—random, routine kicks and cuffings that he saw G.I.s administer to the Vietnamese. Occasionally, official orders were used for justifying gratuitous acts of violence. Thus, early in his tour of duty, Eriksson recalled, G.I.s in his unit were empowered to shoot any Vietnamese violating a 7 P.M. curfew, but in practice it was largely a matter of individual discretion whether a soldier chose to fire at a stray Vietnamese hurrying home a few minutes late to his hootch—the American term for the mud-and-bamboo huts in which most natives lived. Similarly, it was permissible to shoot at any Vietnamese seen running, but, as Eriksson put it, "the line between walking and running could be very thin." The day after the one on which his squad was ambushed and half its members were wounded, several enemy prisoners were taken, and, in retaliation, two were summarily killed, "to serve as an example." A corporal who was still enraged over the ambush tried to strangle another of the prisoners; he had knotted a poncho, nooselike, around the captive's neck and was tightening it when a merciful lieutenant commanded him to desist. 3

Needless to say, Eriksson continued, the kind of behavior he was describing was by no means limited to Americans. The enemy did the same thing, and much of the evidence for this came from the Vietnamese themselves. They constantly reported rapes and kidnappings by the Vietcong; in fact, the Vietcong committed these crimes so indiscriminately that the victims were sometimes their own sympathizers. On one occasion that he knew of, Eriksson said, American troops, attracted by the familiar odor of decomposing bodies, had found a pit piled high with Vietnamese men and women who had been machine-gunned by the V.C. But, as Eriksson pointed out, he could not give me many such firsthand accounts of V.C. depredations. Necessarily, he said, he was in a position to speak only of the behavior of American soldiers, since they were the people he fought and lived with. 4

Ending the first of his brooding silences, Eriksson said, "From one day to the next, you could see for yourself changes coming over guys on our side—decent fellows, who wouldn't dream of calling an Oriental a 'gook' or a 'slopehead' back home. But they were halfway around the world now, in a strange country, where they couldn't tell who was their friend and who wasn't. Day after day, out on patrol, we'd come to a narrow dirt path leading through some shabby village, and the elders would welcome us and the children come running with smiles on their faces, waiting for the candy we'd give them. But at the other end of the path, just as we were leaving the village behind, the enemy would open up on us, and there was bitterness among us that the villagers hadn't given us warning. All that many of us could think at such times was that we were fools to be ready to die for people who defecated in public, whose food was dirtier than anything in our garbage cans back home. Thinking like that—well, as I say, it could change some fellows. It could keep them from believing that life was so valuable—anyone's life, I mean, even their own. I'm not saying that every fellow who roughed up a civilian liked himself for it—not that he'd admit in so many words that he didn't. But you could tell. Out of the blue, without being asked, he'd start defending what he'd done maybe hours ago by saying that, after all, it was no worse than what Charlie was doing. I heard that argument over and over again, and I could never buy it. It was like claiming that just because a drunken driver hit your friend, you had a right to get in your car and aim it at some pedestrian. Of course, I was a foot soldier all this time. I was operating in a forward area and probably seeing the war at its ugliest. In daylight it was search-and-destroy missions, and at night it was setting ambushes for the enemy. I discovered it's not difficult to kill a human being—in combat it's as instinctive as ducking bullets. You never knew whose turn it was to die, and that isn't how it was in rear areas. The farther back you got, the closer you approached the way people lived in civilian life.''   5

        . . . Other soldiers, he said, might just as easily have betrayed the weakness that the four men had betrayed on Hill 192, but it had fallen to Meserve and Clark and Rafe and Manuel* in particular to act as they had. Speakingly evenly, Eriksson said, ''They were among the ones—among the few—who did what everyone around them wanted to do.'' Nor was he himself free of blame, he went on, without pausing—once again referring to the limitations within himself that he had glimpsed in Asia. He had yet to exonerate himself from the self-imposed charge of having failed to save Mao's life. He had no idea how long this feeling would continue, but for the present, he knew, he lived with the charge daily, often wondering how Mao might have fared in a time of peace. Six months ago, he said, he had taken a Minneapolis bus home from work and, being very tired, had dozed off. When he opened his eyes, a new passenger was sitting directly opposite him—a young Oriental woman. Still in the process of waking, and

* The four who took part in the rape-murder of Mao. Lang does not use the actual names of those he writes about here or elsewhere in his book.

not yet thinking clearly, he said, he had transformed her into a peasant woman on her way to do a day's farming, such as he had seen many times in Vietnam; he had envisioned the passenger in a broad, peaked straw hat and black pajamas, carrying the traditional stick across her shoulders, with baskets at either end for holding crops. "Those baskets could get awfully heavy," Eriksson recalled. "Sometimes I didn't see what kept the stick from snapping. They were hard workers, those Vietnamese women, picking little bananas, shinnying up palm trees for coconuts. But on the bus the peasant woman across from me was going to work in paddy fields that were near Mao's hamlet, from which it was a nice walk downhill to a stream that flooded the rice fields. That's where the woman was going in the early morning, but it was peacetime and it wasn't necessary either for her or for the peasant women she was with to smell the bodies that were always rotting for miles around, no one knew where, when I was in the Central Highlands. 6 The only thing these women had to do on their way to the stream was breathe pure mountain air."

2,200 words

Vocabulary

Paragraph
1. predecessors
   vividly
   lush
   towering
   acknowledges
   remote
   reconnaissance
2. legalistic
   bulky
   interminable

depositions
dogged
grillings
strictures
unwarranted
unravel
corporate
impelled
gnaw
3. retrospect
   climactic

impulsive
random
gratuitous
discretion
retaliation
poncho
4. indiscriminately
   depredations
5. brooding
6. exonerate

Stewart Alsop ("Dr. Calhoun's Horrible Mousery") has been a newspaper reporter and columnist for more than twenty-five years. He has co-written a column, "Matter of Fact," with his brother Joseph Alsop, served as specialist in national affairs for *The Saturday Evening Post*, and, since 1968, has written a column for *Newsweek*.

Donald Barthelme ("Game") is a novelist (*Snow White*) and short-story writer whose work appears regularly in *The New Yorker*. His most recent collections of short stories are *Unspeakable Practices, Unnatural Acts* and *City Life*.

Bruno Bettelheim ("Business as Usual"), a psychiatrist and director of the Sonia Shankman Orthogenic School at the University of Chicago, knows about life in a concentration camp firsthand. He was confined in one in the 1930s before he escaped to the United States. Among his books are *Love Is Not Enough, Truants from Life*, and *The Informed Heart*.

Brigid Brophy ("Monogamy") attended Oxford. She is the author of several novels (*The Snow Ball*), critical books on music, and a book on existential philosophy, *Black Ship to Hell*.

Claude Brown ("We Got Soul, Baby, Aren't We Beautiful?") escaped from the Harlem ghetto to become a law student and a successful writer. His autobiography, *Manchild in the Promised Land*, has been widely read and acclaimed.

Art Buchwald's ("A Head Start on Brain Inventory") witty newspaper columns are widely syndicated in the United States and Europe and published, among other papers, by the *New York Post*, the *Los Angeles Times*, and the *Washington Post*.

Estelle Changas (" 'Love Story': A Minority Report") was the first intern appointed to the Rating Board of the Motion Picture Association. She has contributed articles to *Film Quarterly, Cinema, Calendar,* and *Film Comment.*

Shirley Chisholm ("Introduction: *Unbought and Unbossed*") represents the Twelfth Congressional District of Brooklyn in the United States House of Representatives.

Frank Conroy ("Finally Free") is a free-lance writer who contributes regularly to *Life, The New Yorker,* and other periodicals. *Stop-Time,* an autobiography written at the age of thirty-two is the source of "Finally Free."

William Faulkner ("Nobel Prize Award Speech") is one of the great American novelists of this century. Among his novels set in Yoknapatawpha County, Mississippi, are *Light in August, The Sound and the Fury, The Hamlet,* and *Sanctuary.* Faulkner lived most of his life in Oxford, Mississippi. He received the Nobel Prize for Literature in 1950.

Paul Goodman ("A Useful Job") describes himself as "a man of letters in the old sense, one who thinks that the literary process itself, the criticism of life, adds a new and indispensable element." Among his books are *Growing Up Absurd* and two novels, *The Empire City* and *Making Do.*

Mary Haworth's ("Help Me Understand My Wife") advice column is syndicated in newspapers throughout the United States.

Joseph Heller ("Catch 22") currently teaches fiction and dramatic writing at Yale and the University of Pennsylvania. His first novel, *Catch 22,* has been hailed as a masterpiece of comic invention. It served as the basis for the 1970 film *Catch 22.* He scripted the film *Sex and the Single Girl* and wrote a play, *We Bombed in New Haven,* which ran on Broadway. He is currently at work on a novel titled *Something Happened.*

Ernest Hemingway ("I Was Always Embarrassed . . ."), Nobel Prize winner and one of the most influential American writers of this century, is best known for his book of short stories, *In Our Time,* and his novels *The Sun Also Rises, A Farewell to Arms,* and *The Old Man and the Sea.*

Steven Kelman ("You Force the Kids to Rebel") published *When Push Comes to Shove* in 1970.

Martin Luther King, Jr. ("I Have a Dream") was a recipient of the Nobel Prize for Peace. Until his assassination in 1968, he led the Southern Christian Leadership Conference. Among his books are *Why We Can't Wait* and *Stride toward Freedom.*

Daniel Lang ("Casualties of War") writes poetry and short stories as well as nonfiction and is on the staff of *The New Yorker.* In addition to *Casualties of War,* from which the selection in this text is taken, he has published *Early Tales of the Atomic Age, The Man in the Thick Lead Suit, From Hiroshima to the Moon,* and *An Inquiry into Enoughness.*

John Lardner ("Titanic Thompson"), a son of famed humorist Ring Lardner, was born in Chicago in 1912 and died in New York City in 1951. He served as a sports reporter and later foreign correspondent for *The New Yorker* and as a columnist for *Newsweek.* Among his books were *White*

Hopes and Other Tigers, 1951, and *Strong Cigars and Lovely Women,* 1951.

Jeremy Larner's ("Hector Warms Up") novel, *Drive, He Said,* won the First $10,000 Delta Prize Novel Award in 1964. A graduate of Brandeis University, he did graduate work at the University of California at Berkeley.

Jean Mayer ("The Dubious Value of Crop Destruction to Achieve Military Goals") is a professor of nutrition at Harvard University and an authority on the effects of famine on populations.

Marshall McLuhan ("Murder by Television") was born in Edmondton, Canada. He is currently director of the Center for Culture and Technology at the University of Toronto. The center investigates the psychic and social consequences of technological media, which is the subject of his most famous and most influential book, *Understanding Media.* Other books include *The Mechanical Bride* and *The Gutenberg Galaxy.*

Don McNeill ("The Serenos: Linda Cusamano") reported for *The Village Voice.* Shortly after collecting his stories from *The Voice* in a volume titled *Moving through Here,* he died in a drowning accident.

Willie Morris ("I Think I May Have Been Listening") has edited various newspapers as well as *Harper's Magazine.* He is currently at work on a novel, having first published his autobiography, *North toward Home.*

Gordon Parks's ("My Mother's Dream for Me") autobiography, *A Choice of Weapons,* recounts his struggle to succeed as a black man in the United States. His weapon became the camera, and from 1949 on he has been a staff photographer and writer for *Life.* He directed a film version of his novel *The Learning Tree.* He has also composed music and worked as a fashion photographer for *Vogue.*

James Reston ("Joe Namath, the New Anti-Hero"), a longtime chief of the Washington Bureau of the *New York Times,* began his writing career as a sportswriter. Now a vice president of the *Times,* his column appears regularly on the editorial page.

John Riley ("Saga of the Barefoot Bag on Campus") is a newspaper reporter and free-lance writer.

Eugene Schoenfeld ("Kill Speed") writes a medical advice column for underground newspapers. He has collected the most provocative, abrasive, and hip questions and answers from his column in a book titled *Dear Doctor Hippocrates.*

Eric Sevareid ("What Really Hurts . . .") reports regularly from Washington for CBS News. A former war correspondent for CBS and, before that, city editor of the Paris edition of the New York *Herald Tribune,* he has published many magazine articles and several books including *In One Ear* and a personal narrative that became a best seller, *Not So Wild a Dream.*

Gloria Steinem ("What It Would Be Like If Women Win") serves as a contributing editor to *New York* magazine and has long been an advocate of women's liberation.

Studs Terkel ("Cesar Chavez") has been a lawyer, a radio soap-opera actor, a

disk jockey, a sports commentator, and a television master of cere-
monies. Currently he has a daily radio program on WFMT Chicago. He
has published *Division Street: America*, *Giants of Jazz*, and *Hard Times:
An Oral History of the Great Depression*.

Mark Twain (Samuel Clemens) ("The War Prayer") wrote many books, among
them *Huckleberry Finn* which Ernest Hemingway called the "first modern
American novel." Twain is one of the greatest writers in United States
literary history.

John Updike ("Central Park") is one of the established writers of firm reputation in American letters today. He served on the staff of *The New Yorker*
from 1955 to 1957. His novel *The Centaur* won the National Book Award
for fiction in 1964. Among his other novels are *The Poorhouse Fair*,
Rabbit Run, and *Couples*. He has also published verse and a collection
of short stories, *Pigeon Feathers*.

Katherine Whitehorn ("A Fine Time to Be Alive") is a wife and mother living in
London, where she writes a weekly column for the London Sunday
Observer.

Martin Weinberger ("The Double Standards") publishes a prize-winning bi-
weekly newspaper, *The Claremont Courier*, in Claremont, California.

Frances Weismiller ("To Ralph Nader with Love . . .") is a free-lance writer,
sometimes under the name A. R. Quentin. "To Ralph Nader with
love . . ." is part of a work in progress which deals with ". . . a complicated theory of the timing of prerevolutionary turmoil, which appears
whenever youth seriously outnumbers young adults."

Tom Wolfe ("Clean Fun at Riverhead") has written for *New York*, *Esquire*,
Harper's Bazaar, and other periodicals. One of the central ideas thread-
ing through the essays in his books *The Kandy-kolored Tangerine-flake
Streamline Baby* and *The Pump-house Gang* is the suggestion that many
recent forms and styles of life—from the "twist" to the Beatles to
surfing to hard rock—express the ordinary American's sense of form
and beauty. His most recent book is *The Electric Kool-Aid Acid Test*.

Experiencing a photograph involves recognition of the pattern the picture makes, study of the details that make up the pattern, and the personal response of each viewer based on the associations evoked by the picture. Typical responses might begin with, "That reminds me of..." or "That makes me feel...." A person sees what he brings to an experience. Each individual will "see" different elements in the same photo. Each will impose aspects of his own experience on the photo to determine its meaning for himself. It is this personal response, this individual evocation that makes photographs apt subjects for visual discussion and writing assignments.